7 Projects ♥ 20 So Elegant Kiss Lock Purses

Simplistic yet Sew Amazingly Elegant

This Book Belongs To

_____

_____

Sew Amazingly Elegant
Copyright © 2020 by Jacine Wang
All rights reserved.

No part of this product may be reproduced in any form, unless otherwise stated, in which case reproduction is limited to the use of the purchaser. The written instructions, photographs, designs, projects, and patterns are intended for the personal, noncommercial use of the retail purchaser and are under federal copyright laws; they are not to be reproduced by any electronic, mechanical, or other means, including informational storage or retrieval systems, for commercial use. Permission is granted to photocopy patterns for the personal use of the retail purchaser.

ISBN: 978-1-7333503-2-7 (eBook)
ISBN: 978-1-7333503-3-4 (Paperback)
Library of Congress Control Number: 2020913690

The information in this book is presented in good faith, but no warranty is given nor results guaranteed. Since the author and/or the publisher have no control over choice of materials of procedures, the author and/or the publisher assume no responsibility for any consequences arising from the information, advice or instructions given in this publication.

By purchasing this book, you agree not to share, upload elsewhere, or resell the pattern either as a digital download or printed pattern. You are prohibited from giving or selling any of the patterns in this book to a magazine, blog, or book publisher. You are not allowed modifying the pattern slightly and sell it as your own creation.

Readers are permitted to reproduce any of the items/patterns in this book for their personal use, or for the purposes of selling for charity, free of charge, or home industry and without the prior permission of the author. Any use of the items/patterns for commercial purposes is not permitted without the prior permission of the author. Properly attribute each item (and online listing) that is being made using the patterns in this book is welcome, but not required.

Attention Teachers: The author encourages you to use this book for teaching, subject to the restrictions stated above.

Attention Copy Shops: Please note the following exception - publisher and author give permission to photocopy pattern page for personal use only.

The author and/or publisher are not affiliated with or sponsored by the licensed fabrics used and presented in this book.

Photographs, illustrations, interior and cover designed by Jane J. Wang

Published in 2020 by EZ2Sew Design Studio, a division of EZ Shop & Design
Plano, Texas USA

For further inspiration, visit website: www.ezshopdesign.com

Printed in the United States of America

10 9 8 7 6 5 4 3 2 1

7 Projects ♥ 20 So Elegant Kiss Lock Purses

Simplistic yet Sew Amazingly Elegant

Jacine Wang

Table of Contents

Dedication
Preface
Acknowledgements

Introduction
About the Author

Essential Tools 1
Fabric & Interfacing 5
Hardware & Accessory 11
Understand the Pattern 17
Basic Bag Construction 25
Install the Purse Frame 39
Project 1 - Helena-I, Pearl, Irene 49
    Helena-I 51
    Pearl 51
    Irene (V1 & V2) 52
Project 2 - Quiana 67
    Quiana (III_O_V1) 69
    Quiana (IV_O_V1) 75
Project 3 - Lacy, Natalie, Unice (V2) 80
    Lacy 81
    Natalie 81
    Unice (V2) 82
Project 4 - Helena-II, Unice (V1) 97
    Helena-II (V1 & V2) 100
    Unice (V1) 106

Table of Contents

Project 5 - Sally 119
      Sally (V1 & V2) 125

Project 6 - Helena-III, Janelle-I, Janelle-II, Melody 135
      Helena-III 139
      Janelle-I 144
      Janelle-II 149
      Melody 152

Project 7 - Tamia 159
      Tamia (V1) 161
      Tamia (V2) 167

Pattern Index

Helena-I 50	Pearl 61
Helena-II (V1) .... 111~112	Quiana (III_O_V1) 74
Helena-II (V2) 113	Quiana (IV_O_V1) 79
Helena-III 137	Sally (V1 & V2) .... 120~121
Irene (V1) .... 62~64	Sally (V1) 122
Irene (V2) .... 64~66	Sally (V2) .... 123~124
Janelle-I .... 147~148	Taima (V1) .... 176~179
Janelle-II .... 150~151	Taima (V2) .... 180~185
Lacy .... 88~90	Unice (V1) .... 114~118
Melody .... 155~158	Unice (V2) .... 94~96
Natalie .... 91~93	

Dedication

In memory of my grandmother who passed away in August 2020 at the age of 103. You have left marks of grace in our lives. You will not be forgotten.

Preface

Do you have a list that has all the things you want to try and things you want to achieve? "Sewing" was not in my list and I would have never thought about it. The reason I avoided sewing in the past was because I was always afraid of pricking myself with the needle (even though it still happens) and rarely sewed unless I absolutely needed to.

Well, never say "Never", right?!

I started my "sewing" journey after our family adopted two super cute kittens since our kids went to college; they became my inspiration. I wouldn't have imagined that sewing would bring me so much joy and am unable to go a day without it.

Handmade stuff is such a wonderful thing. Join me, start sewing and have fun!

Jaine

07.01.2020

Acknowledgements

I can't believe that I finished my 2nd book within a year after publishing the 1st book "Sew Amazing Cute" in 2019. None of this would have been possible without my family's support and encouragement.

The most important thing is to thank you for purchasing my book, providing amazing feedback and encouraging me to continue to write more!

Even though I am not affiliated with or sponsored by the trademark owner of the fabrics, I still want to thank you for those who created and designed the beautiful fabrics that I used and presented in my book.

Introduction

After I made and designed many projects, I found out that I had lots of fabric scraps left. If you have my book "Sew Amazingly Cute", you might know that I fell in love with making these small, adorable, and elegant frame purses, so the scraps have found their place.

In this book, I will continue sharing my patterns and instructions for making frame purses by using different sizes, shapes and materials for the frame. It's very easy to learn and make.

There is something for everyone to make, from an amateur sewing a one-piece pattern to veteran sewing the most difficult pattern in the book. No matter which pattern you work on, always make sure you have the correct frame to match the pattern.

With the addition of the purse frame, it can modernize the look of your purse with elegance, suitable for all ages. Let's make something "Simplistic yet Sew Amazingly Elegant".

About the Author
Jacine Wang

"Sew Amazingly Cute"

She is a self-learner starting from scratch and now enjoys designing handbag patterns and sewing as well. While she is sewing, her two pretty kitties, Asti and Celine, are on or under her sewing table, napping or playing, sometimes lying on the fabrics to get her attention while she works. If she, who knew nothing about sewing, can sew, "sew" can you.

Jacine lives in Plano, Texas with her husband, Charles, and they have two kids, Christine and Johnathan.

Essential Tools

Craft Shears
A good pair of craft scissors can be used to cut the patterns.

Fabric Cutting Shears
Fabric cutting shears are used for cutting fabric.

Pinking Shears
Pinking shears have blades with serrated edges. They leave a zigzag pattern after cutting. They are useful for trimming off excess material on a curved seam to reduce the bulk.

Rotary Cutters
There are different sizes of rotary cutters: 60mm, 45mm, 28mm and 18mm. The 18mm and 28mm are more helpful for the patterns mentioned in this book because of the size of the pattens you will be cutting and the accuracy required to cut them.

Craft Knife
There are some markings from the patterns that need to be transferred onto the fabric after cutting. The craft knife is useful for this but could also use a marking pen or tailor's chalk instead.

Cutting Mat
The cutting mat is used to protect the table while you cut the fabric and transfer the markings.

Clear Ruler
A ruler is used for drawing straight lines.

Seam Gauge
The seam gauge is useful for adding seam allowance around the patterns if the pattern doesn't include seam allowance.

Tape Measure
The tape measure for sewing is a flexible ruler used to measure length, width, and height.

Essential Tools

Essential Tools

Thread Snips

Thread snips, thread nippers, or thread clippers are a must in a sewing kit. They cut threads quickly in tight corners that larger scissors can't reach.

Seam Ripper

The seam ripper is used for removing stitches. You will need this tool if you accidentally forget to leave an opening for turning the purse right side out.

Awl

This tool is optional. If you feel the piece is too small to feed through the presser foot using your fingers, it can act as an assistant to feeding the fabric.

Fabric Marking Pencils
Tailor's Chalk
Erasable Gel Pens

These are used to trace patterns, draw seam allowances, and make markings on the wrong side of the fabric. If you need to make markings on the right side of the fabric, use a heat or water erasable pen.

Sewing Pins

Sewing pins are used to temporarily hold the fabric in place while cutting several layers or sewing.

Clips

If you don't like using pins to hold the fabric in place while sewing, clips will do the same job. I use sewing pins while cutting several layers of fabric and use clips while sewing.

Pin Cushion

A pin cushion is used to store pins or needles.

Sewing Machine

You don't need a fancy or complicated sewing machine. Any sewing machine that can sew a straight line will get the job done.

Iron and Ironing Board

The iron is used to press the seam allowance, flatten the fabric and apply the interfacing. It can also shape the finished purse. The ironing board is used to protect the surface under the iron.

Hand Sewing Needles

A lot of the projects included in this book required hand sewing. It is possible to hand-sew entire projects without the sewing machine. Thus, it's very important to have a few good sewing needles.

I would also recommend using a *Thimble* while installing the frame on the purse. This tool is used to push the needle throughout layers of fabric without hurting your fingers.

Seam Roller

This tool is very useful for pressing the seams flat without using iron.

Beacon 3-In-1 Advanced Craft Glue / Gutermann HT2 Textile Fabric Glue

Crystal clear, permanent adhesive. If you are going to use Glue-in frame, you need glue to finish the job.

Flat head screw driver

This tool is useful for tucking the fabric into the purse frame channel.

Essential Tools

Fabric & Interfacing

Fabric

What type of Fabric can we use?

Any kind of fabric from light to medium weight, such as cotton, quilting cotton, linen, micro-suede, corduroy, nylon and cork could be used. We will try to avoid any fabric that is too thick or too heavy.

Cotton
(light weight)

Used for:
Exterior; Interior;

Quilting Cotton
(light to medium weight)

Used for:
Exterior; Interior;

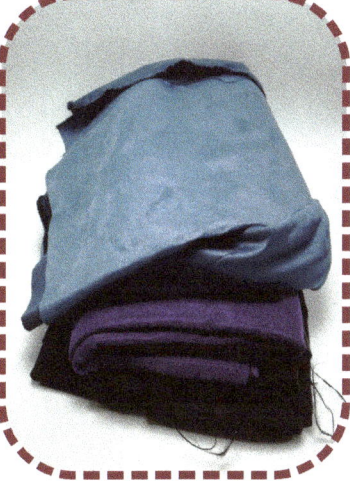

Micro-Suede
(medium weight)

Used for:
Exterior;

Cork
(medium weight)

Used for:
Exterior;

Corduroy
(medium weight)

Used for:
Exterior;

Nylon
(light to medium weight)

Used for:
Interior;

Interfacing

> **NOTE:** Always follow the manufacturer's directions for applying any interfacing to the fabric.
>
> Test before applying to any main fabric. You can also mix and match two or three different kinds of interfacing onto the fabric.

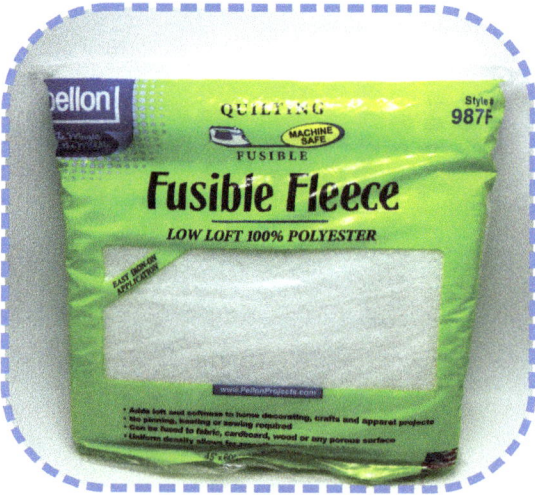

Pellon 987F Fusible Fleece

Used for:
Exterior; Interior;

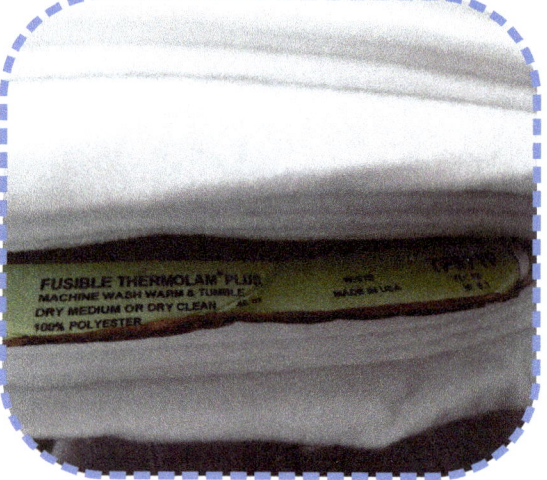

Pellon TP971F Fusible Thermolam Plus

Used for:
Exterior;

by Annie's Soft and Stable

Used for:
Exterior;

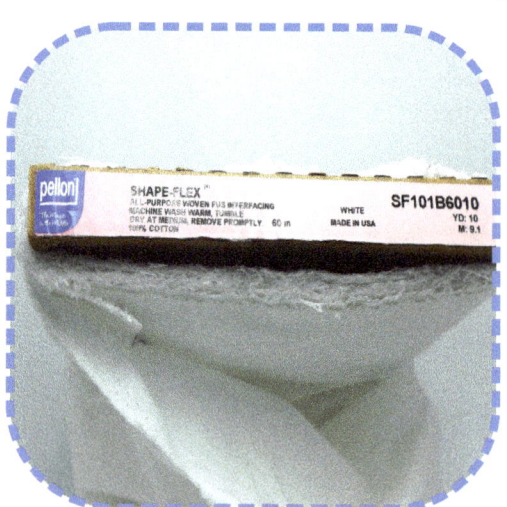

Pellon SF101 Shape-Flex Woven Fusible Cotton

Used for:
Exterior; Interior;

Interfacing

> **NOTE:** Always follow the manufacturer's directions for applying any interfacing to the fabric.

Test before applying to any main fabric. You can also mix and match two or three different kinds of interfacing onto the fabric.

Pellon 910 Sew-in Featherweight

Used for:
Exterior; Interior;

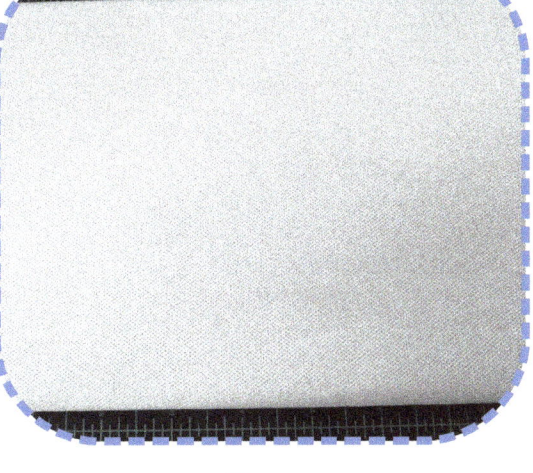

Pellon 520 Deco-Fuse

Used for:
Exterior (for reinforcement);

HTC 422 Fusible Non-Woven Interfacing

Used for:
Exterior; Interior;

Heat & Bond High Loft Iron-On Fusible Fleece

Used for:
Exterior;

Fabric & Interfacing

Apply Interfacing

*E*ven if you don't apply any interfacing on the fabric, the finished piece still might have some structure, and stand on its own. But after installing the metal frame onto the top, the whole piece could fall and collapse because of the weight of the metal frame.

Applying the appropriate interfacing is very important and it will make the whole piece have a soft and structured feel, but not stiff.

<u>ALWAYS</u> test the interfacing on a small piece of the fabric before applying to the main fabric and <u>ALWAYS</u> follow manufacturer's directions for applying any interfacing to the fabric.

Applying Fusible Interfacing

① Place the fabric wrong side up on the ironing board;

② Place the fusible interfacing on top, with the adhesive side (bumpy side) faced down on the wrong side of the fabric;

③ Cover the fabric and interfacing with a press cloth or a heat resistant craft sheet, and press the iron onto it.

④ Make sure the interfacing attached well onto the fabric.

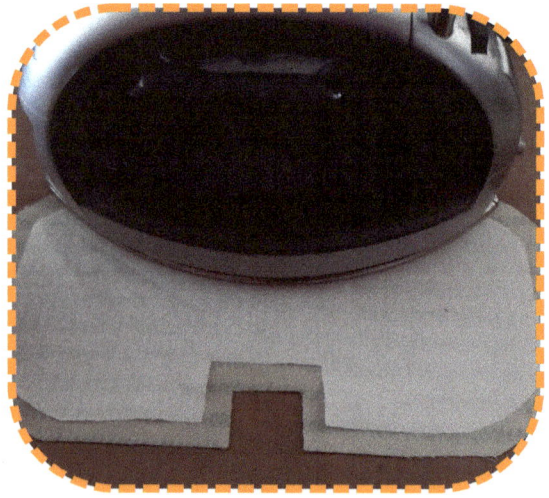

Apply Interfacing

Layering Fusible Interfacing

Exmaple Interfacings:
- ❶ *Pellon 987F* - Pellon 987F Fusible Fleece
- ❷ *Pellon SF101* - Pellon SF101 Shape-Flex Woven Fusible Cotton

① Place the fabric wrong side up on the ironing board;

② Place the fusible interfacing ❶ on top, with the adhesive side (bumpy side), faced down onto to the wrong side of the fabric; Cover the fabric and interfacing with a press cloth or a heat resistant craft sheet, and press the iron onto it.

③ Place the fusible interfacing ❷ on top of the fusible interfacing ❶ with the adhesive side faced down; Cover the fabric and interfacing with a press cloth or a heat resistant craft sheet, and press the iron onto it.

④ Make sure both layers of interfacing attached well onto the fabric.

Applying Sew-in Interfacing

① Place the fabric wrong side up;

② Place the sew-in interfacing on top of the wrong side of the fabric;

③ Baste stitching all the way around at the center of (or smaller than) the seam allowance to attach both fabric and sew-in interfacing together (Figure 1). Make sure the interfacing attached well onto the fabric.

④ You may quilt the fabric with the thicker sew-in interfacing (Figure 2).

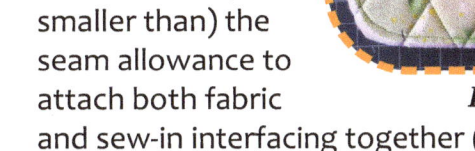

Figure 1

Figure 2

Hardware & Accessory

Purse Frame

*P*urse Frames play a leading role in all of the projects mentioned in this book. There are many shapes (rectangular, curved/arch, m-shape, single frame and double frames), sizes (from mini, small to large), materials (metal, plastic, wire) and colors (gold, silver, bronze, black) of purse frames out there and three types of installation methods: sew-in, glue-in and slide-in. There are many different kinds of lock shapes on top of the frames that you can choose from as well.

Throughout this book, we will be using purse frames with different sizes, shapes, and installation processes. The pattern will indicate the type of purse frame that will be used to complete the purse piece. ***Do NOT install a frame with the wrong size and shape***, otherwise it won't fit properly (check the examples below). Most of the projects in this book use sew-in style frames. If you prefer not to use this, you could also use a glue-in frame. But make sure the SIZE and SHAPE match the pattern.

Correct Fit

Incorrect Fit

 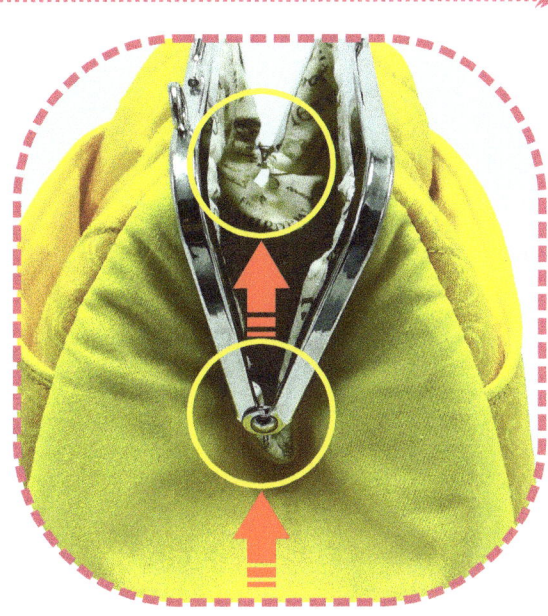

Top: The perimeter of the finished purse piece is _shorter_ than the frame perimeter.
Right: The perimeter of the finished purse piece is _longer_ than the frame perimeter.

Hardware & Accessory

Purse Frame

Measuring conversion rate: 1 inch = 2.54 cm (1" * 2.54 = 2.54 cm)
SIZE - **W**: *Frame width*; **H**: *Frame height (**NOT** including the kiss lock)*; **P**: *Perimeter of the frame*;
SHAPE - **O**: *Oval*; **R**: *Round*; **Rect**: *Rectangle*; **DB**: *Double*; MATERIAL: **MeT**al / **PL**astic;
Used for: the <<*Pattern name*>> used in this book;

SIZE: Mini to Small

 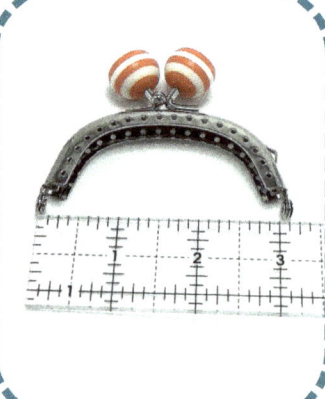 

W: 2.56" (6.5 cm)　　　　W: 3.15" (8 cm)　　　　　W: 3.3" (8.5 cm)
H: 1.5" (3.8 cm)　　　　　H: 1.77" (4.5 cm)　　　　H: 1.75" (4.45 cm)
P: 4.5" (11.5 cm)　　　　 P: 2.125" (5.4 cm)　　　　P: 5.5~5.75" (14~14.6 cm)
Shape: Rect / MT　　　　Shape: O / MT　　　　　 Shape: Rect / MT
Used for: The Pearl　　　 Used for: The Quiana　　　Used for: The Helena-I, III

SIZE: Mini to Small　　　　## SIZE: Small to Medium

W: 3.35" (8.5 cm)　　　　W: 4.13" (10.5 cm)　　　　W: 4.9" (12.5 cm)
H: 1.625" (4.13 cm)　　　 H: 2" (5.08 cm)　　　　　H: 2" (5.08 cm)
P: 4.3" (10.9 cm)　　　　 P: 7.0" (17.8 cm)　　　　 P: 8" (20.32 cm)
Shape: O / PL　　　　　　Shape: Rect / MT　　　　Shape: Rect / MT
Used for: The Helena-II　 Used for: The Irene　　　　Used for: The Janelle-I

*** Please allow 1/16"~1/8" (0.15~0.3 cm) differences at all measurements above. ***

Purse Frame

SIZE: Small to Medium

W: 4.9" (12.45 cm)
H: 2.625" (6.67 cm)
P: 8.25" (20.95 cm)
Shape: Rect / MT
Used for: The Janelle-II

W: 5.9" (15 cm)
H: 2" (5.08 cm)
P: 9.5" (24.1 cm)
Shape: Rect / MT
Used for: The Lacey

W: 5.3-4.5" (13.5-11.5 cm)
H: 2.375-1.45" (6-3.65 cm)
P: 7.7-5.8" (19.55-14.7 cm)
Shape: DB / MT
Used for: The Sally

SIZE: Medium to Large

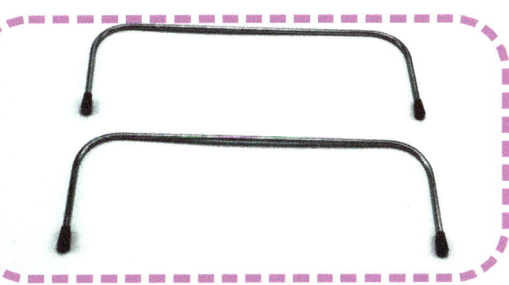

W: 6.3" (16cm); H: 2.625" (6.67cm)
P: 8.5" (21.6 cm)
Shape: O / PL
Used for: The Unice

W: 7.1" (18 cm); H: 2.4" (6 cm)
P: 11.5" (29 cm)
Shape: Rect / MT
Used for: The Tamia

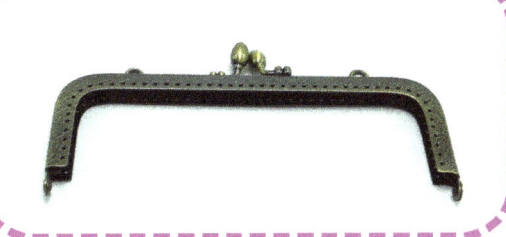

W: 6.3" (16 cm); H: 2.85" (7.24 cm)
P: 9.45" (24 cm)
Shape: R / MT
Used for: The Melody

W: 7.1" (18cm); H: 2.56" (6.5cm)
P: 10.75" (27.3 cm)
Shape: Rect / MT
Used for: The Natalie

** Please allow 1/16"~1/8" (0.15~0.3 cm) differences at all measurements above. **

Accessories

We are going to use several accessories mentioned in this section. Not all of the patterns in this book will require accessories, so check the pattern instructions for details and add them at your discretion.

Hardware & Accessory

Purse Feet
There are different sizes, shapes and colors to choose from.

D-Ring
Size: 0.5" (1.25 cm)
Color: match other hardware

Magnetic Snap Button
Size: 0.75" (2 cm)

Zipper
Size: #4.5, single or double zipper pull(s)
Length: 16"

Zipper Ends
Color: match other hardware

Beads
Size: 4mm and 6mm
Color: match fabric or hardware

Accessories

** There are different sizes, shapes, colors and materials to choose from. **

Handmade Tag

Shoulder Strap

Buttons

Lobster Clasp

Lace

Zipper Pull

Tassel

Elastic

Size: 1/2" width
Color: upon to the fabric color

Hardware & Accessory

Understand the Pattern

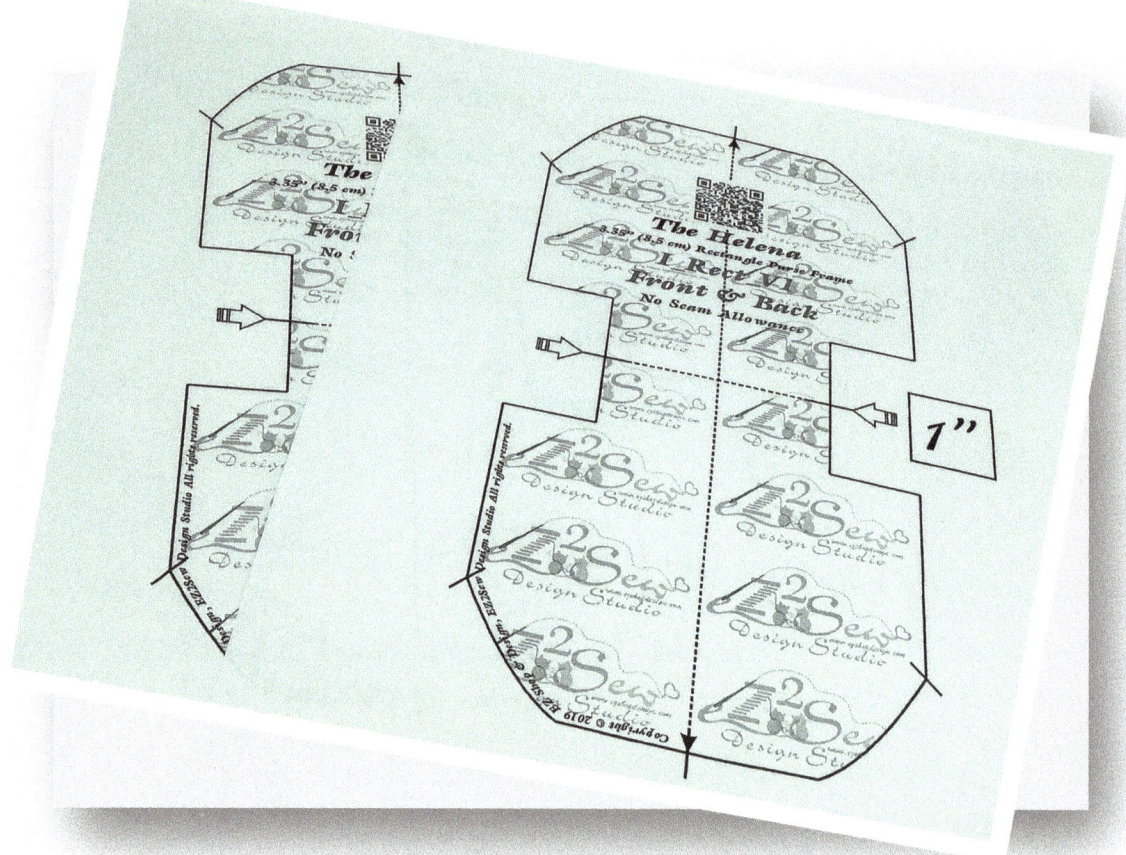

How to Use

$\mathcal{L}$et's get the pattern ready so we can start sewing our project. *All the patterns in this book have NO SEAM ALLOWANCE included.* Before we start to cut the fabric, we need to do some preparations.

How to Use the Pattern

1 **Print out or Trace the Pattern onto paper.** Trace the pattern by using tracing paper from the pattern page, or print out the pattern from the pattern page (check the Printing Instructions below). Make 2 copies of each piece of the pattern.

2 **Gather the Tools.** You need the following tools: a straight line ruler with 1/8" interval markings, a seam gauge and a pencil. And, of course, a good pair of craft shears for cutting the paper patterns.

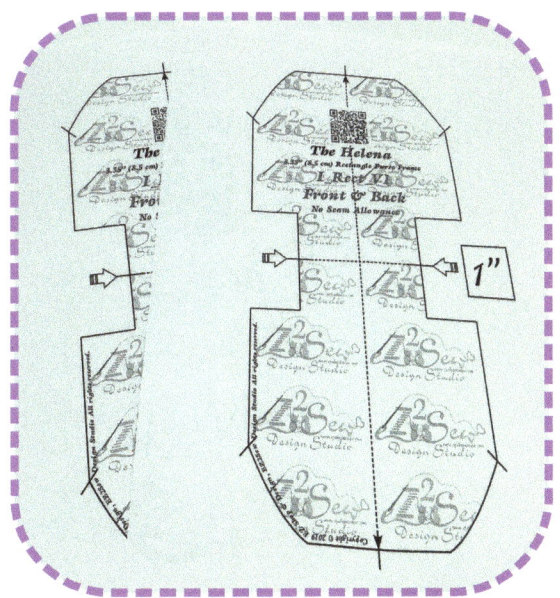 

Printing Instructions

$\mathcal{P}$lease make sure your printer's scaling is set to "none," "actual size" or "100%". Do NOT check the "scale to fit paper size" option. Once the pattern is printed out, make sure it printed correctly. Check the "1 inch Square" and it should measure 1" x 1". If the square is not the correct size, check the printer settings again.

How to Use

How to Use the Pattern (Continued)

3 **Add Seam Allowance and transfer all the markings.** You should have 2 copies of the paper patterns, put one copy aside. Since the pattern does **NOT** have seam allowance, we need to add seam allowance around the pattern before cutting the fabric.

 Add seam allowance: 1/4", 3/8" or 1/2" (0.7 cm, 1 cm or 1.25 cm) around the paper pattern, to your preference. (refer to the pictures below)

Use the Seam Gauge to draw the seam allowance on the curve area; use the Straight Line Ruler to draw the seam allowance on the straight line. Extend the center markings or other markings to the seam allowance as well.

4 **Cut the pattern.** Cut both patterns out using craft scissors: one with seam allowance and the other without. Now, you should have 2 cutouts of the patterns above.

 The pattern *with* seam allowance (*Pattern B*) is used for cutting the fabric (main and lining) or the sew-in interfacing. The pattern *without* seam allowance (*Pattern A*) is used for cutting the fusilbe interfacing.

 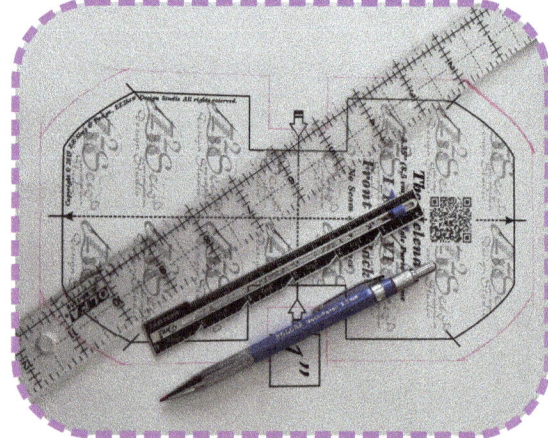

Pattern B With Seam Allowance   *Pattern A Without Seam Allowance*

The Pattern

Before starting to cut the fabric, we need to understand the meaning of all the markings and texts on the pattern. Especially, if you are using directional fabric, you have to make sure they are facing in the right direction.

Understand the Pattern

1 *The <Pattern Name>.* Each pattern has its own unique name. Gather all the pattern pieces which have the same name on the pattern before cutting fabric or interfacing. Do not mix pattern pieces with different names on it.

2 *The <Size>, <Shape>, and/or <Material> of the Purse Frame.* This line will indicate the purse frame size, shape and/or material of the purse frame is going to be used for the pattern. **Do NOT install the wrong size or shape purse frame to the project.**

3 *I_Rect_V1.* This line consists of three separate parts: "I", "Rect", and "V1". What do they represent?

I the roman numeral indicates the number of piece(s) required to construct the purse piece. In the example below, you need to cut out ONE piece as shown.

R ect/PL-Rect/O/R means the frame shape. Do NOT install the wrong shaped frame onto the purse piece, otherwise you won't get the expected result.

V v1 means "variation 1". Some purse frames may have more than one variation pattern with the same pattern name. The example below shows **Variation 1**.

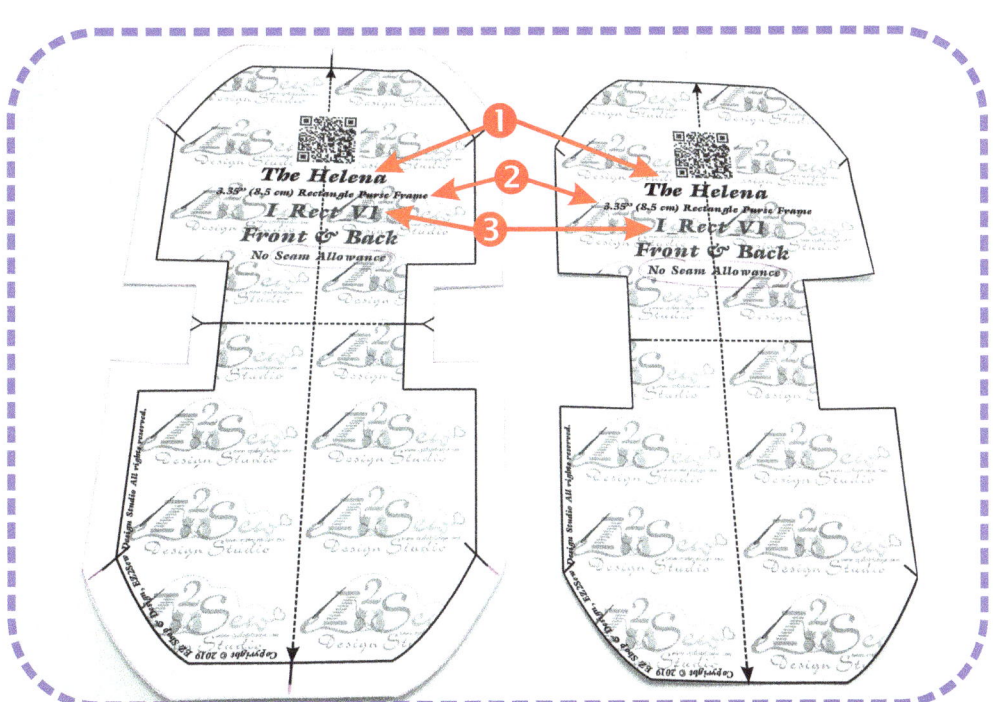

The Pattern

Understand the Pattern (continue)

4 *Front & Back.* This tells you where to connect and construct the purse piece. "Front & Back" means the purse "Front" and/or "Back"; "Side Gusset" means the side of the purse; "Bottom" means the bottom of the purse. "Pocket (Front/Back, Side Gusset or…)" means the pocket and where to place.

5 *Seam Allowance.* All the patterns provided in this book have NO SEAM ALLOWANCE. Because of this, we will require two sets of the pattern: one without seam allowance (Pattern A) and one with seam allowance drawn in (Pattern B). To make sure you don't mix up the two, circle "**No Seam Allowance**" on "**Pattern A**" and "**Seam Allowance**" on "**Pattern B**".

6 *Arrow Markings.* The arrows on the pattern indicate direction. If you are using directional fabric, you need to make sure that it's facing the correct direction. Some of the patterns only need one piece of fabric, but with directional fabric, two pieces must be cut and connected to each other.

7 *Markings.* There are markings in all the patterns. You have to transfer them **ALL** to the fabric's seam allowance. Use a craft knife or chalk to mark them onto the fabric.

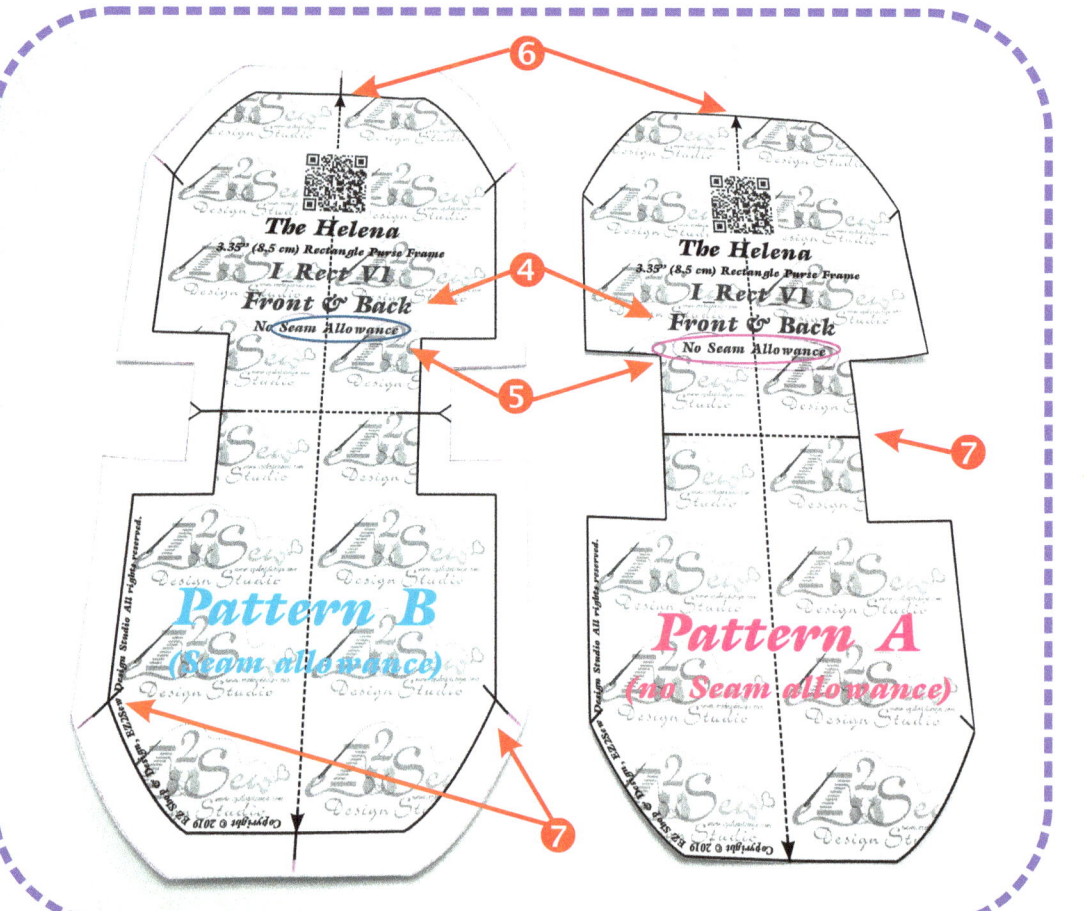

The Pattern

Understand the Pattern (continue)

8 *Other Markings.*

 The **double half circle** marking indicates the place where to join/connect the fabric.

★ For **NON-Directional** fabric: **FOLD** the fabric in half and line up the double half circle marking along the folded edge. Add seam allowance all the way around, except the edge with the double half circle. Cut the fabric as ONE piece. (Figure 2)

★ For **Directional** fabric: Add seam allowance all the way around on the pattern, and then cut two pieces of the fabric. Connect two pieces of fabric at the special marking with the seam allowance of your choice. Now, the fabric becomes ONE piece. (Figure 3)

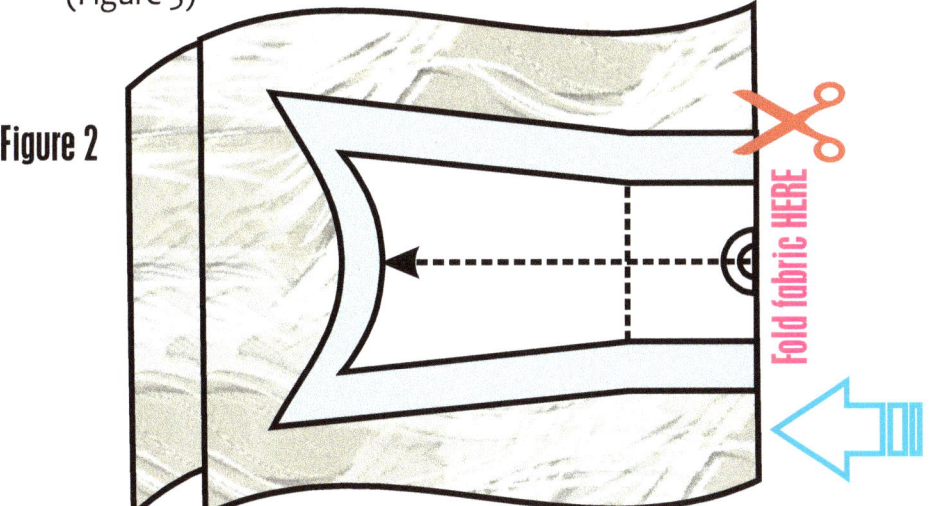

Figure 1

Figure 1 is NOT an actual size of the pattern.

Figure 2 — Fold fabric HERE

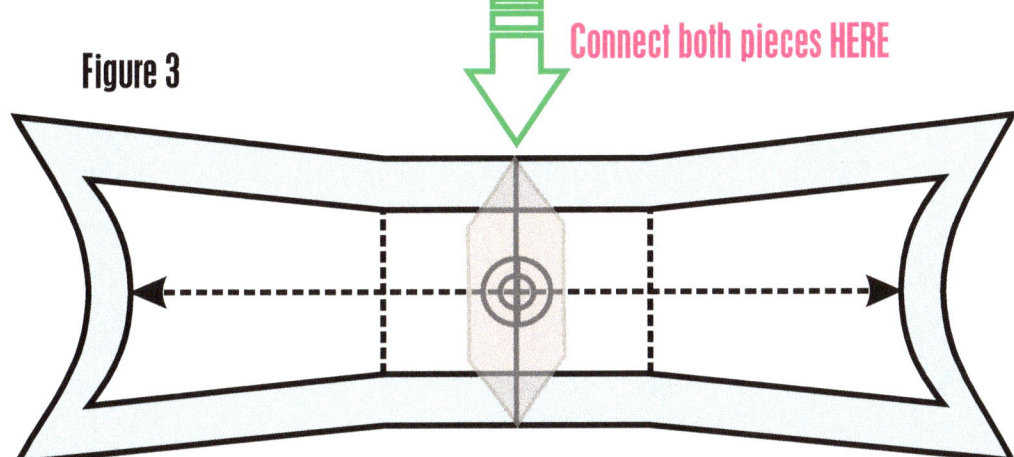

Figure 3 — Connect both pieces HERE

The Pattern

Understand the Pattern (continue)

8 *Other Markings.* (continue)

 The **diamond** shape marking indicates where you join/connect the pattern pieces together.

★ **Half diamond** (Figure 1):

Figure 1

1. Print 2 copies of the same pattern piece.
2. Cut out both copies and turn one of the pattern pieces to the reverse side (Figure 2).
3. Line up both pieces to form the diamond.
4. Use clear tape to connect both pieces together.
5. The new pattern will be Pattern A (Figure 3) which has NO seam allowance. Add seam allowance of your choice all the way around to make the Pattern B before cutting any fabric.

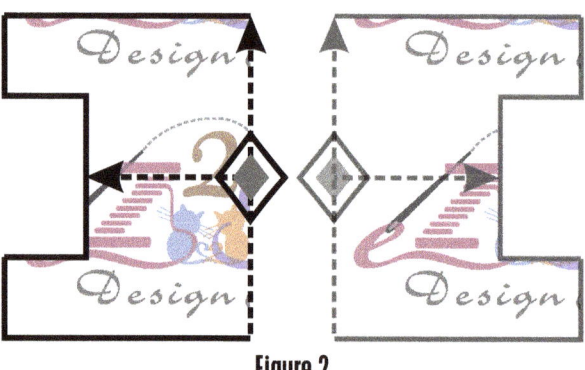

Figure 2

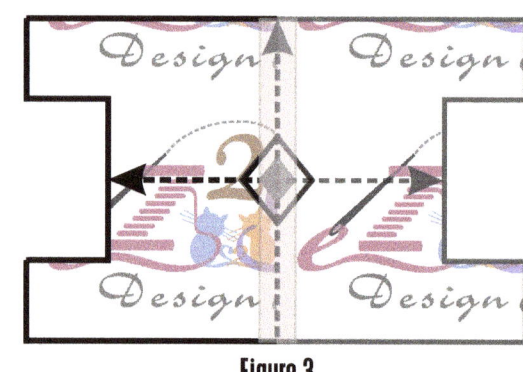

Figure 3

** NOT an actual size of the pattern. Do NOT use it for cutting the fabric. **

★ **1/4 diamond** (Figure 4):

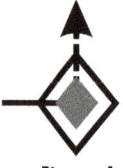

Figure 4

1. Print 4 copies of the same pattern piece.
2. Cut out all the copies and flip one of the pattern pieces horizontally (refer to next page Figure 5).
3. Line up the top two quarters to create the top half. (Refer to next page Figure 6)
4. Use clear tape to connect both pieces together.
5. Join the other two pieces by repeating the same steps above.

The Pattern

Understand the Pattern (continue)

 Other Markings. (continue)

 ★ **1/4 diamond** (Figure 4):

Figure 4

6 Flip one of the joined patterns vertically and line up the two pieces to form the complete diamond.

7 The new pattern will be Pattern A (Figure 7) which has no seam allowance. Add seam allowance of your choice all the way around to make the Pattern B before cutting any fabric.

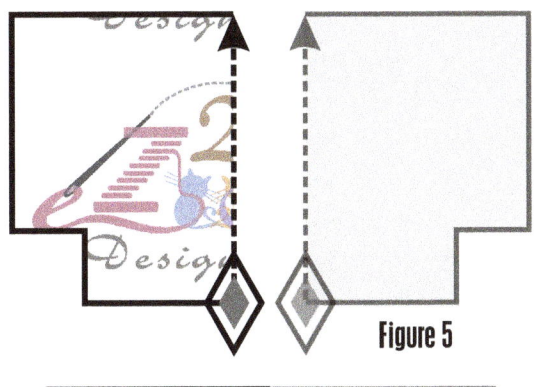

Figure 5

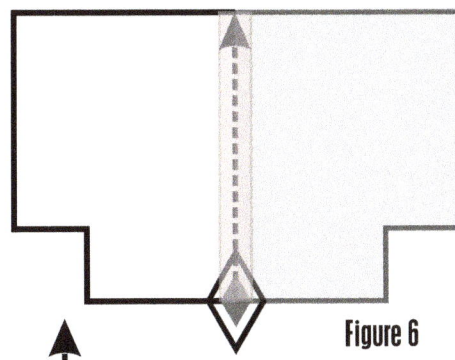

Figure 6

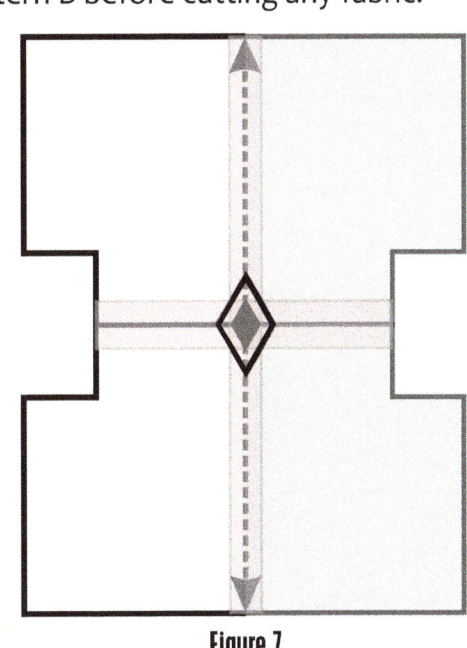

Figure 7

** NOT an actual size of the pattern. **
** Do NOT use them for cutting the fabric. **

The **dotted circle** marking indicates where you install the magnet closure hardware.

The **dotted rectangle with gray shade** marking indicates where you sew the tag (optional).

The **special** marking indicates where you fold the 3D pocket.

The **dot circle** marking indicates where to install the purse feet.

The **double doted rectangle** marking at the **"Bottom"** pattern piece indicates where to quilt (optional).

Basic Bag Construction

Curved Seam

Some basic bag construction that will be used in the patterns will be introduced in this chapter. The elements include curved seams, slip pockets, 3-D pocket, handle, zipper flap, bag feet installation and etc.

Construct a Curved Seam

1 *Trace the Pattern.* Trace the pattern with **NO** seam allowance by using chalk or erasable pen on the wrong side of both connecting fabrics. This will be the seam line and will help you focus on the fabric while sewing, regardless if you are hand sewing or using a sewing machine.

2 *Match the center markings.* Match the center markings, then use clips or pins to hold them in place. Place the piece with the curved seam under the piece with the straight seam, right side facing each other.

3 *Sew the center to hold them in place (Optional, but Recommended).* You might want to sew the center of the straight seam first to hold both pieces in place.

4 *Snips in Curves.* Near the curved areas where both pieces will be joined, cut a few slits on the top piece with the straight seam, so that the fabric will become more flexible to match the bottom fabric with curved seams.

5 *Match the rest of the Markings.* Match the side markings on both sides, use pins or clips to hold them all the way around.

6 *Sew all the way around.* If you did step 3, sew halfway until you meet the straight seam, and then finish the other half.

7 *Repeat.* Repeat the same steps above on other side of the piece.

Slip Pocket

We all love pockets inside or outside our handbags to organize the stuff we carry. There are several different pocket styles when making a handbag. In this book, I will use the following: a slip pocket (with a curved or flat top), a rectangular slip pocket, and a 3D slip pocket with or without an elastic top slip pocket. You can make as many pockets as you want or as few pockets as you need in your handbags to create your own unique style. Please refer to the individual pattern instruction for details.

Modify the Curved Top Slip Pocket Pattern

Most of the pocket patterns included in this book have a curved top. You can definitely make a flat top slip pocket if you prefer to have a flat top slip pocket while making your own bag, as shown below. Making both the flat and curved top pockets have the same steps, so let's get started.

You may have the pocket pattern pieces similar to the one show here (Figure 1). If you prefer to have a flat top pocket instead of curved one, then cut the pattern piece at ❶ or ❷, or any straight line in between. Since the pattern does not include seam allowance, after cutting the pattern out, do NOT forget to add the seam allowance of your choice all the way around the pattern before cutting any fabric.

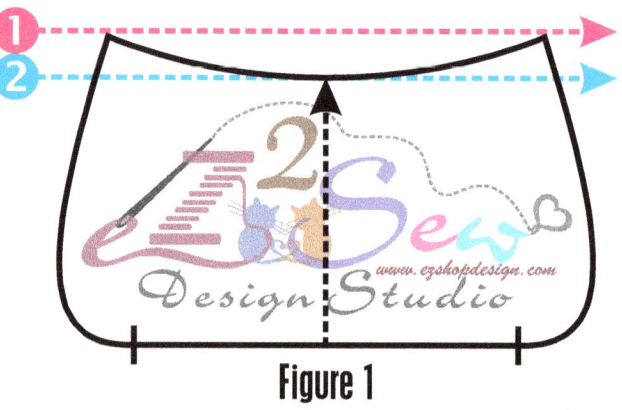

Figure 1

Construct the Slip Pocket - Style A

1 *Right side facing each other.* Place both the pocket Main and Lining fabric Right side facing each other. Align all the markings, top and bottom, especially the center.

2 *Sew the top of the pocket.* Sew the straight or curved line by using the seam allowance of your choice at the top of the pocket ONLY, do NOT sew all the way around.

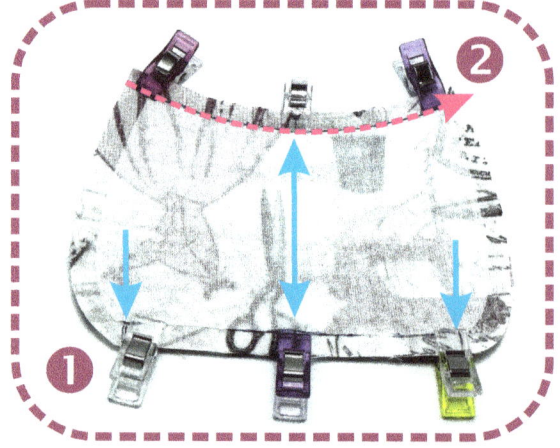

Slip Pocket

Construct the Slip Pocket - Style A (continue)

3 *Make notches.* Use pinking shears to make notches at the curved seam allowance. **NOTE:** *Skip to the next step if you are making the straight top pocket.*

4 *Turn Right side out.* Flip the joined pieces Right side out and align all the markings at the bottom if there are any, especially the centers. Smooth the curved seam with your finger tip, using the iron to press the pocket flat if needed.

5 *Topstitching.* Top stitch at the top of the pocket after flipping the pocket piece Right side out.

6 *Attach to the base piece.* Attach the pocket piece to the base piece, align all the markings, especially the centers. Baste stitch the pocket to the base piece all the way around (except the top).

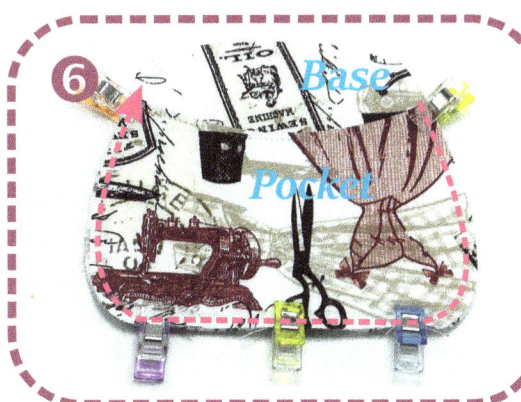

Construct the Slip Pocket - Style B

1 *Get both the pocket Main and Lining pieces ready to connect.* Place the pocket Main and Lining pieces Right sides facing each other. Align the center markings.

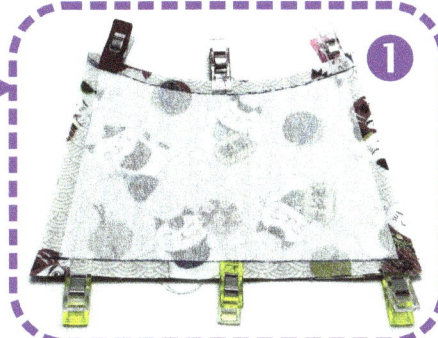

Basic Bag Construction

28

Slip Pocket

Construct the Slip Pocket - Style B (continue)

2. Sew both top and bottom edges. Sew only the top and bottom edges by using the seam allowance of your choice and leave both side edges open.

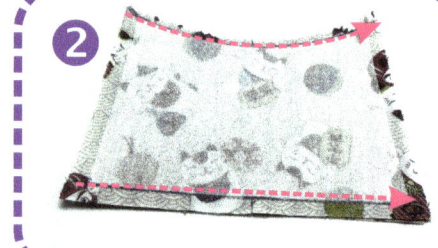

3. Turn Right side out. Turn the pocket piece Right side out through one of the side edges. Press well if necessary.

4. Topstitching. Top stitch the top edge ONLY by using the seam allowance 1/16" (2 mm).

5. Connect the pocket piece to the base piece. Place the pocket Main fabric Right side facing up on top of the base piece, align all the centers, the pocket top, right, and left corners, and the bottom center to the marking on the base piece.

6. Attach to the base piece. Sew to close the pocket bottom and attach to the base piece (please refer to the "Pocket" pattern).

Construct the Slip Pocket - Style C

1. Cutting the fabric. If you would like the Main and Lining of your pocket to have the same fabric, fold the fabric in half. Line up the pattern on your fabric where ⌒ is aligned with the folded side. Add seam allowance all the way around except for the side with the marking. Cut this piece out. Or, if you want different fabric for the Main and Lining, cut 2 pieces out adding the seam allowance all the way around the pattern.

📢 **NOTE:** Add the seam allowance of your choice before cutting any fabric.

Slip Pocket

Construct the Slip Pocket - Style C (continue)

2 *Fold the pocket in half at the longer side.* Align the centers.

 NOTE: If you are using 2 pieces of fabric, connect both pieces at the top first.

3 *Sew both sides.* Sew both sides by using the seam allowance of your choice. Do NOT sew the bottom.

4 *Turn Right side out.* Trim both top seam allowances, like a triangle, to reduce the bulk, be careful to not cut the thread. Turn Right side out through the bottom opening.

5 *Topstitching.* Top stitch at the top of the pocket **BEFORE** attaching to the base piece.

6 *Attach to the base piece.* Attach the pocket piece to the base piece, align all the markings, especially the center. Topstitch the pocket to the base piece all the way around (except the top).

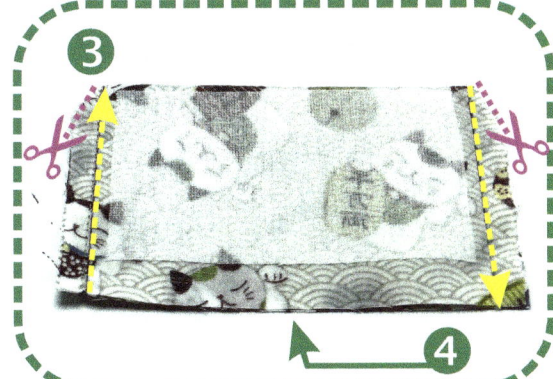

Construct the Slip Pocket - Style D

1 *Cutting the fabric and apply the interfacing.* Add seam allowance all the way around the pocket pattern. Cut 1 x Main and 1 x Lining using **non-directional** fabric for the pocket pieces. Apply the interfacing if needed.

Basic Bag Construction

Construct the Slip Pocket – Style D (continue)

2 *Place the Main and Lining pieces Right sides facing each other.* Align center markings and all the other markings. Place the Main and Lining pieces Right sides facing each other.

3 *Sew both pieces together.* Sew both pieces by using the seam allowance of your choice together. **Leave an opening** on one of the longer sides.

4 *Turn Right side out.* Trim all 4 corners to reduce the bulk. Turn the whole piece Right side out through the opening.

5 *Topstitching.* Top stitch at both shorter sides **BEFORE** attaching to the base piece.

6 *Attach to the base piece.* Align all the center markings, use pins to hold the pocket in place. Sew the pocket to the base piece all the way around and sew everything except the top sides by using the seam allowance 1/16" (2 mm), please refer to the photo below.

divide the pocket into 2 (optional)

Slip Pocket

Construct the Slip Pocket - Style E

1 **Cutting the fabric.** Fold the **non-directional** fabric in half, lining up ⌒ to the folded edge. Add seam allowance all the way around except for the side with ⌒. Cut out the piece and unfold. Apply the interfacing, if needed.

📢 **NOTE:** Add the seam allowance of your choice before cutting any fabric.

2 **Fold the pocket in half at the longer side.** Align both top centers.

3 **Sew the top only and leave an opening.** Sew the top by using the seam allowance of your choice. Leave an opening in the center. Press the seam flat.

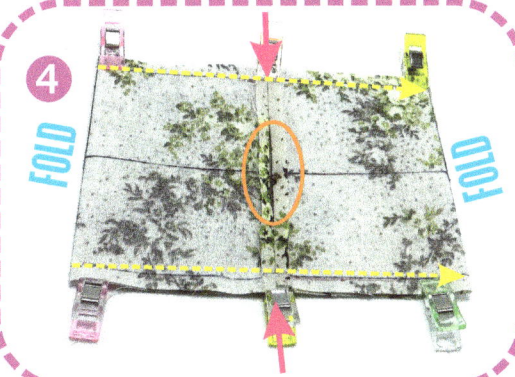

4 **Align the seam to the folded center and sew both sides.** Please refer to the photo.

5 **Turn Right side out.** Trim the 4 corners to reduce the bulk. Be careful not to cut the thread. Turn Right side out through the center opening.

6 **Topstitching.** Top stitch at both tops of the pocket **BEFORE** attaching to the base piece.

✍ For **Directional** fabric: Before constructing the Slip Pocket - Style **D** and/or Style **E**, make sure the pattern on the Main and Lining fabric are facing the correct direction, if not, cut 2 pieces and connect them to become one piece first. Note: Add seam allowance all the way around before cutting.

Slip Pocket

Construct the Slip Pocket - Style E (continue)

7 *Attach to the base piece.* Place the base piece Right side up and the pocket piece Right side up on top of the base piece, which means the opening of the pocket will face to the Right side of the base piece. Use pins to hold the pocket piece to the base piece, align all the markings, especially the centers. Sew the pocket to the base piece all the way around by using the seam allowance 1/16" (2 mm), except both tops of the pocket (please refer to the photo).

Construct the 3-D Pocket

If you see this special marking at the bottom of the pattern piece, this will be the 3-D Pocket piece. Let's understand what this special marking means before starting to construct it.

Understand the Special Marking

*P*inch marking ❶ and fold it over on top of marking ❷. Align both markings and use clips to hold them in place.

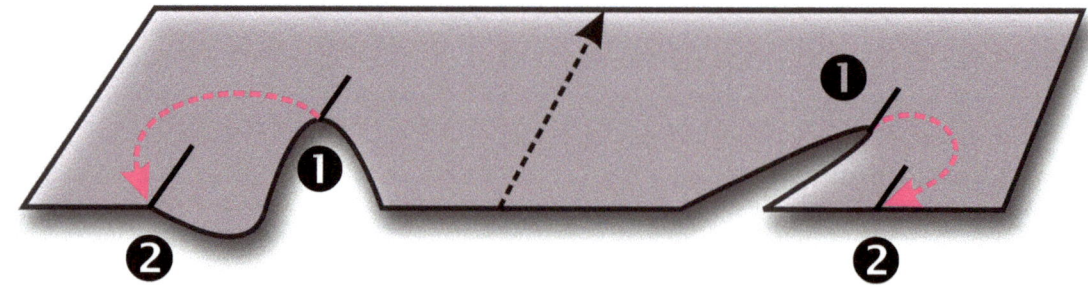

3-D Pocket

Construct the 3-D Pocket (continue)

1 *Follow Steps 1 to 5 from how to constructing the "Slip Pocket".* Please refer to the section "**Construct the Slip Pocket - Style A**".

2 *Create a casing for the elastic.* After top stitching at the top of the pocket, sew a curved (for curved top) or straight (for flat top) line away from the top stitching seam to create a casing (1/16" wider than the width of the elastic you are using) for inserting the elastic.

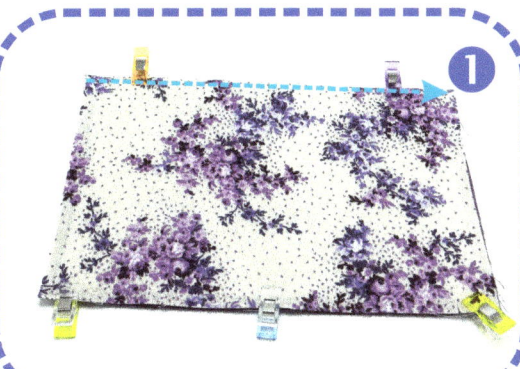

3 *Feed the elastic through the casing.* Mark the desire width on the elastic as the pattern instruction. Attach the bodkin or a large safety pin to the edge of one end of the elastic and insert through the casing.

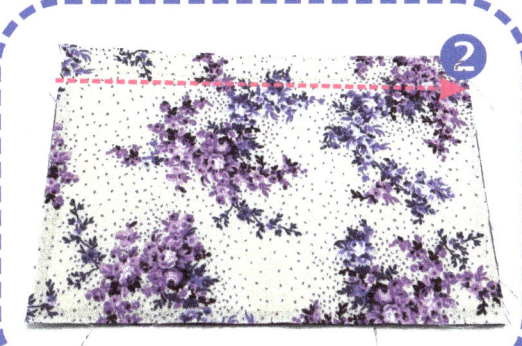

4 *Adjust the gathers evenly and hold both ends in place.* Gently feed the elastic through one side of the casing, use pin or clip to hold the tail in place once reaching the marking. Adjust the gathers as you go. Stretch the elastic until you match the width markings on both ends.

5 *Make 3-D folds at the bottom of the pocket.* Please refer to the previous page "**Understand the Special Marking**" to make 3-D folds at the bottom of the pocket on both sides.

6 *Attach to the base piece.* Align the bottom markings at both the pocket and base pieces. Use pins or clips to hold both pieces in place. Topstitch both pieces to join them together by using 1/16" (2 mm) seam allowance, and then trim the excess elastic at both sides.

Handle
Construct the Handle and D-Ring Tab

There are many ways to construct the handle. You can use pre-made handles if you like, but I am going to use the simple way to make the handle which is the same as making the D-ring tab. There are many different materials you could use for the handle, for instance: quilting cotton, cork, PU leather, leather, vinyl and etc..

1 **Cut the fabric.** Please follow the pattern instruction to cut the fabric, but you do **NOT** need to add seam allowance.

2 **Fold the fabric in half at the longer side.** Place the fabric Wrong side up on the iron board and fold the fabric in half, Iron flat the center of the fabric. (Figure 1 & 2)

Figure 1

3 **Fold both the longer edges inward to align the center and iron flat.** (Figure 2)

Figure 2

4 **Fold in the center and iron flat.** (Figure 3 & 4)

5 **Topstitch the longer edges.** Top stitching both longer edges by using 1/16" (2 mm) seam allowance.

Figure 3

6 For the D-Ring tab, fold the tab in half and slide the D-ring through.

Figure 4

D-Ring tab

Basic Bag Construction

Purse Feet

Install the Purse Feet

1 *Get the Bottom piece ready and apply the interfacing.* You may use a thicker fabric or apply more than one layer of interfacing (for example: Fusible Fleece, Deco-Fuse and Shape-Flex Woven Fusible Cotton) as the Bottom piece.

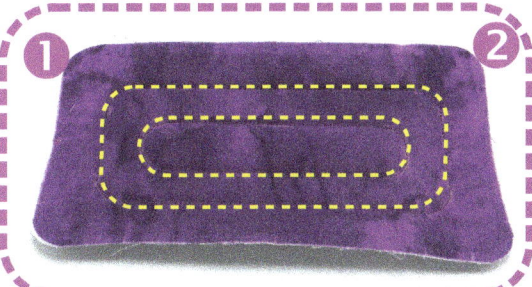

2 *Quilt the bottom piece (optional).* This is an optional step, you may quilt the bottom if you would like to.

3 *Poke the holes.* Use the pattern as a guide and use the awl or seam ripper to poke the hole through all the layers.

4 *Insert the purse feet into the hole.* Insert the purse feet into the holes through the Right side of the bottom.

5 *Flatten the purse feet.* Flatten the purse feet at the Wrong side of the bottom.

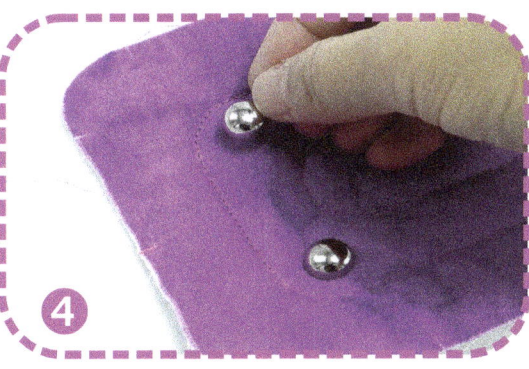

6 *Apply a layer of the woven fusible cotton interfacing.* Apply a layer of interfacing to cover the pure feet for protecting the metal feet against the fabric.

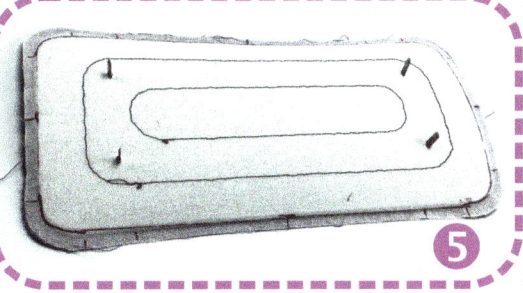

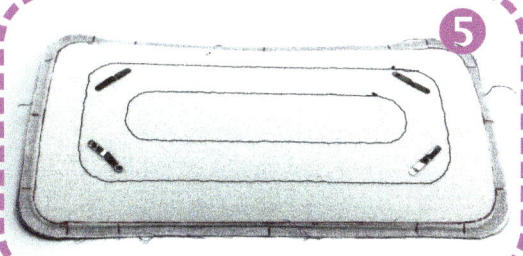

Basic Bag Construction

Zipper Flap

Construct the Zipper Flap Casing

*P*repare the materials and follow the instructions for sewing the zipper flap casing. The casing is for installing the metal frame to the purse. You will need a zipper, 2 x Main and 2 x Lining flaps and a zipper presser foot if your sewing machine has it.

1 **Fold the shorter edge's seam allowance inward to the Wrong side.** Fold the seam allowance on the shorter edges inward to the Wrong side of the fabric and iron flat. You may sew down or use pins/clips to hold them in place.

2 **Align the centers.** Find the centers of the zipper, 1 x Main and 1 x Lining. Place the zipper Right side up and one of the Main pieces Wrong side up at the top of the zipper, align the center, sew by using the seam allowance of your choice. Then, place one of the Lining pieces Right side up at the bottom of the joined piece, sew by using the same seam allowance of your choice.

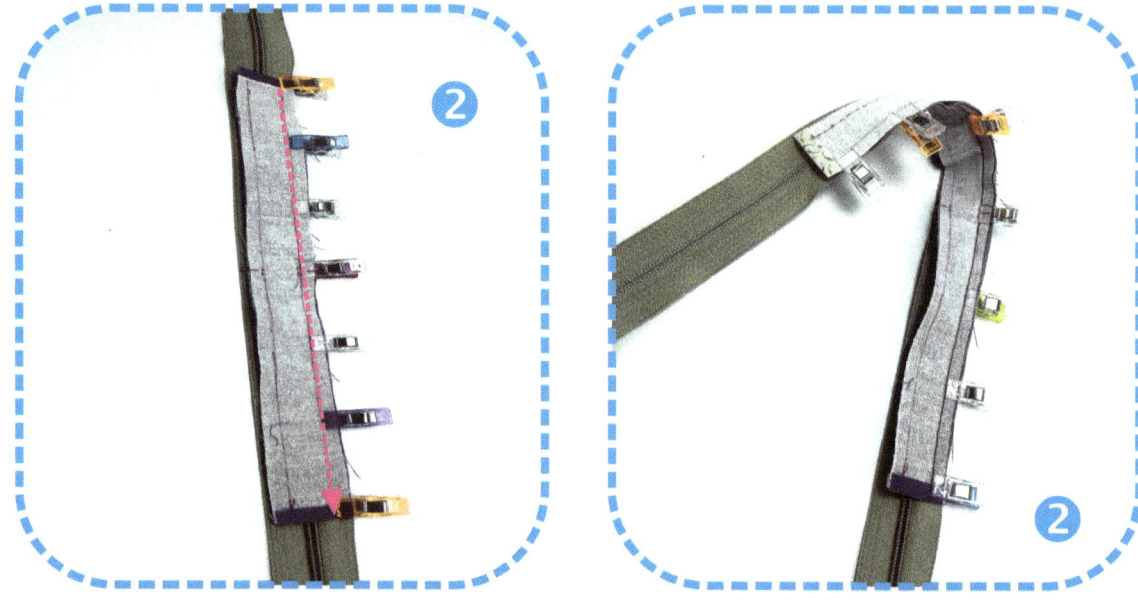

Zipper Flap

Construct the Zipper Flap Casing (continue)

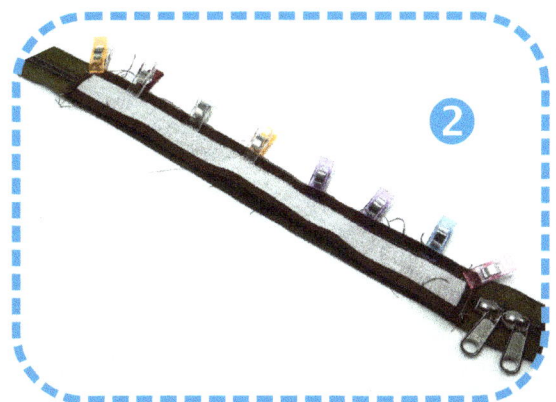

 You may sandwich three pieces together and sew to join them: Place the Lining piece Right side up, the Zipper Right side up at the top of the Lining, then the Main piece Wrong side up at the top of the zipper. Center align all three pieces and sew by using the seam allowance of your choice.

3 *Flip the Main and Lining pieces Wrong sides facing each other.* After joining the three pieces all together, flip the Main and Lining pieces Wrong sides facing each other.

4 *Topstitch and LEAVE AN OPENING.* Top stitch 3 sides only and **LEAVE AN OPENING** on one of the shorter edges for installing the metal frame later.

5 *Repeat on the other side of the zipper.* Align both flaps on the shorter edges instead of the center. Repeat the steps 2 to 4 on the other side of the zipper.

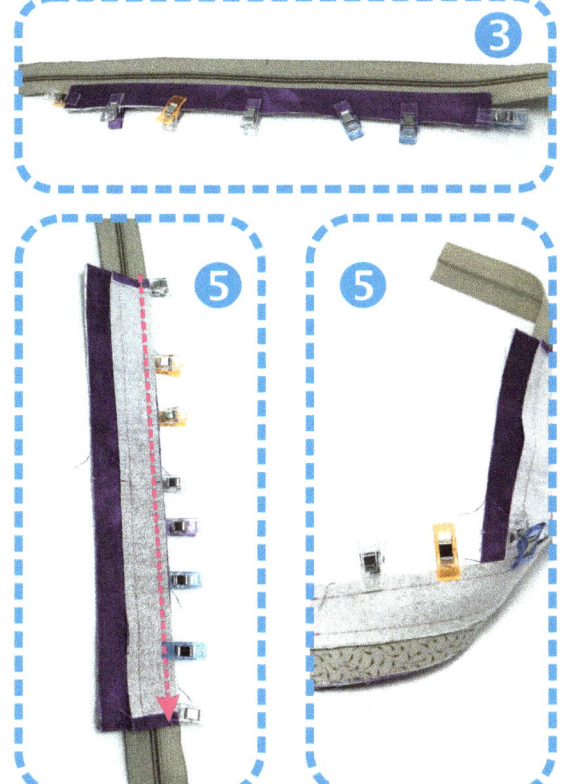

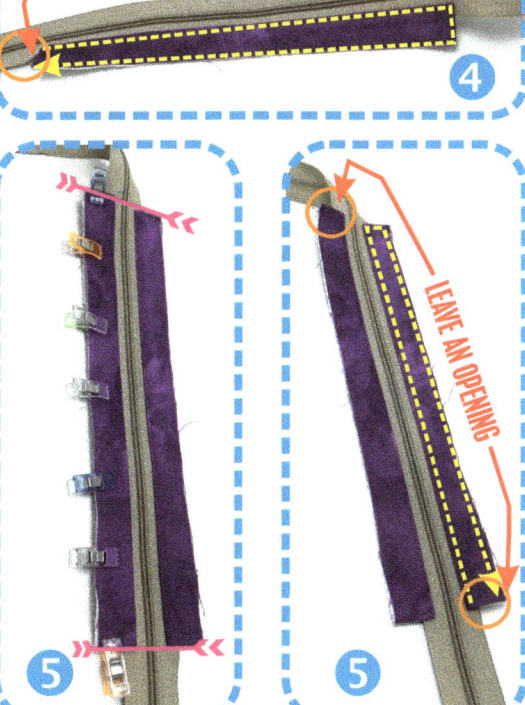

Install the Purse Frame

Frames

There are three kinds of frame styles which will be covered in this book. They are - "Sew-in", "Glue-in" and "Slide-in" purse frames. Most of the projects are finished by using "Sew-in" frames in this book, if you prefer to use the "Glue-in" style, you have to find a frame with the same size to replace it. 2 patterns in this book will need 2 "Slide-in" frames as a "pair" for installation and have to match the exact same width and length as the pattern instruction, otherwise the finished piece won't look as expected.

Slide-in Purse Frame

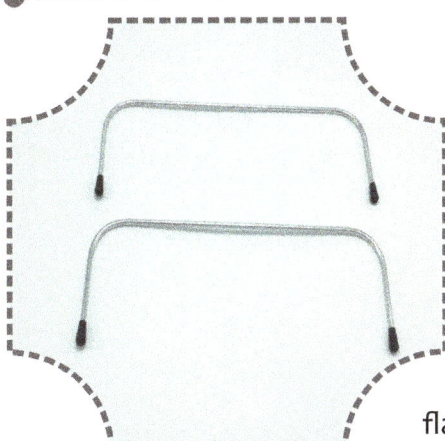

*Y*ou have to use 2 "Slide-in" frames as a "set/pair" for installation and have to match the exact same width and length as the pattern instruction.

❶ **Leave an opening** at both sides of the zipper flap while sewing the zipper flap onto the zipper.

❷ **Slide the purse frame into** both sides of the casing **through the openings**, one frame at each side.

❸ **Adjust and align** both sides of the frames to the purse center.

❹ Hand sew to **close the openings** on both sides by using blind stitches.

It's very easy to install the "Slide-in" purse frame. If you can't find the frames that match the size of the pattern, you could make a pair by using wire hangers instead. Cut the length needed and bend the wire into the same shape and size as the pattern mentioned, cover the wire ends by using tape to prevent the sharp edges poking through the fabric.

Glue-in Purse Frame

★ The "Glue-in" purse frame does not have holes on the frame, unlike the "Sew-in" purse frame.

★ After installation, it will **permanently** attach to the purse piece. It's difficult to remove and can't be reused.

★ Since it needs glue to install, it will get messy during installation and needs time to dry on each side of the frame as well.

Install the Purse Frame

Install the Purse Frame

Glue-in Purse Frame (continue)

You will need the following to install the "Glue-in" purse frame:

- The finished purse piece
- A "Glue-in" purse frame with the correct dimensions
- A flat head screwdriver
- Beacon 3-In-1 Advanced Craft Glue or Gutermann HT2 Textile Fabric Glue
- Fabric Marking Pencils, Tailor's Chalk or Erasable Gel Pens
- A few wet paper towels for wiping the excess glue, if needed

Let's install the "Glue-in" purse frame onto the finished purse piece.

❶ Mark 4 centers on the finished purse piece.

❷ Squeeze the glue into the purse frame track and apply evenly with a toothpick.

❸ When the glue starts to get tacky, use the screwdriver to tuck one side of the purse piece into the frame track by aligning all the centers. Move it around to adjust until it is in the right place.

❹ Wipe off excess glue with some wet wipes, if necessary.

❺ Wait until the glue dries and then do the same on the other side.

❻ Use the flat nose pliers to bend the frame inwards near the hinges to hold the purse piece in place.

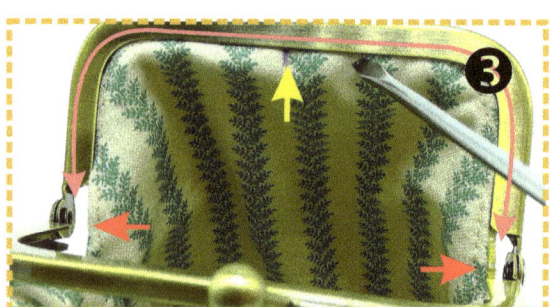

Basic Stitches

efore we start installing the "Sew-in" purse frame to the purse piece, we need to know some basic hand sewing stitches.

Running Stitch

The running stitch is a basic and very simple stitch that most beginners should know how to do. The running stitch can sew straight and curved lines in hand sewing and embroidery. If you don't want to or don't know how to use a sewing machine, using the running stitch with a small interval between stitches works as well.

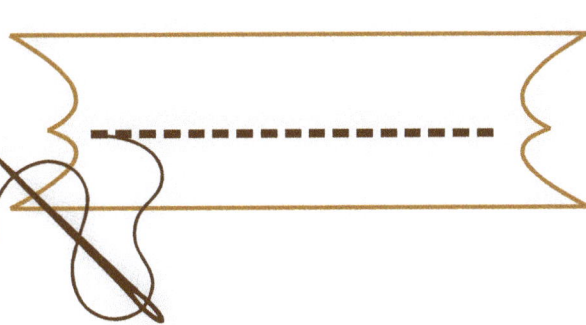

Ladder Stitch

It also called the Blind/Slip/Invisible stitch which is very useful for closing gaps and the opening after turning the purse right side out.

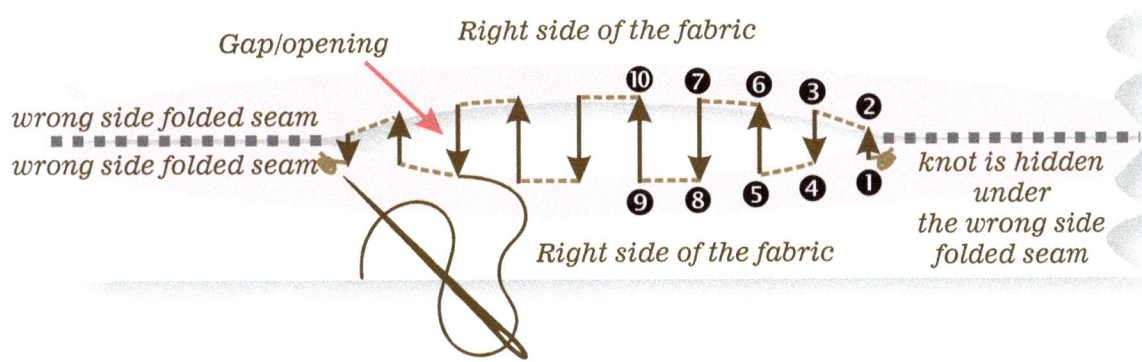

Back Stitch

① If you are using a sewing machine, please remember to backstitch at the beginning and the end of all seams to secure the threads.

② If you are hand sewing, this is another useful stitch to use.

③ A simple Back stitch can be used for starting and ending the installation of the purse frame on each side of the purse frame.

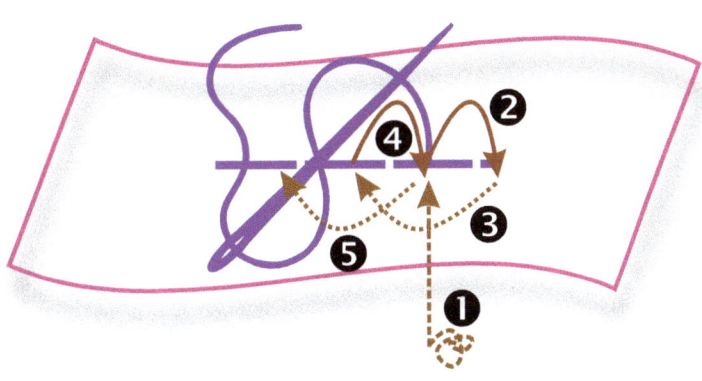

Install the Purse Frame

Install the Purse Frame

Frames

Basting Stitch

The basting stitch is a longer version of a running stitch, sometimes with or without tying a knot at the beginning or end. We are going to use the basting stitch for temporarily holding the frame to the top of the finished purse piece while installing the purse frame onto it. You may use other solutions (using pins or clips) to temporarily hold the purse frame while installing.

Like my book "**Sew Amazing Cute**" mentioned, there are many ways to install the sew-in purse frame. If you are interesting in learning other methods, please refer to the chapter "*Install Sew-in Purse Frame*" for more details. In this book, I will focus on one of my favorite sewing methods, the "Slip stitch". Now, let's get everything ready and start to install.

Sew-in Purse Frame

★ The "Sew-in" purse frame has holes on the frame, so it is sewn onto the purse piece.

★ It can be re-used even after installation. Just tear of the threads and sew it to another purse piece.

★ It is not messy like the "Glue-in" frame.

★ It takes time to sew the frame onto the purse piece by hand.

★ Optional: You can add some beads while installation.

Get the Tools Ready

1 **Needle Puller:** Use on finger to grip and pull needles.

2 **Thimble:** Finger protector. Use on finger to push the needle into several layers of fabric.

3 **Thread Nippers/Snips:** For snipping threads.

Frames

Sew-in Purse Frame (continue)

4 *Screwdriver:* A small flat head screwdriver is used for tucking the purse piece into the frame track.

5 *Needle:* A good strong hand-sewing needle is used for sewing the frame and purse piece together.

6 *Pin and Pin Cushion:* The pin is used for temporarily holding the purse piece and frame in place. The pin cushion is used for storing your needles and pins.

7 *Threads:* There are many types of threads you can choose from, for instance, Cotton threads, Nylon/Rayon threads, Polyester threads and invisible threads to complete the project.

Color of the threads:

★ *Invisible threads -* It won't leave noticeable threads at the exterior and interior. Some of the invisible threads are very slippery. If you are installing the purse frame for the first time, I would recommend using non-slippery types of threads until you are familiar with how the installation works.

★ *Coordinating threads -* You may coordinate the color of the Main/Exterior or Lining/Interior fabric.

★ *Contrasting threads -* If you would like a more colorful project, any contrasting color or rainbow color will work as well.

Before installing the purse frame

1 Get your completed purse piece and the purse frame ready for the next step.

❶

2 Find the centers of each side (4 sides) and make markings by using a fabric pen or pencil on the completed purse piece.

3 Align all 4 centers on both the purse piece and the frame. Tuck the top of the purse piece into the frame track.

4 Use pins to hold them in place. Make adjustment until all 4 sides are aligned into their center positions. Use the Basting stitch to hold both pieces together temporarily, so it won't move around while installing. *Remove the basting stitches after completing installation.*

Frames

Sew-in Purse Frame (continue)

Since installing the sew-in style purse frame is a bit challenging, it wouldn't be an issue if you practiced slowly and patiently.

1 Starting from the inside of the 1st hole, pull the needle through the fabric and all the way through to the outside.

2 From the outside, push the needle through the 2nd hole.

3 Loop the needle back into the 1st hole again from inside.

Optional: Add a bead through the needle before going to step 4.

4 Push the needle through the 2nd hole again, ending with the thread on the inside.

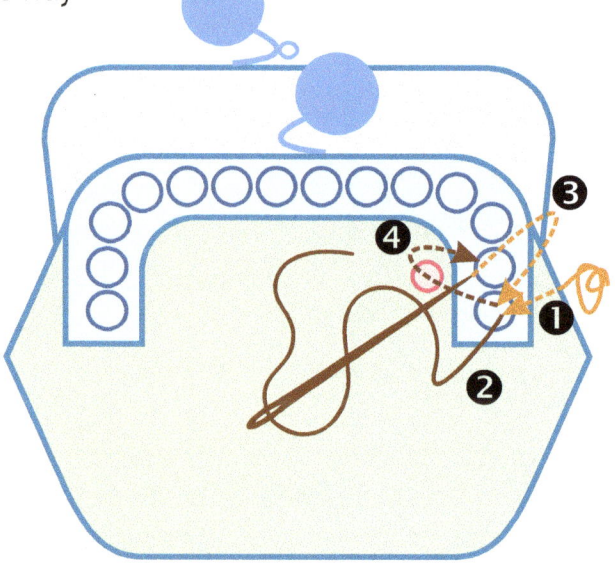

The steps above are called "Back" stitching, securing the thread. We will do these steps again when we reach the last 2 holes on the same side of the purse frame.

 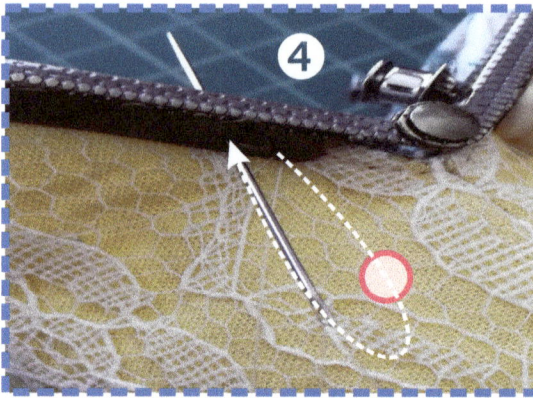

Install the Purse Frame

Frames

Sew-in Purse Frame (continue)

After step 4, the needle should be on the inside of the 2nd hole.

5 Now, place the needle next to the last stitch about 1/16" (1~2mm) away from it, then from the same hole, pull the needle through to the outside.

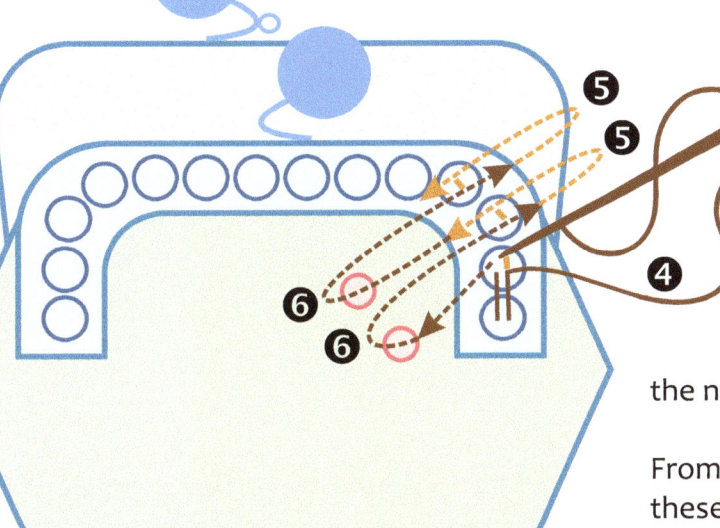

✎ **Optional:** Add a bead through the needle before going to the next step.

6 Moving to the next hole, push the needle through to the inside.

From inside the 3rd hole, repeat these 2 steps until reaching the last 2 holes.

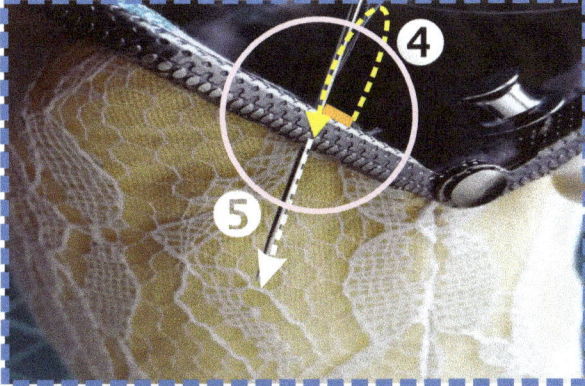
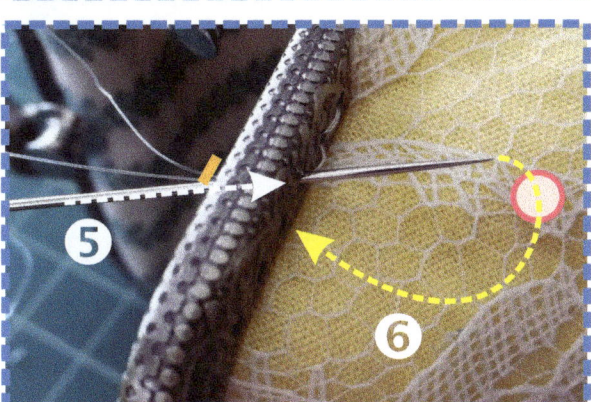
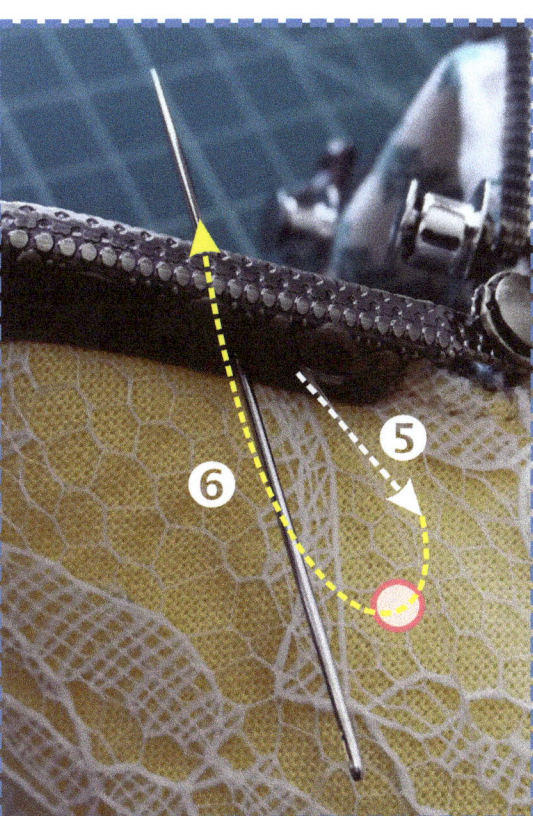

Install the Purse Frame

Frames

Sew-in Purse Frame (continue)

After repeating steps 5 and 6 several times, finally, we reach last two holes.

Optional: Add a bead through the needle before going to the next step.

7 Now, the needle should be on the outside of the 2nd to last hole. Push the needle into the last hole from the outside.

8 We need to secure the thread and do the "Back" stitch, like we did with the first 2 holes. Loop the needle back into the 2nd to last hole again, ending up on the outside.

9 Push the needle back into the last hole, ending up on the inside. Move on to step 10, or repeat steps 8 and 9 one more time.

10 Tie a knot and cut the remaining thread tail.

Repeat steps 1~10 with the other side of the frame. Remove Basting stitches if you used them.

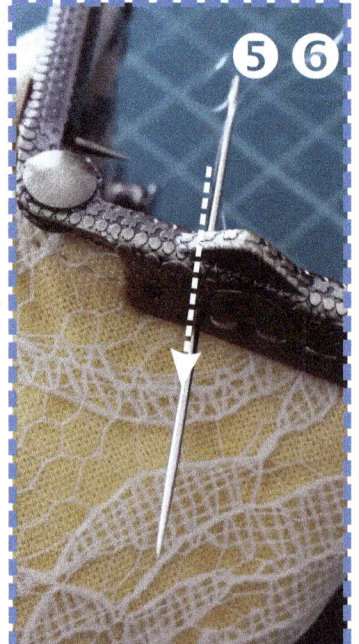 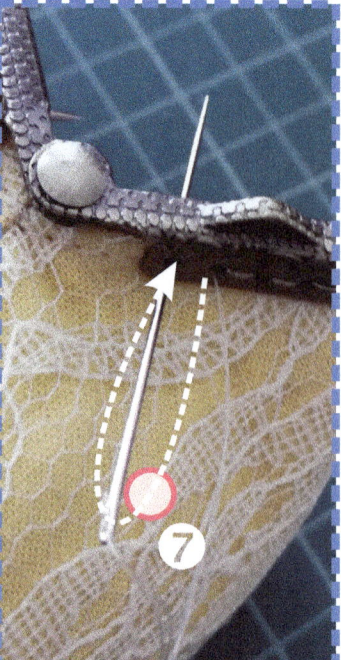 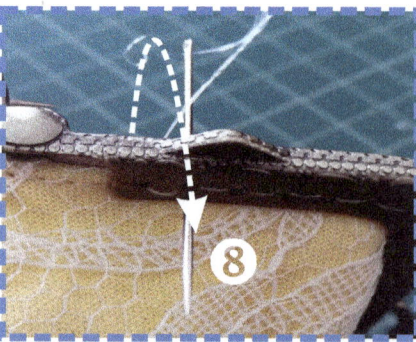 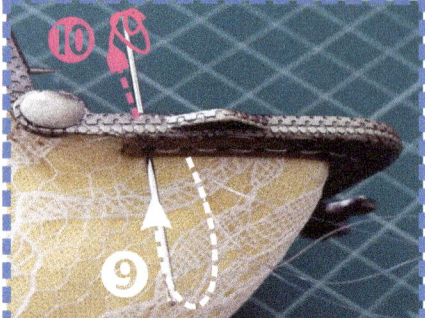

Frames

Sew-in Purse Frame (continue)

By using the **Slip Stitch** to install the frame to the purse piece, the interior will appear like dots under the frame and the exterior will have dashes that connect each hole.

If you are interesting in using other stitches, like the **Running Stitch** or **Back Stitch** to install the frame, please check the book "<u>Sew Amazingly Cute</u>" for more information.

By using the Slip Stitch to install the frame, it will leave small dots in the interior and dashes on the exterior.

Type of Thread
★ *Invisible/Nylon threads*

Color of Thread
★ *Invisible*

There are many ways to install the purse frame. You may start sewing from the center, left or right, depending on your preference and the installing method you choose.

Install the Purse Frame

EXHIBIT

Helena I

I_Rect_V1

4" (Top W) x 2.5" (Bottom W)
3.5" (H) x 2" (D)

Top W: the widest part; H: not including the frame;

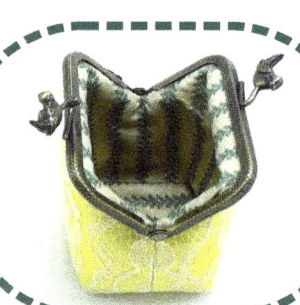

** Finished Size: (approximate measurements) **

Pearl

I_Rect_V1

3" (Top W) x 2.5" (Bottom W)
3" (H) x 1.5" (D)

Top W: the widest part; H: not including the frame;

EXHIBIT
Irene

I_Rect_V1 & V2

V1: 5.5" (Top W) x 4.5" (Bottom W) x 3.5" (H) x 2.5" (D)
V2: 5.25" (Top W) x 4.25" (Bottom W) x 4.5" (H) x 2" (D)
* Top W: the widest part; H: not including the frame;

** Finished Size: (approximate measurements) **

These three patterns were grouped together because they use the same steps to construct the Exterior and Interior. The difference between these three patterns are the size of the frame and the finished purse piece. *"The Irene V1 & V2"* patterns have interior pockets, but the other two don't.

 "The Pearl" - if you have difficulty fitting the fabric into the presser foot on the sewing machine due to the size of the piece, you may hand sew the whole piece using the Running Stitch or Back Stitch.

 "The Irene V1 & V2" - (1) If you would like to add some decorations onto the exterior (like the photos shown above), you might need to prepare the laces and buttons. (2) For adding pockets to the interior - you need to prepare the pocket fabric and interfacing. For details about how to construct the Interior Pocket, please refer to the chapter **"Basic Bag Construction"**, section **"Construct the Slip Pocket - Style D or Style E"** and later in this chapter as well.

PREPARATION

PREPARING ALL THE MATERIALS

 **For NON-Directional Fabrics**

Exterior/Interfacing:

- **Main** fabric - "Front & Back" (Pattern B) x 1;
- **Interfacing** - "Front & Back" (Pattern A) x 1; (no seam allowance needed, unless it's a sew-in interfacing)

Interior/Interfacing:

- **Lining** fabric - "Front & Back" (Pattern B) x 1;
- **Interfacing** - "Front & Back" (Pattern A) x 1; (no seam allowance needed, unless it's a sew-in interfacing)

 **For Directional Fabrics**

Exterior/Interfacing:

- **Main** fabric - "Front & Back" (Pattern B) x 2;
- **Patchwork:** "Top" (Pattern B) x 2; "Bottom" (Pattern B) x 1; Optional: Lace x 2;
- **Interfacing** - "Front & Back" (Pattern A) x 1; (no seam allowance needed, unless it's a sew-in interfacing)

 Tip: Do **NOT** apply the interfacing until all the Main pieces are connected together.

Interior/Interfacing:

- **Lining** fabric - the same as above;
- **Interfacing** - the same as above;

★ Please refer to the Chapter "**Understand The Pattern**" before cutting any fabric and interfacing.

★ **Pattern A** - the original pattern which has "NO Seam Allowance"

★ **Pattern B** - the pattern which has the "Seam Allowance" of your choice (1/4", 3/8" or 1/2")

DIRECTIONS

For Directional Fabrics

 The following steps are for those who will be using directional fabrics and/or making patchwork. If you are using non-directonal fabrics and don't want to make patchwork, you may skip these steps.

Construct the Exterior

1 **Cut the fabrics.** Fold the pattern in half or cut it in 3 pieces, add seam allowance all the way around before cutting the fabrics.

2 **Connect the fabrics together.**

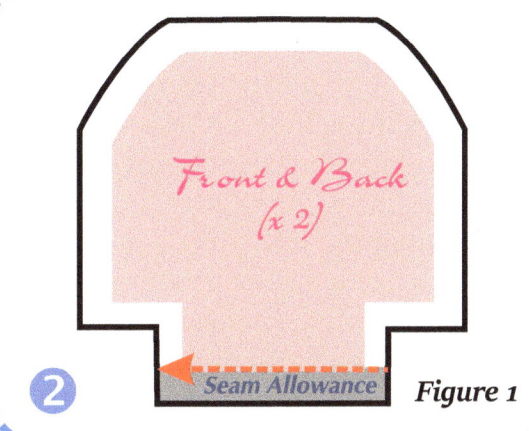

Figure 1

✂ If you cut the fabric in 2 pieces (Figure 1) - 2 x "Front & Back": Connect both pieces at the bottom, Right side facing together. Sew by using the seam allowance of your choice.

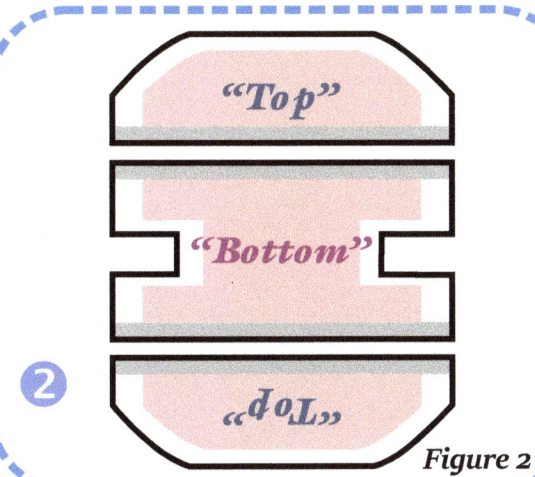

Figure 2

 If you cut the fabric in 3 pieces (Figure 2) - 2 x "Top" and 1 x "Bottom": Place the bottom of the "Top" and one of the flat edges of the "Bottom", Right side facing each other. If you want to add lace (optional), put it in between the two pieces and sew using the seam allowance of your choice.

3 **Press seam allowances open.** Press seam allowances open flat at the Wrong side. The lace can be placed upward or downward, depending on the lace you use and if the lace has direction. Now the Exterior is ONE piece.

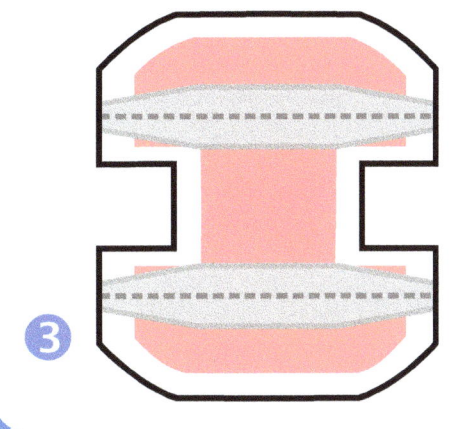

DIRECTIONS

Construct the Exterior

4 **Get the fabrics ready.** You should have one piece of Main/Exterior, one piece of Lining/Interior and both interfacings ready.

5 **Fusing the fabrics.** Apply interfacing to the Wrong side of the main and lining fabrics, following the manufacturer's instructions. Please refer to the Chapter "Fabric & Interfacing", Section "Apply Interfacing" for more details.

 For those using directional fabric and/or make patchwork, you may top stitch 1/8" or 1/16" away from the connecting edge **AFTER** applying the interfacing to the fabric.

DIRECTIONS

Construct the Exterior

6. Fold the Main fabric in half. Fold the Main fabric in half, Right side facing together; Align all the markings, top-centers and bottom-centers.

 Use pins or clips to hold them in place. Make sure all the markings are aligned.

7. Sew both sides. Sew both sides by using the seam allowance of your choice. Press open the side seam allowances.

8. Sew box corners. Fold the box corner, align the center of the side seam and the center marking of the bottom; sew both box corners by using the seam allowance of your choice.

9. Turn the Main piece Right side out. We just completed constructing the exterior piece. Turn it Right side out and put it aside.

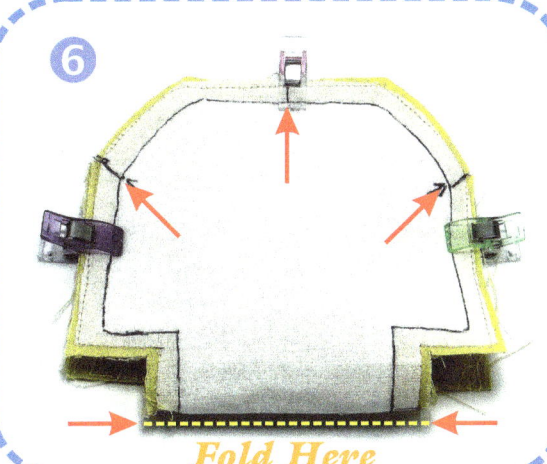

Fold Here

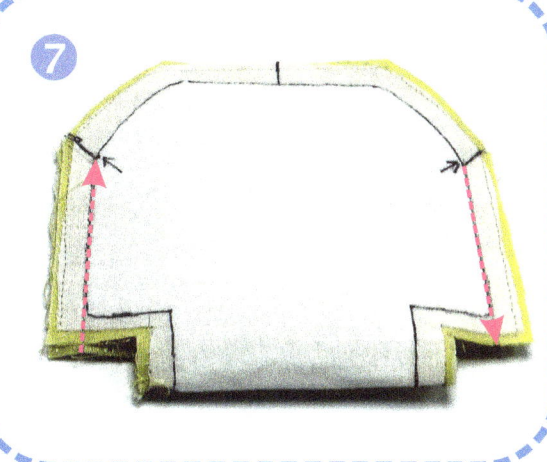

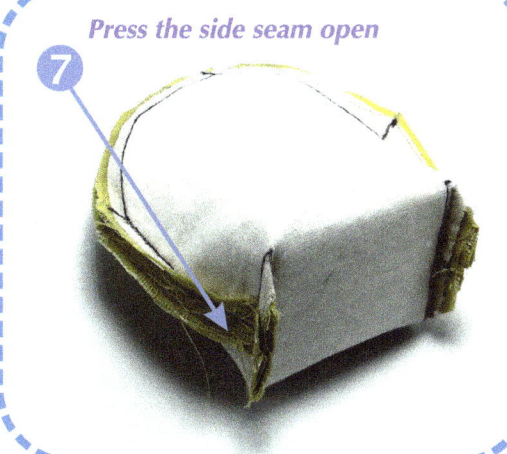

Press the side seam open

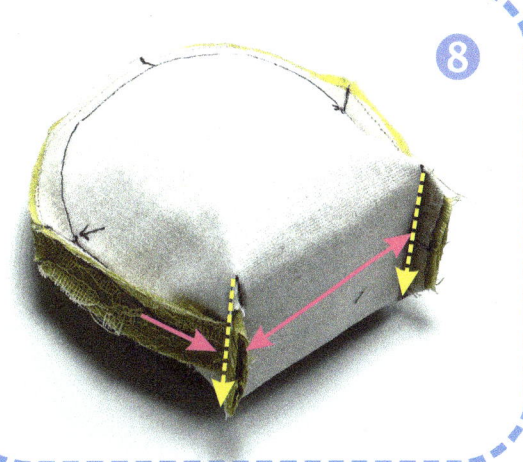

DIRECTIONS

Construct the Interior

1 **Fold the Lining fabric in half.** Fold the Lining fabric in half, Right side facing together; Align all the markings, top-centers and bottom-centers.

2 **Sew both sides.** Sew both sides by using the seam allowance of your choice. Press open the side seam allowances.

 *You may either leave an opening here or do it later while connecting both the exterior and interior. The opening is for turning the whole piece Right side out.*

3 **Sew box corners.** Fold the box corner, align the center of the side seam and the center marking of the bottom; sew both box corners by using the seam allowance of your choice.

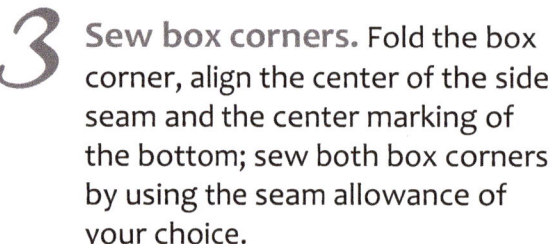

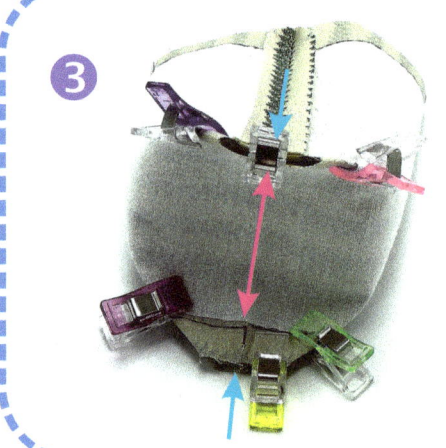

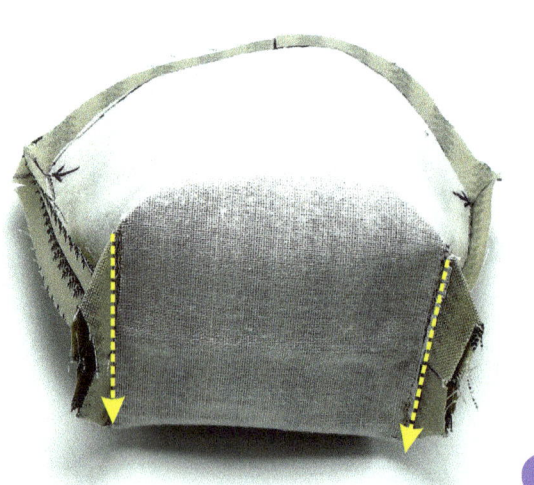

DIRECTIONS

Complete the Purse piece

1 **Connect both Main and Lining pieces.** You should have both Main and Lining pieces ready to complete the purse piece. Place the Main piece (Right side out) into the Lining piece (Wrong side out), with the Right sides of both pieces facing each other. Align all 4 center markings.

✏️ *Use chalk or erasable pen to draw the seam line on the Wrong side of the Lining before sewing.*

2 **Sew all the way around the top and leave an opening** to connect both pieces with the seam allowance of your choice. Use Pinking Shears to trim the excess or cut notches on the curved seam. Clip the tops of both side seams.

3 **Turn Right side out.** Turn the whole purse piece Right side out through the opening. Use your finger tip or something pointy (but not sharp) to round out the top curved seam.

4 **Press well.** Use an iron to press the purse piece with a bit of steam to remove wrinkles if necessary.

DIRECTIONS

Complete the Purse piece

5 Fold the opening seam allowance inward. Use clips or pins to hold it in place.

6 Topstitching. Top stitch all the way around the top edge by using 1/16" seam allowance.

 Do NOT use a seam allowance larger than 1/8", even though the top edge will be under the frame; using a seam allowance smaller than 1/8" will work well.

7 Mark all 4 centers. Press well if needed. Use chalk or erasable pen to mark all 4 centers.

Install the purse frame

1 Install the purse frame. Get the correct size and shape purse frame ready to install to the completed purse piece.

 Please refer to the Chapter "Install the Purse Frame".

DIRECTIONS

Construct the Interior Pocket

There are two ways to construct "*The Irene*" "Interior Pocket" depend on how you cut the fabric.

 Cut 2 pieces: (1) Add seam allowance all the way around the "Interior Pocket" pattern (Figure 1); (2) cut 2 of Figure 1, one for the main piece and the other for the lining; (3) apply interfacing at the Wrong side of the main piece if necessary; (4) follow the instruction in the chapter "Basic Bag Construction", section "Construct the Rectangular Shape Slip Pocket - **Style D**" for more information; (5) attach the finished pocket piece onto the Lining (Figure 3).

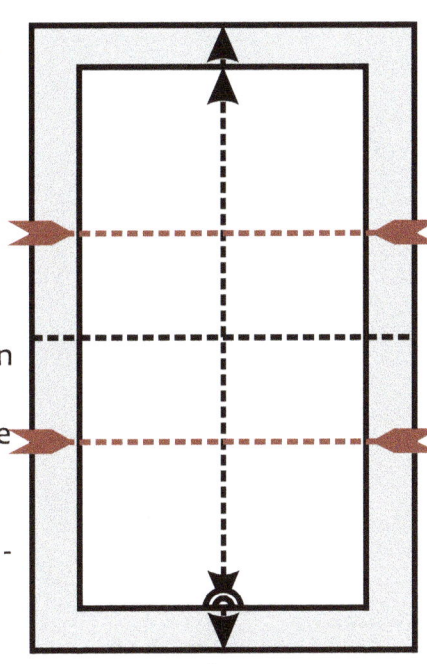

Figure 1

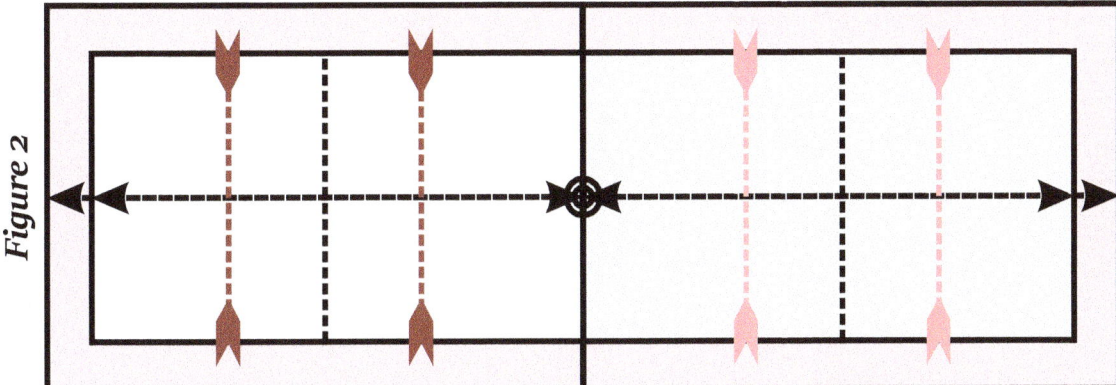

Figure 2

 Cut 1 piece: (1) Please refer to the chapter "Basic Bag Construction", section "Construct the Rectangular Shape Slip Pocket - **Style E**" for more details (Figure 2); (2) attach the finished pocket piece onto the Lining (Figure 3).

Figure 3

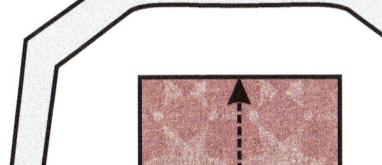

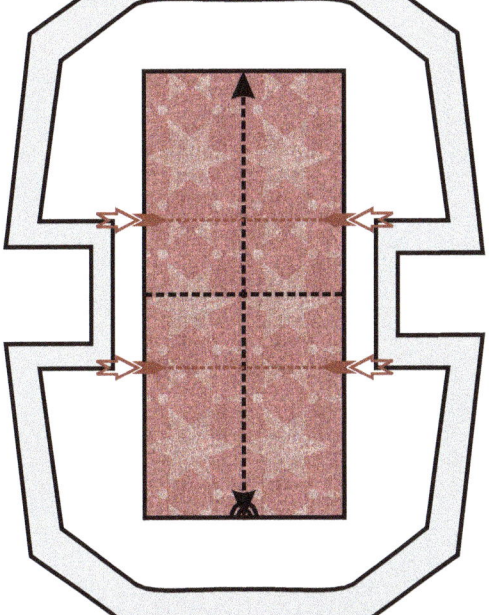

 "The Irene" - Please refer to the chapter **"Basic Bag Construction"**, section **"Construct the Slip Pocket - Style D or Style E"** for details about how to construct the Interior Pocket before cutting and sewing.

> ★ **NOTE:** *The attached pattern has <u>NO</u> seam allowances included. Refer to the Chapter "Understand The Pattern" completely before cutting or sewing!* ☺

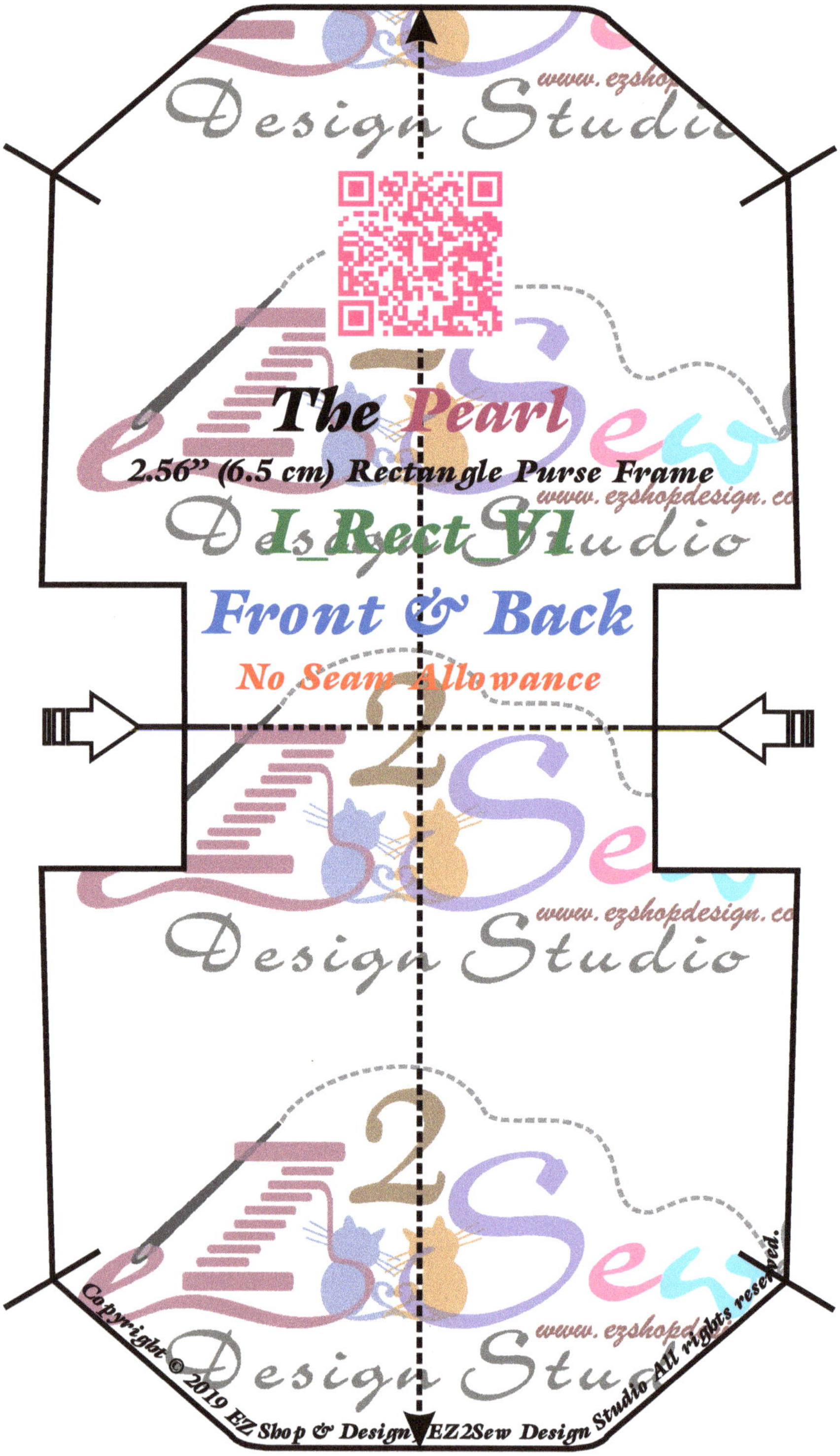

The Pearl
2.56" (6.5 cm) Rectangle Purse Frame

Is_Rect_V1
Front & Back
No Seam Allowance

`1"`

`3 cm`

Printing Instructions

*P*lease make sure your printer's scaling is set to "none," "actual size" or "100%". Do NOT check the "scale to fit paper size" option. Once the pattern is printed out, make sure it printed correctly. Check the "1 inch Square" and it should measure 1" x 1". If the square is not the correct size, check the printer settings again.

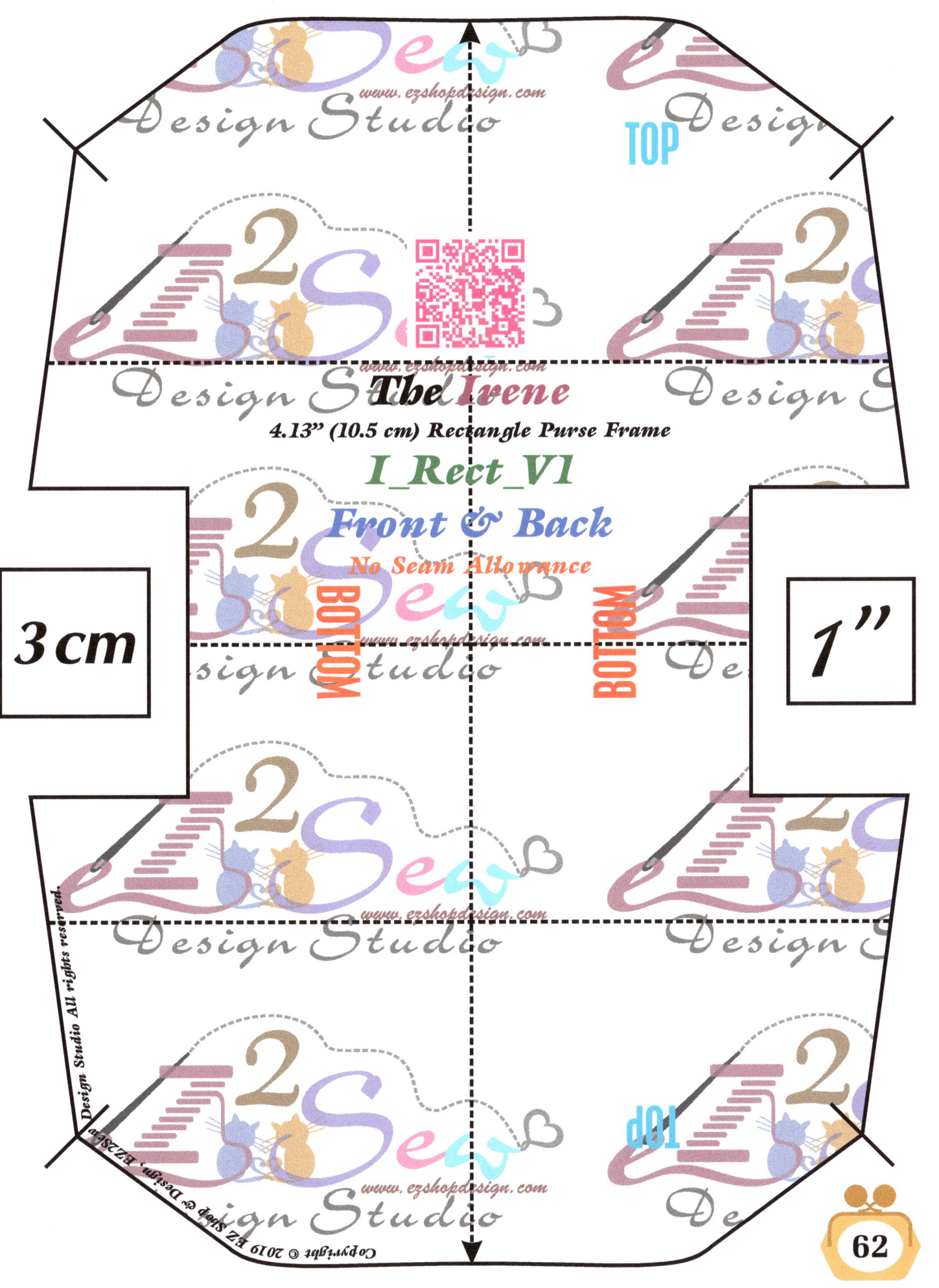

☆ **NOTE:** The attached pattern has **NO** seam allowances included. Refer to the Chapter "Understand The Pattern" completely before cutting or sewing! ☺

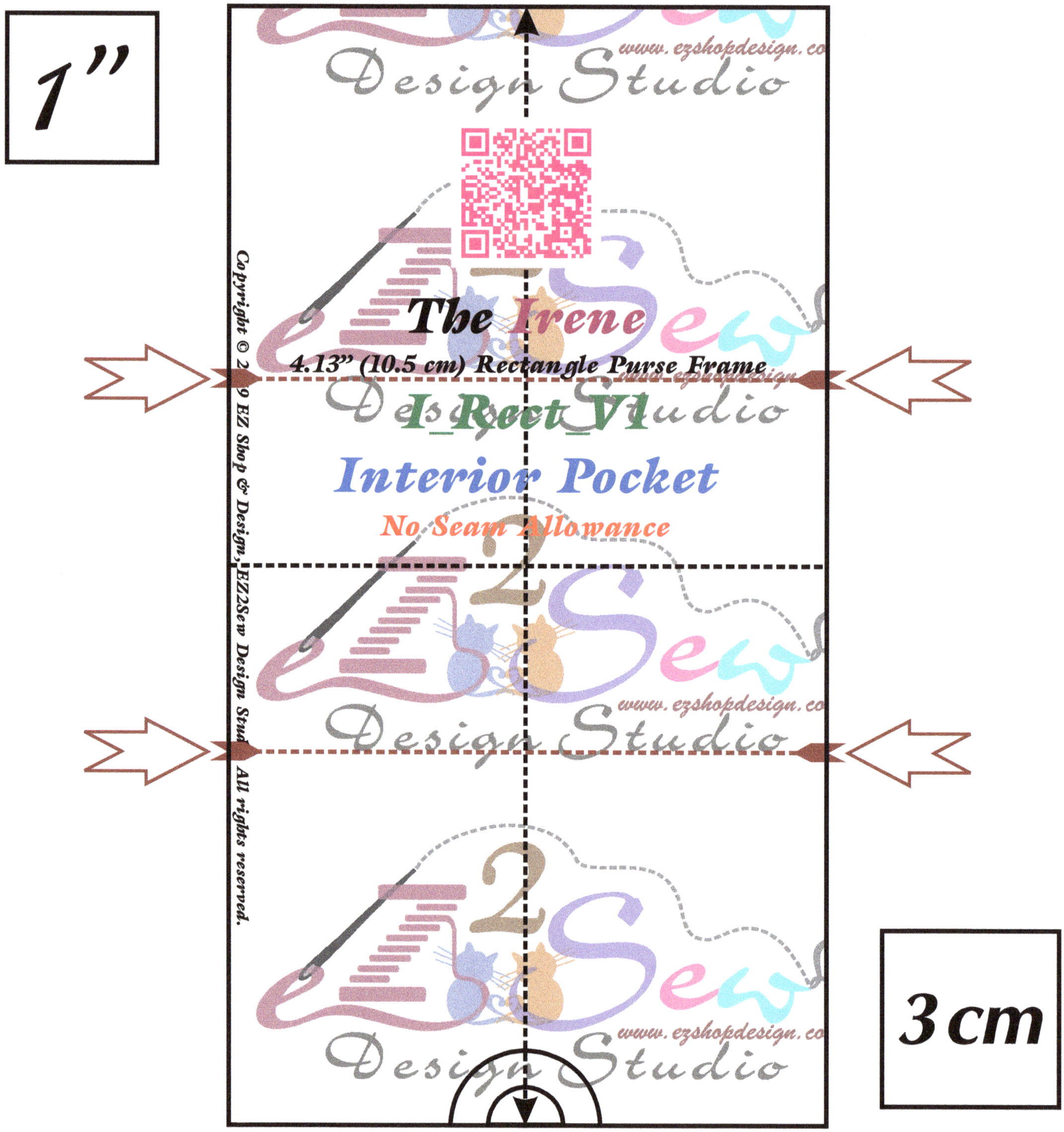

1"

The Irene
4.13" (10.5 cm) Rectangle Purse Frame

I_Rect_V1

Interior Pocket

No Seam Allowance

Copyright © 2019 EZ Shop & Design, EZ2Sew Design Studio. All rights reserved.

3 cm

Printing Instructions

63

𝒫lease make sure your printer's scaling is set to "none," "actual size" or "100%". Do NOT check the "scale to fit paper size" option. Once the pattern is printed out, make sure it printed correctly. Check the "1 inch Square" and it should measure 1" x 1". If the square is not the correct size, check the printer settings again.

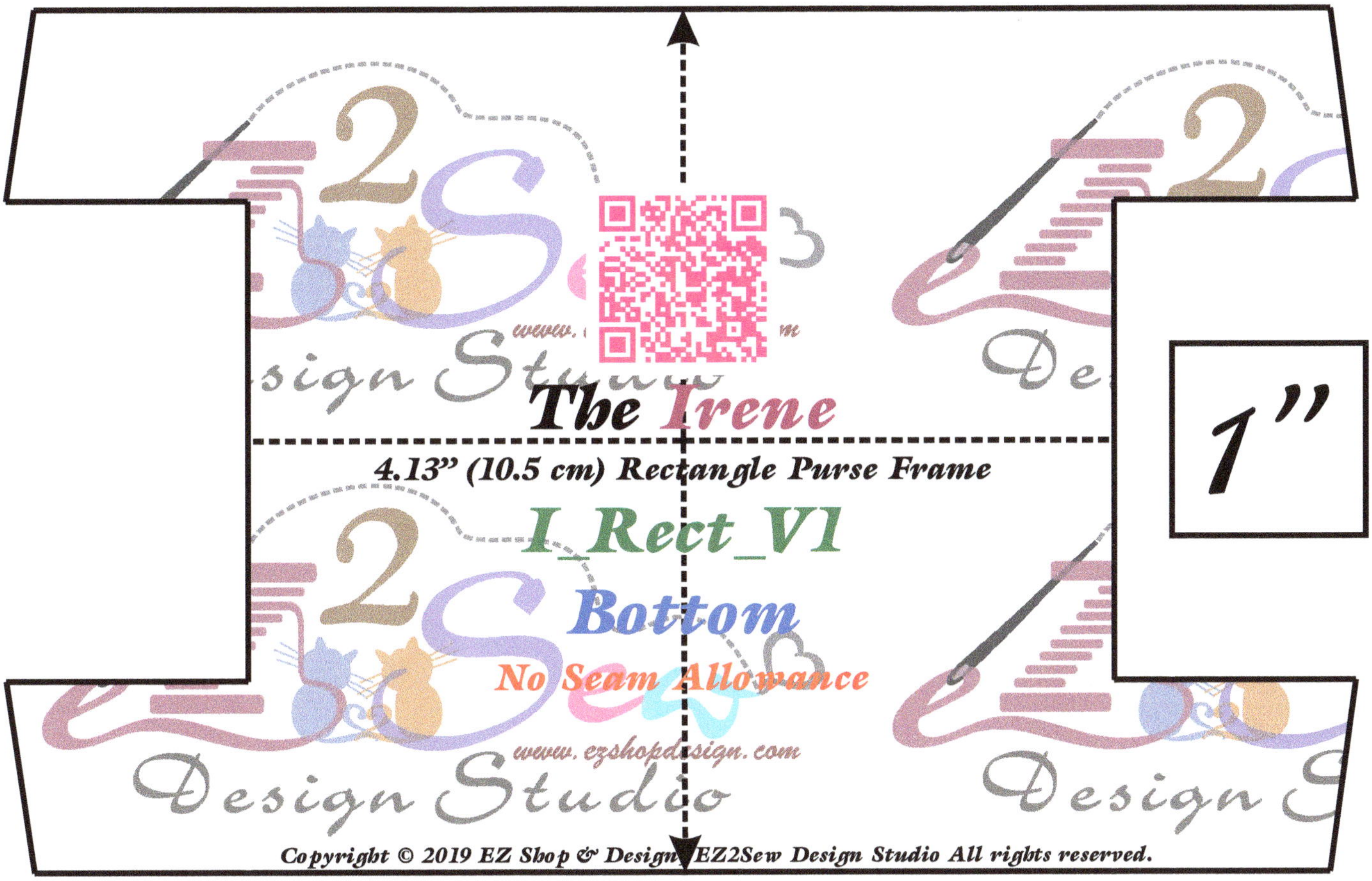

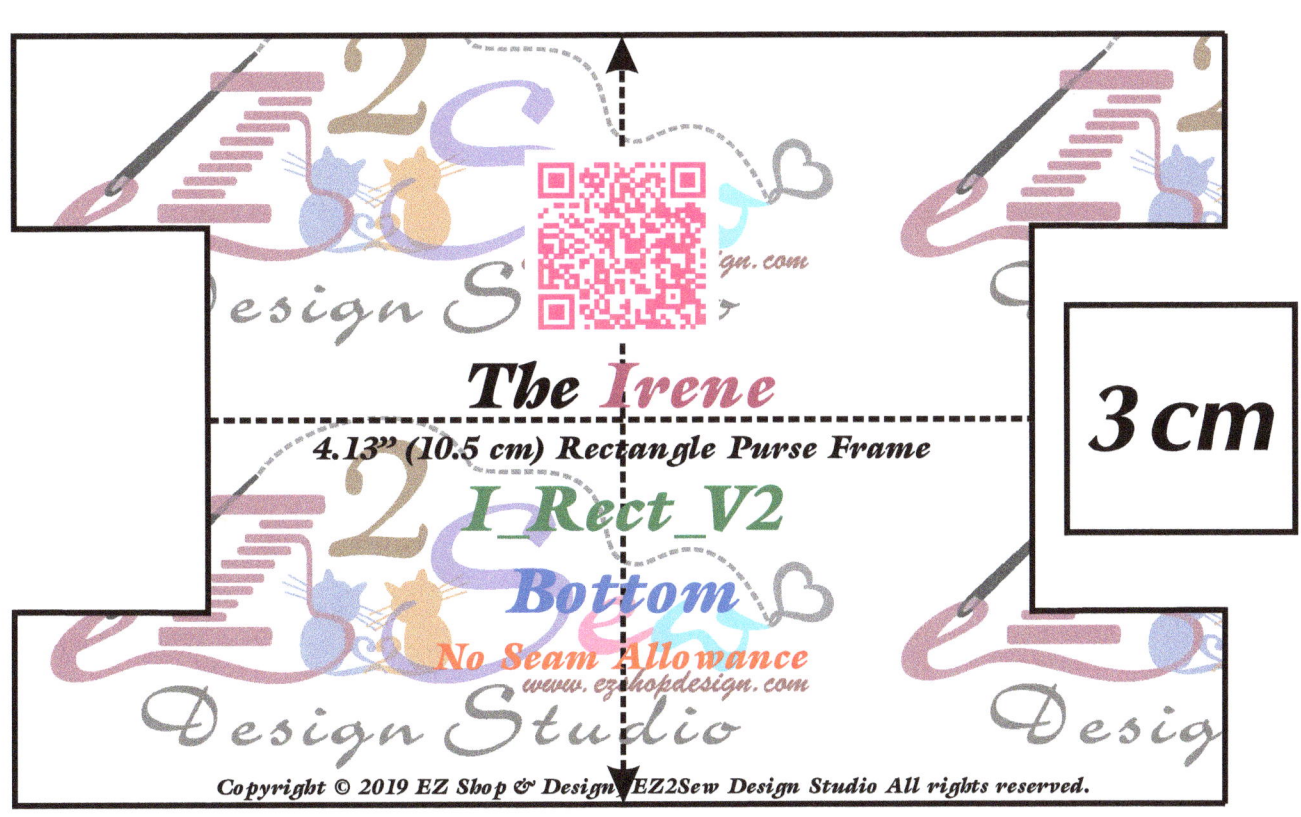

✯ **NOTE:** The attached pattern has **NO** seam allowances included. Refer to the Chapter "Understand The Pattern" completely before cutting or sewing! ☺

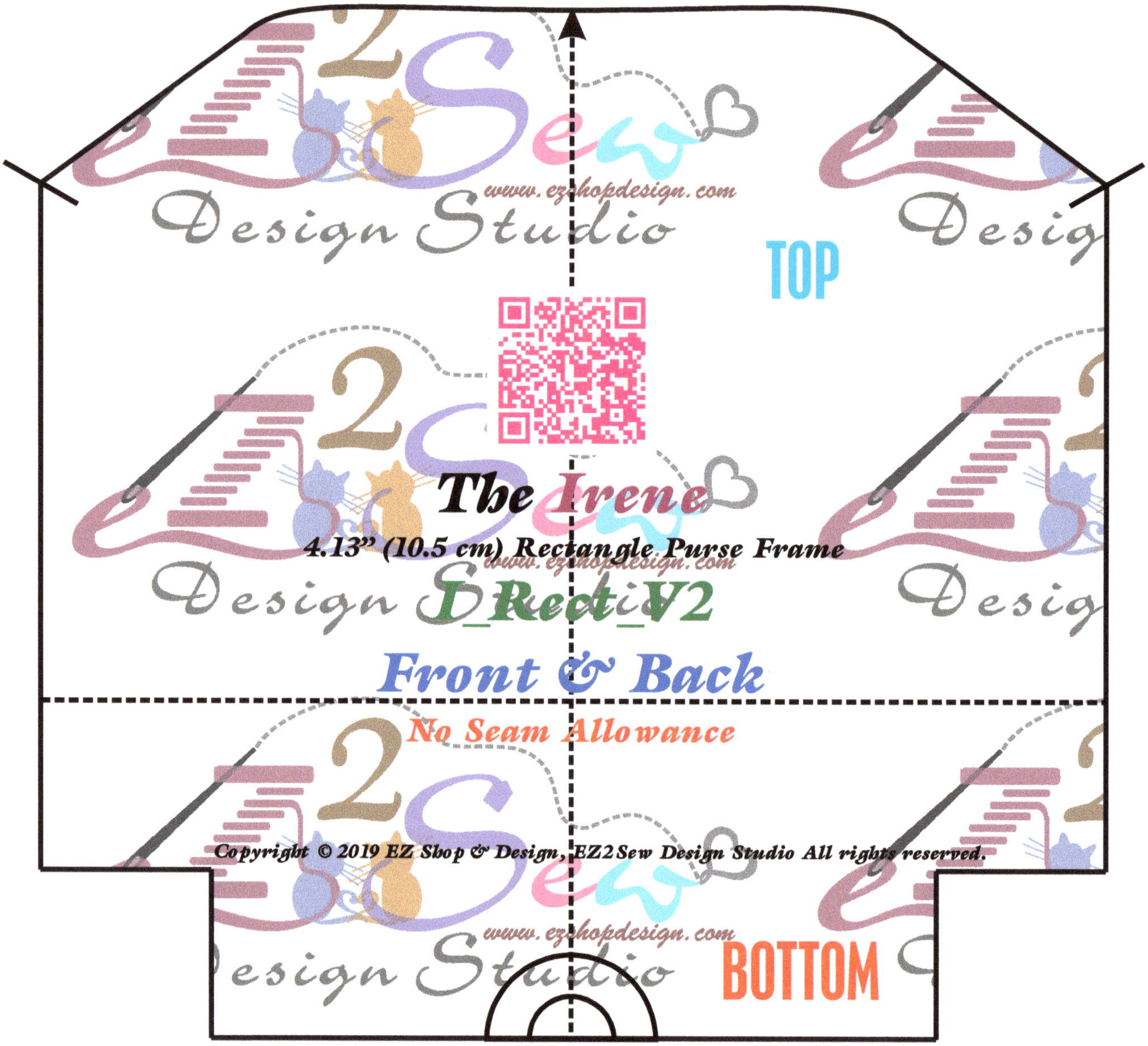

TOP

The Irene
4.13" (10.5 cm) Rectangle Purse Frame
D_Recti_V2
Front & Back
No Seam Allowance

Copyright © 2019 EZ Shop & Design, EZ2Sew Design Studio All rights reserved.

BOTTOM

1"

3 cm

Printing Instructions

𝒫lease make sure your printer's scaling is set to "none," "actual size" or "100%". Do NOT check the "scale to fit paper size" option. Once the pattern is printed out, make sure it printed correctly. Check the "1 inch Square" and it should measure 1" x 1". If the square is not the correct size, check the printer settings again.

> ★ **NOTE:** The attached pattern has **NO** seam allowances included. Refer to the Chapter "Understand The Pattern" completely before cutting or sewing! ☺

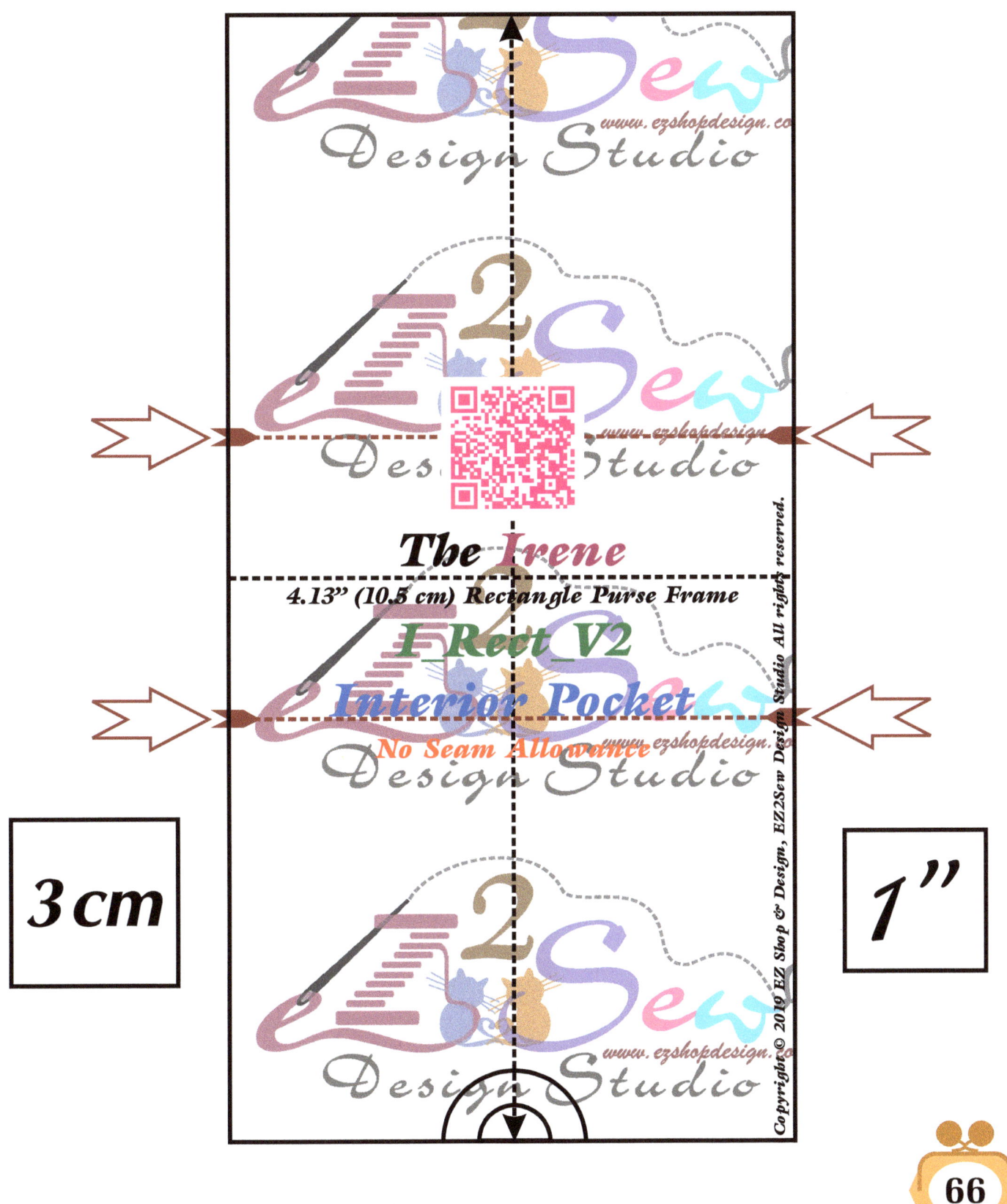

EXHIBIT

Quiana

III_O_V1

3" (Top W) x 2.75" (Bottom W)
2.75" (H) x 2" (D)

Top W: the widest part; H: not including the frame;

** Finished Size: (approximate measurements) **

Quiana

IV_O_V1

IV: 3" (Top W) x 2.25" (Bottom W)
2.5" (H) x 2.5" (D)

Top W: the widest part; H: not including the frame;

PREPARATION
PREPARING ALL THE MATERIALS

Quiana: III_O_V1

✂ For NON-Directional Fabrics

Exterior/Interfacing:

- **Main** fabric - "Front & Back" (Pattern B) x 2; "Side Gusset & Bottom" (Pattern B) x 1;

- **Interfacing** - "Front & Back" (Pattern A) x 2; "Side Gusset & Bottom" (Pattern A) x 1; (no seam allowance needed, unless it's a sew-in interfacing)

Interior/Interfacing:

- **Lining** fabric - "Front & Back" (Pattern B) x 2; "Side Gusset & Bottom" (Pattern B) x 1;

- **Interfacing** - "Front & Back" (Pattern A) x 2; "Side Gusset & Bottom" (Pattern A) x 1; (no seam allowance needed, unless it's a sew-in interfacing)

✂ For Directional Fabrics

Exterior/Interfacing:

- **Main** fabric - "Front & Back": the same as non-directional fabrics;

- ✂ **"Side Gusset & Bottom":** [Option 1] Fold "Side Gusset & Bottom" (Pattern A) in half, add seam allowance all the way around (Pattern B) x 2;

- ✂ **"Side Gusset & Bottom":** [Option 2] "Side Gusset" (Pattern B) x 2; "Bottom" (Pattern B) x 1;

- **Interfacing** - the same as above;

 *Tip: Do **NOT** apply the interfacing until the "Side Gusset & Bottom" pieces are connected together and become ONE piece.*

Interior/Interfacing: the same as above;

★ *Please refer to the Chapter "**Understand The Pattern**" before cutting any fabric and interfacing.*

★ **Pattern A** - the original pattern which has "NO Seam Allowance"

★ **Pattern B** - the pattern which has the "Seam Allowance" of your choice (1/4", 3/8" or 1/2")

DIRECTIONS

For Directional Fabrics

 The following steps are for those who will be using directional fabrics and/or making patchwork. If you are using non-directonal fabric and don't want to make patchwork, you may skip these steps.

Prepare the Materials

1 **Cut the fabrics.** Please refer to the Chapter "Understand The Pattern", before cutting and sewing.

2 **Connect "Side Gusset & Bottom" together.** If you are using directional fabric on the "Side Gusset & Bottom" and/or making patchwork, you need more than one piece to connect them together. (Figure 1)

✂ If you cut the fabric in 2 pieces (fold in half at ①) - 2 x "Side Gusset & Bottom": Connect both pieces at the bottom edge, Right side facing together. Sew by using the seam allowance of your choice. (Figure 2)

✂ If you cut the fabric in 3 pieces (fold pattern at ②) - 2 x "Side Gusset" and 1 x "Bottom": Place the bottom of the "Side Gusset" and one of the shorter edges of the "Bottom", Right side facing each other, and sew by using the seam allowance of your choice. (Figure 3)

3 **Press the seam allowances open.** Press the seam allowances open at the Wrong side. Now, the "Side Gusset & Bottom" is ONE piece.

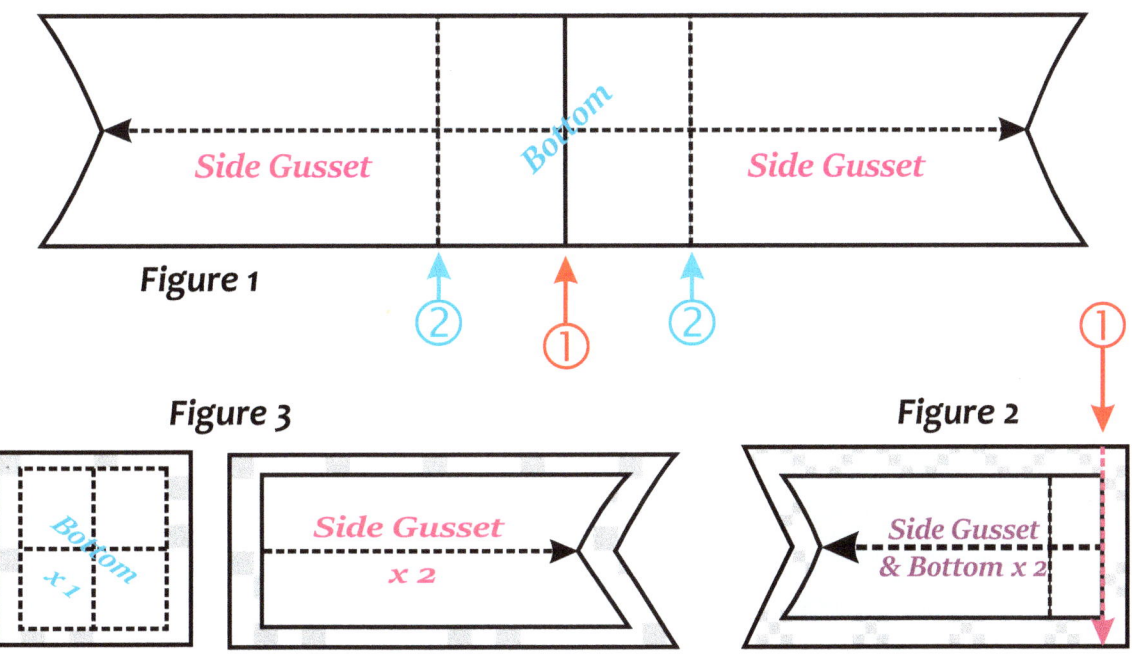

Figure 1

Figure 3

Figure 2

DIRECTIONS

Prepare the Materials

4 **Get the fabrics ready.** You should have three pieces of Main/Exterior, three pieces of Lining/Interior and all the interfacing ready.

5 **Fusing the fabrics.** Apply interfacing to the Wrong side of the main and lining fabrics, following the manufacturer's instructions. Please refer to the chapter "Fabric & Interfacing", section "Apply Interfacing" for details.

 (Optional) For those who use directional fabric and/or make patchwork, you may top stitch 1/8" or 1/16" away from the connecting edge **AFTER** applying the interfacing to the fabric.

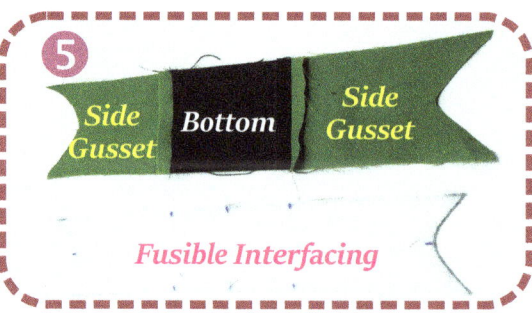

Fusible Interfacing

"Front & Back"
"Side Gusset & Bottom"
Sew-in Interfacing

Construct the Interior

 Please refer to the chapter "**Basic Bag Construction**", section "**Construct a Curved Seam**" to construct the Interior. **Please refer to the photos below as well.** The circular number indicates the instruction steps which mentioned at the section "Construct a Curved Seam".

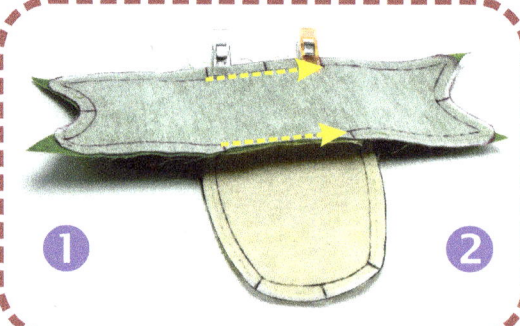

71

DIRECTIONS

Construct the Exterior

 Using the same steps as you construct the Interior.

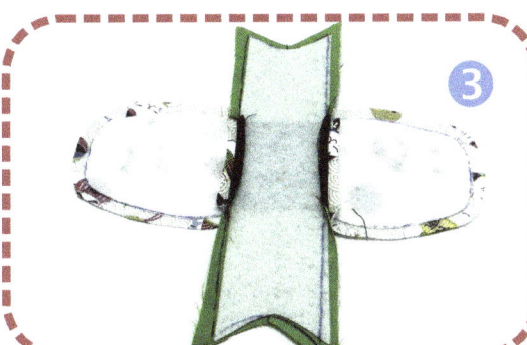

Complete the Purse piece

1 **Get Main and Lining pieces. Connect both pieces.** You should have both Main and Lining pieces ready to complete the purse piece. Place the Main piece (Right side out) into the Lining piece (Wrong side out), with the Right sides of both pieces facing each other. Align all 4 center markings.

 *Use chalk or erasable pen to draw the seam line on the Wrong side of the Lining before sewing.*

2 **Sew all the way around the top and leave an opening** to connect both pieces with the seam allowance of your choice. Use Pinking Shears to trim the excess or cut notches on the curved seam. Make a clip on both side gussets where the valley of the "V" shape is; do not cut the thread.

3 **Turn Right side out.** Turn the whole purse piece Right side out through the opening. Use your finger tip or something pointy (but not sharp) to round out the top curved seam.

4 **Press well.** Use an iron to press the purse piece with a bit of steam to remove wrinkles if necessary.

DIRECTIONS

Complete the Purse piece

5 **Fold the opening seam allowance forward to the inside.** Use clips or pins to hold it in place.

6 **Topstitching.** Top stitch all the way around the top edge by using 1/16" seam allowance.

> *Do NOT use a seam allowance larger than 1/8", even though the top edge will be under the frame; using a seam allowance smaller than 1/8" will work well.*

7 **Mark all 4 centers.** Press well if needed. Use chalk or erasable pen to mark all 4 centers.

Install the purse frame

1 **Install the purse frame.** Get the correct size and shape purse frame ready to install to the completed purse piece.

> *Please refer to the Chapter "Install the Purse Frame".*

⭐ **_NOTE:_** The attached pattern has **NO** seam allowances included. Refer to the Chapter "Understand The Pattern" completely before cutting or sewing! ☺

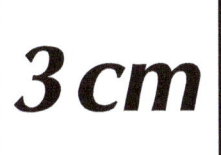

3 cm

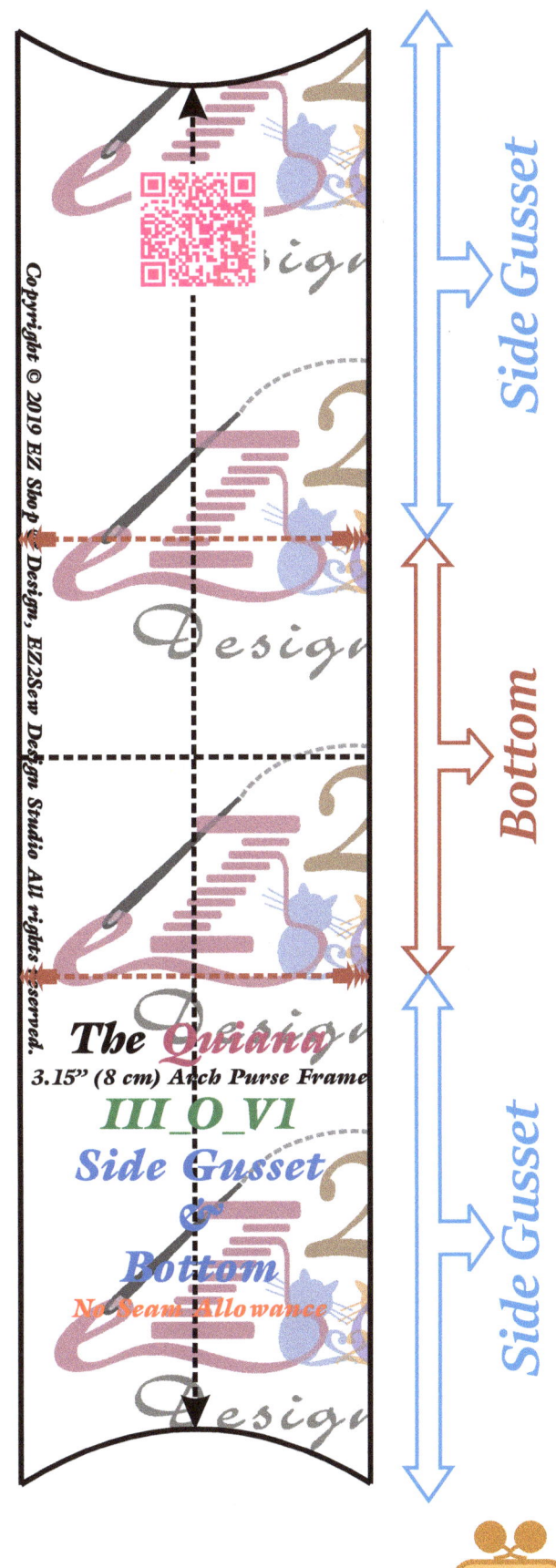

1"

Printing Instructions

*P*lease make sure your printer's scaling is set to "none," "actual size" or "100%". Do NOT check the "scale to fit paper size" option. Once the pattern is printed out, make sure it printed correctly. Check the "1 inch Square" and it should measure 1" x 1". If the square is not the correct size, check the printer settings again.

PREPARATION

PREPARING ALL THE MATERIALS

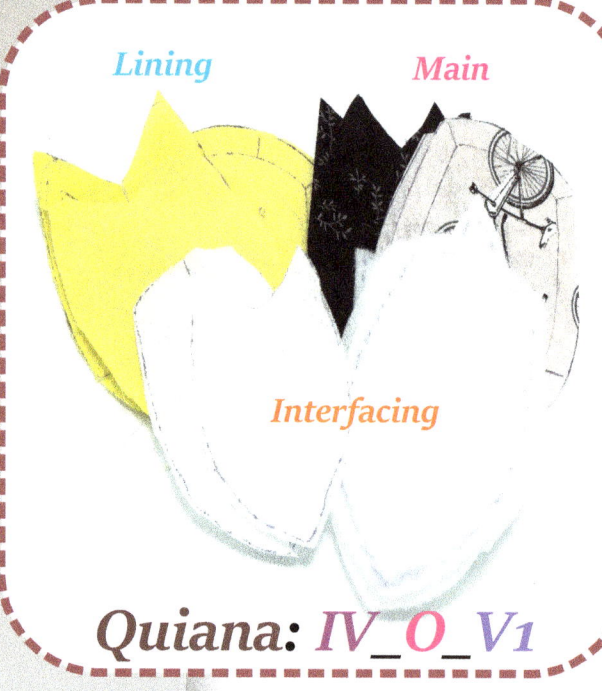

Quiana: **IV_O_V1**

✂ For NON-Directional Fabrics

<u>Exterior/Interfacing:</u>

- **Main** fabric - "Front & Back" (Pattern B) x 2; "Side Gusset" (Pattern B) x 2;

- **Interfacing** - "Front & Back" (Pattern A) x 2; "Side Gusset" (Pattern A) x 2; (no seam allowance needed, unless it's a sew-in interfacing)

<u>Interior/Interfacing:</u>

- **Lining** fabric - "Front & Back" (Pattern B) x 2; "Side Gusset" (Pattern B) x 2;

- **Interfacing** - "Front & Back" (Pattern A) x 2; "Side Gusset" (Pattern A) x 2; (no seam allowance needed, unless it's a sew-in interfacing)

✂ For Directional Fabrics

<u>Exterior/Interfacing:</u>

- **Main** fabric - the same as non-directional fabrics;

- **Interfacing** - the same as above;

<u>Interior/Interfacing:</u>

- **Main** fabric - the same as non-directional fabrics;

- **Interfacing** - the same as above;

 *Please refer to the Chapter "Fabric & Interfacing" for details on how to "Apply Interfacing".*

Reference

★ *Please refer to the Chapter "Understand The Pattern" before cutting any fabric and interfacing.*

★ <u>**Pattern A**</u> - the original pattern which has "NO Seam Allowance"

★ <u>**Pattern B**</u> - the pattern which has the "Seam Allowance" of your choice (1/4", 3/8" or 1/2")

DIRECTIONS

Construct the Interior

1 **Trace Pattern A on the Wrong side of the fabric.** Trace Pattern A (with NO seam allowance) to all the pieces on the Wrong side of the fabric and transfer all the markings as well.

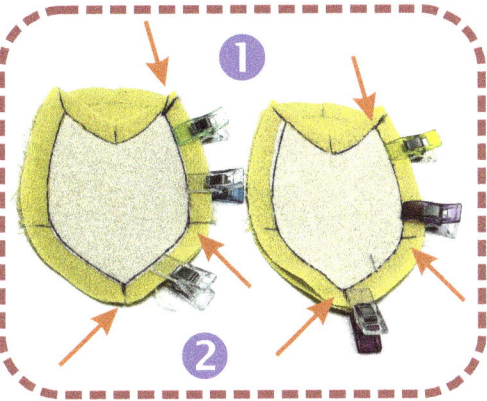

2 **Align Markings.** Place one of the "Front & Back" pieces, Right side up, under one of the "Side Gusset" pieces, Wrong side up. Align both bottom-centers at marking ②, and marking ①. Repeat the same step on the other "Front & Back" and "Side Gusset".

 Use pins or clips to hold them in place. Make sure all the markings are aligned.

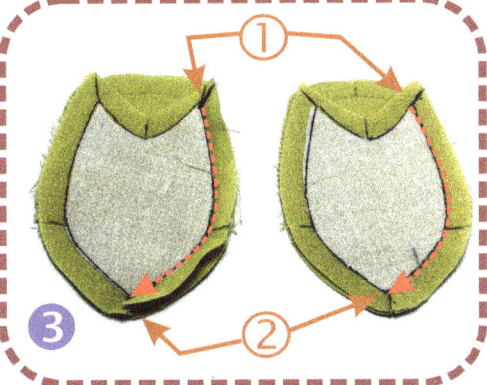

3 **Sew.** Start from ① and stop at ② by using the seam allowance of your choice on both pairs of "Front & Back" and "Side Gusset".

4 **Connect.** Now, you should have two pairs of connected "Front & Back" and "Side Gusset" pieces. Press the seam allowances open. Place both pieces Right side facing each other, align all the markings, especially the center seam at the bottom of both pieces.

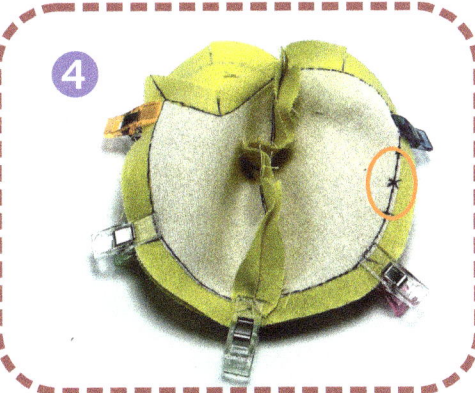

 Make sure all the markings are aligned, especially the center connected seam. If both center seams did not align well, the bottom will look crooked.

5 **Sew all the way around.** Sew all the way around by using the seam allowance of your choice. Start from marking ①, **leave an opening**, and end at marking ②.

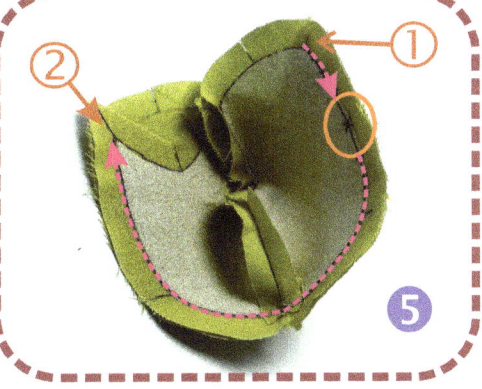

DIRECTIONS

Construct the Interior

 LEAVE AN OPENING at the side that has the **straight** seam for turning the whole piece Right side out later.

6 **Make notches and Press well.** Cut notches or clips at all the curved seams. Press all the seam allowances open, trim the excess if necessary. Put aside the completed Lining piece.

Construct the Exterior

1 **Construct the exterior** using the same process as you did with the lining, except you do **NOT** need to *leave an opening*. Sew the exterior by using the seam allowance of your choice.

 NO need to leave an opening. **SEW SLOWLY** *on the curved seam.*

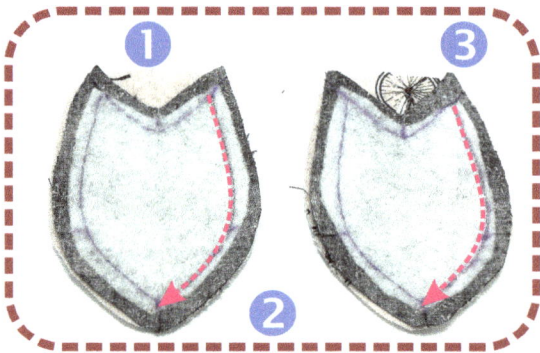 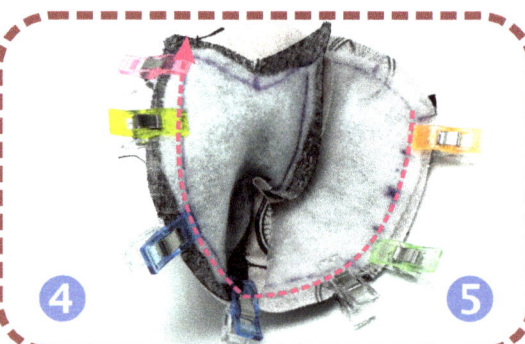

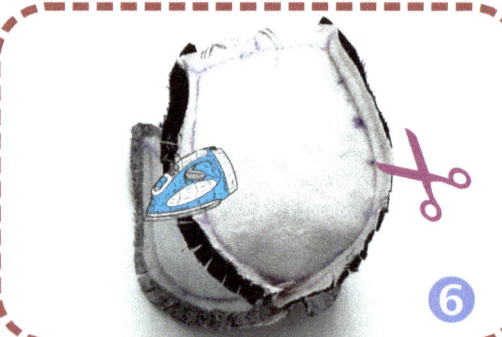 

Complete the Purse piece

1 **Get both Main and Lining pieces ready to connect.** You should have both Main and Lining pieces ready to complete the purse piece. Place the Main piece (Right side out) into the Lining piece (Wrong side out), with the Right sides of both pieces facing each other. Align all 4 center markings.

Use chalk or erasable pen to draw the seam line on the Wrong side of the Lining before sewing.

DIRECTIONS

Complete the Purse piece

2 **Sew all the way around.** Sew all the way around the top edge to connect both pieces with the seam allowance of your choice.

3 **Trim.** Use Pinking Shears to trim the excess or make notches at the curved seam allowances. Make a clip on both side gussets where the valley of the "V" shape is; do not cut the thread.

4 **Turn Right side out.** Turn the whole purse piece Right side out through the opening. Use your finger tip or something pointy (but not sharp) to round out the top curved seam.

5 **Press well.** Use an iron to press the purse piece well with a bit of steam to remove the wrinkles if necessary.

6 **Close the opening.** Use Ladder/Blind stitches to close the opening.

7 **Topstitching.** Top Stitch all the way around the top edge by using 1/16" seam allowance.

Do NOT use a seam allowance larger than 1/8", even though the top edge will be under the frame; using a seam allowance smaller than 1/8" will work well.

8 **Mark all 4 centers.** Press well if needed. Use chalk or erasable pen to mark all 4 centers.

Install the purse frame

1 **Install the purse frame.** Get the correct size and shape purse frame ready to install to the completed purse piece.

Please refer to the Chapter "Install the Purse Frame".

☆ **NOTE:** The attached pattern has **NO** seam allowances included. Refer to the Chapter "Understand The Pattern" completely before cutting or sewing! ☺

Printing Instructions

Please make sure your printer's scaling is set to "none," "actual size" or "100%". Do NOT check the "scale to fit paper size" option. Once the pattern is printed out, make sure it printed correctly. Check the "1 inch Square" and it should measure 1" x 1". If the square is not the correct size, check the printer settings again.

3 cm

1"

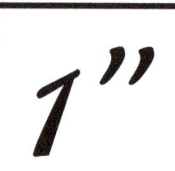

EXHIBIT

Lacy

III_Rect_V1

9" (Top W) x 7" (Bottom W)
6" (H) x 4" (D)

* Top W: the widest part; H: not including the frame;

** Finished Size: (approximate measurements) **

Natalie

III_Rect_V1

6" (Top W) x 8.5" (Bottom W)
3.5" (H) x 4.5" (D)

* Top W: the widest part; H: not including the frame;

EXHIBIT

Unice

III_PL-Rect_V2

8.5" (Top W) x 6.5" (Bottom W)
6" (H) x 3.5" (D)

* Top W: the widest part; H: not including the frame;

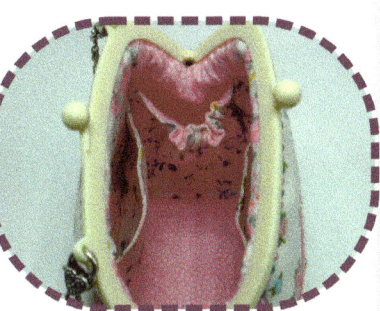

** Finished Size: (approximate measurements) **

These three patterns were grouped together because they use the same directions to construct the Exterior and Interior. The differences between these three patterns are the size/shape of the frame, the size of the finished purse piece and different styles of the exterior and/or interior pockets. You might want to start from the easiest in difficulty to the more challenging of the three - the Lacy, the Natalie and the Unice (V2).

 "The Lacy" - Please refer to the chapter **"Basic Bag Construction"**, the section **"Construct the Slip Pocket - Style A"** to construct the exterior and/or interior pockets.

 "The Natalie" - For details about how to construct the interior pockets, please refer to the chapter **"Basic Bag Construction"**, the section **"Construct the Slip Pocket - Style A and Style B"** and later in this chapter as well.

 "The Unice (V2)" - Please also refer to the chapter **"Basic Bag Construction"**, the section **"Construct the Slip Pocket - Style A"** to construct the exterior and/or interior pockets. For details about how to construct the interior side gusset 3-D pockets, please refer to the section **"Construct the 3-D Pocket"**.

PREPARATION

PREPARING ALL THE MATERIALS

✂ **For NON-Directional Fabrics**

Exterior/Interior/Interfacing:

- **Main/Lining** fabric (Pattern B) - "Front & Back" x 2; "Side Gusset & Bottom" x 1;

- **Interfacing** (Pattern A) - "Front & Back" x 2; "Side Gusset & Bottom" x 1;

Pocket/Interfacing: Each pocket is constructed in pairs (Main x 1, Lining x 1)

- **Slip Pocket (Style A, B)**: Main x 1, Lining x 1; Interfacing x 1;

- **3-D Pocket**: Main x 1; Lining x 1; Interfacing x 1; Elastic 8" (20 cm) x 1;

Natalie

Lacy

Unice (V2)

✂ **For Directional Fabrics**

- **"Front & Back"**: the same as non-directional fabrics;

✂ **"Side Gusset & Bottom":**

  ☞ [Option 1] Fold "Side Gusset & Bottom" (Pattern A) in half, add seam allowance all the way around (Pattern B) x 2;

  ☞ [Option 2] "Side Gusset" (Pattern B) x 2; "Bottom" (Pattern B) x 1;

✎ *Tip: Do **NOT** apply the interfacing until all the "Side Gusset & Bottom" pieces are connected together. If you are using different fabric for the Bottom piece, for example: cork, apply interfacing of each piece individually.*

✎ NOTE: Add seam allowance before cutting any fabric. No seam allowance needed for cutting the interfacing, unless using a sew-in interfacing.

Reference

★ Please refer to the Chapter "**Understand The Pattern**" before cutting any fabric and interfacing.

★ **Pattern A** - the original pattern which has "NO Seam Allowance"

★ **Pattern B** - the pattern which has the "Seam Allowance" of your choice (1/4", 3/8" or 1/2")

DIRECTIONS

$\mathcal{F}$ollow the simple steps below to construct these three patterns. All the pockets are optional and you can construct as many as you like for both the exterior and interior.

1 **Prepare all the materials and apply interfacing to the fabric.** Add seam allowance around the patterns before cutting any fabric.

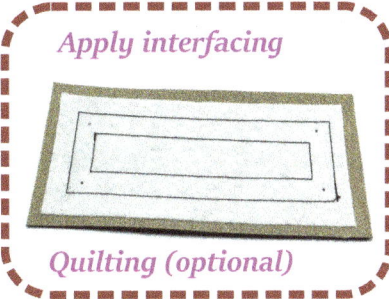
Apply interfacing
Quilting (optional)

2 **Install the purse feet at the exterior "Bottom" piece.** If you would like to install the purse feet, please refer to the chapter **"Basic Bag Construction"**, the section **"Construct the Purse Feet"** for details.

Install purse feet

3 **Connect the exterior "Side Gusset & Bottom".** For those who will be cutting the "Side Gusset & Bottom" into more than one piece, please refer to the pattern directions of **"The Quiana: III_O_V1"** for how to connect the "Side Gusset" & "Bottom" pieces to become ONE piece.

Apply another layer of interfacing

4 **Construct the exterior "Pocket(s)".** Please refer to the chapter **"Basic Bag Construction"**, the section **"Construct the Slip Pocket - Style A"**. You may construct one or two pockets and attach to the "Front & Back" piece, or no pocket on the exterior if you prefer. Cut the pocket fabric in pairs (1 x main, 1 x lining and 1 x interfacing) for each one you construct.

 **"The Natalie":** There is no pocket on the exterior.

Bottom
Side Gusset

5 **Complete the exterior construction.** Please refer to the chapter **"Basic Bag Construction"**, the section **"Construct a Curved Seam"** to complete the exterior construction.

Construct a Curved Seam

Connect the "Side Gusset" & "Bottom" pieces
Bottom
Side Gusset

DIRECTIONS

6 Construct the interior "Side Gusset & Bottom". Do the same as step 3.

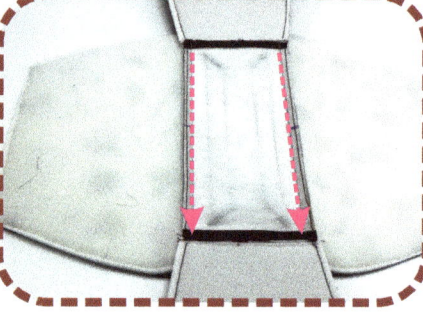

 "The Unice (V2)" - If you would like to construct the 3-D pocket at both side gussets, you <u>have to cut the "Side Gusset & Bottom" into 3-piece</u>. Construct the 3-D pockets before connecting the "Side Gusset & Bottom" and become one piece. For details about how to construct the interior side gusset 3-D Pocket, please refer to the chapter **"Basic Bag Construction"**, the section **"Construct the 3-D Pocket"** and photos at the end of this chapter for reference.

Construct a Curved Seam

7 Construct the interior "Pocket(s)". For patterns "**The Lacy**" and "**The Unice (V2)**" do the same as step 4.

Construct a Curved Seam

 "The Natalie" - For details about how to construct the Interior Pocket, please refer to the chapter **"Basic Bag Construction"**, the section **"Construct the Slip Pocket - Style A and Style B"** and the photos below.

Turn Right side out

 **"The Natalie"** - **Attach Pocket(1) and Pocket(2) to the Lining "Front & Back" piece** - Place Pocket(2) on top of Pocket(1) which has already been attached (Figure 1); Align the centers; Baste stitch all the way around, except the top; You may also divide the pocket from the center, please refer to the photo (Figure 2).

Figure 1

Figure 2

DIRECTIONS

8 Complete the interior construction. Do the same as step 5.

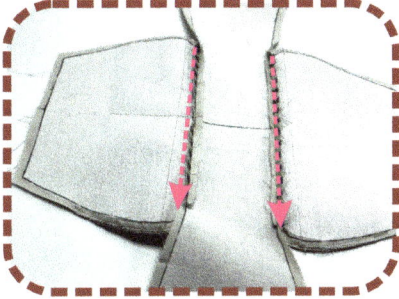

9 Complete the purse piece and install the purse frame. Please refer to the Pattern "**The Quiana: III_O_V1**" for details.

 *Please refer to the Pattern "**The Quiana: III_O_V1**" directions for details of the "Complete the Purse piece", "Install the purse frame" and photos below.*

The Unice (V2): Construct the 3-D Pocket

Connect main and lining

Flip the Pocket to the Right side
Topstitching

Create a casing

DIRECTIONS

The Unice (V2): Construct the 3-D Pocket (continue)

Mark 4" from center on the elastic

Push the elastic through the casing

Create a 3-D fold

Create a 3-D fold

Hold both folds in place

Place the 3-D pocket on top of the Side Gusset

Attach the pocket to the Side Gusset

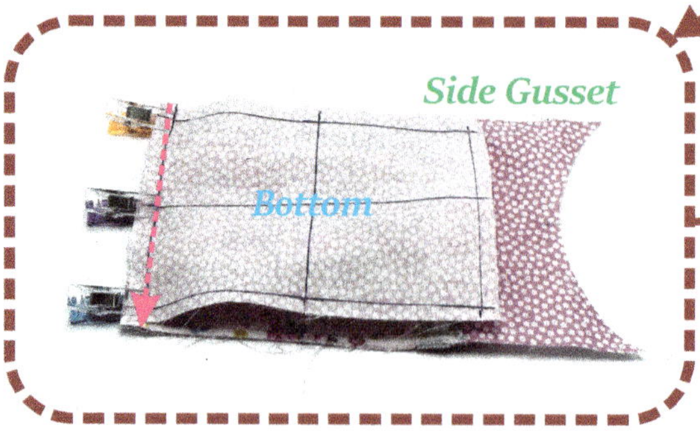

Side Gusset

Bottom

Side Gusset

Bottom

Connect both "Side Gussets" with the 3-D Pocket attached to the "Bottom"

> ★ **NOTE:** The attached pattern has **NO** seam allowances included. Refer to the Chapter "Understand The Pattern" completely before cutting or sewing! ☺

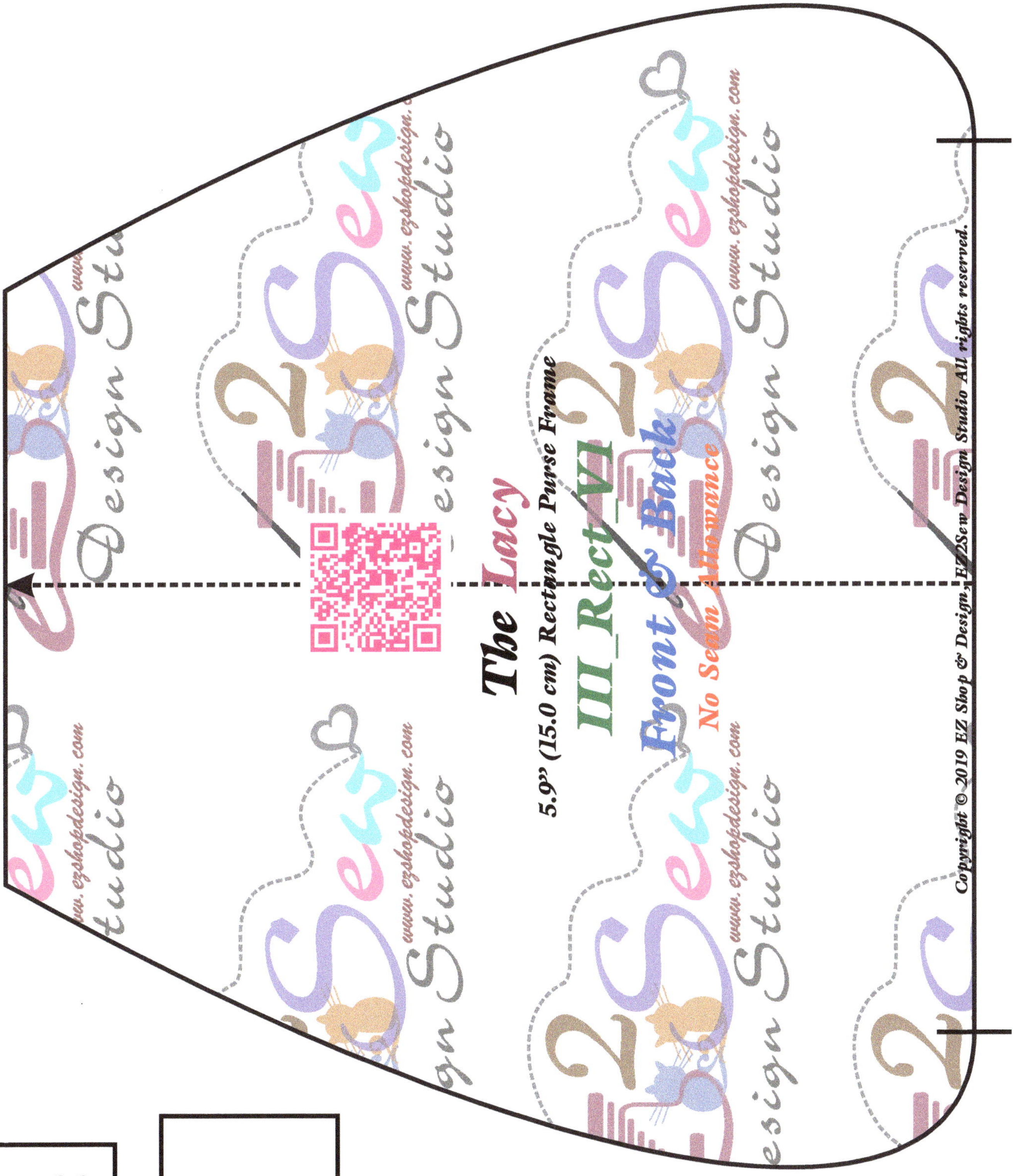

The Lacy
5.9" (15.0 cm) Rectangle Purse Frame
III_Rect_VI
Front & Back
No Seam Allowance

Copyright © 2019 EZ Shop & Design, EZ2Sew Design Studio All rights reserved.

| 1" | 3 cm |

> ★ **NOTE:** The attached pattern has **NO** seam allowances included. Refer to the Chapter "Understand The Pattern" completely before cutting or sewing! ☺

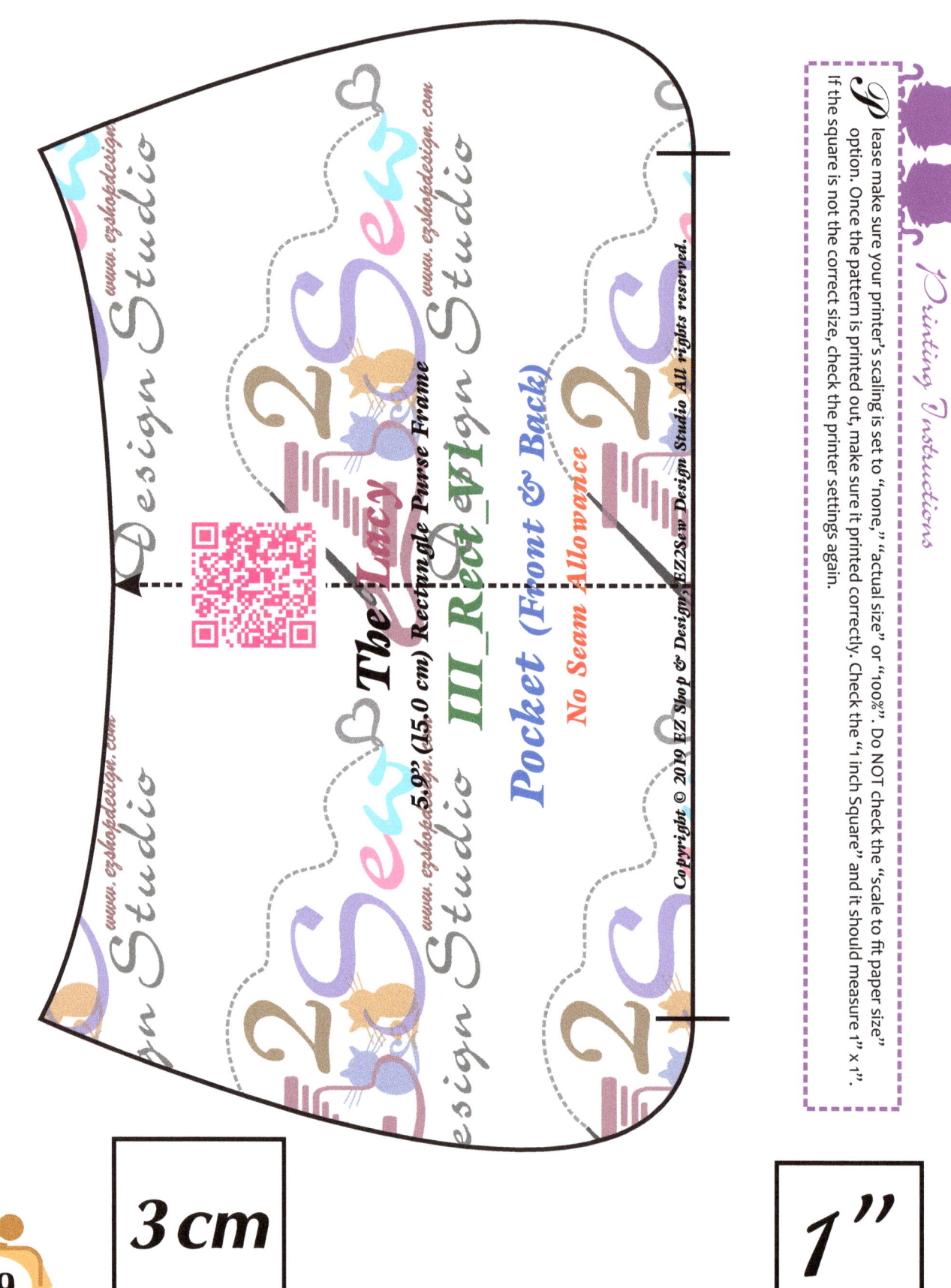

3 cm

1"

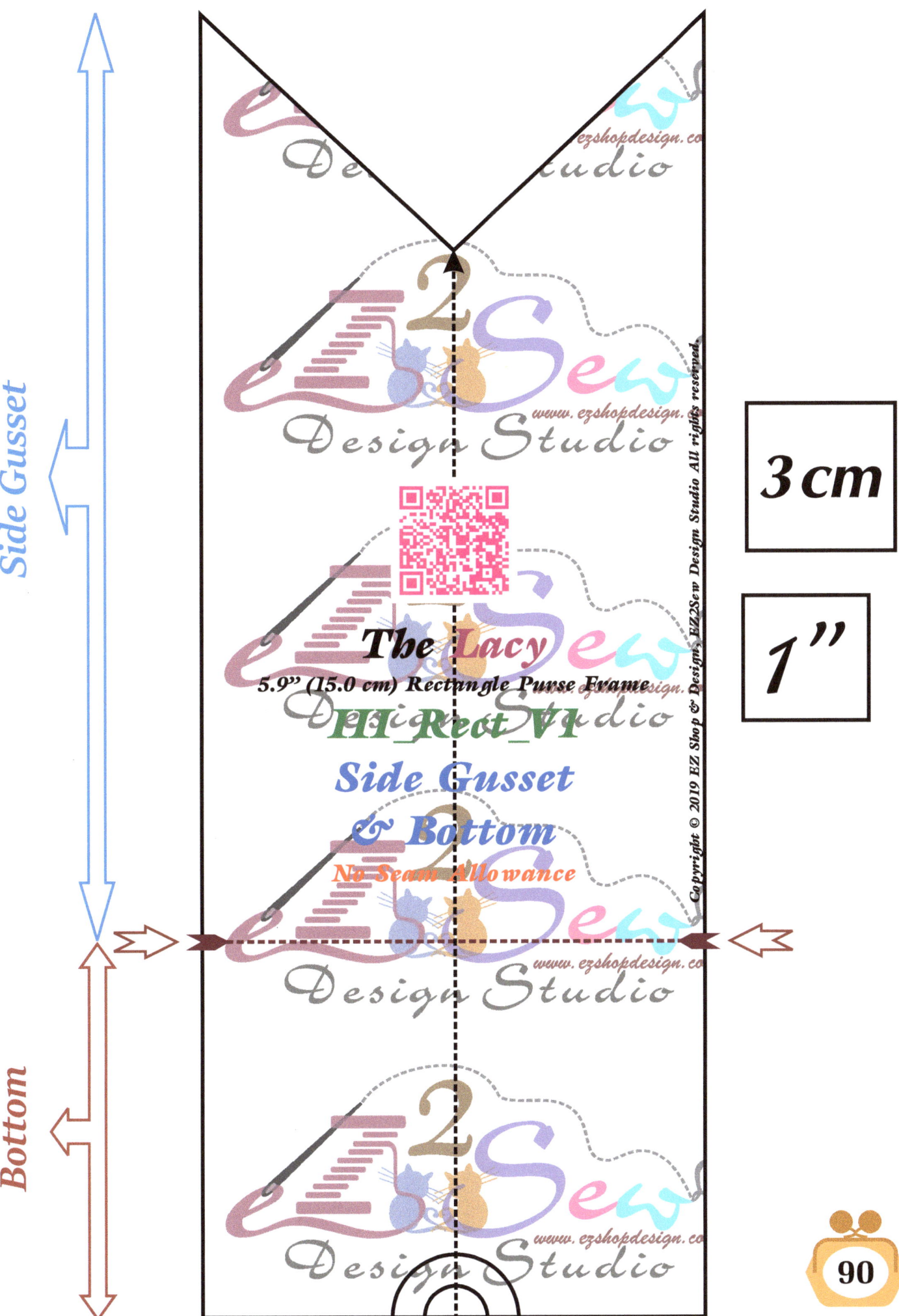

> ★ **NOTE:** The attached pattern has **NO** seam allowances included. Refer to the Chapter "Understand The Pattern" completely before cutting or sewing! ☺

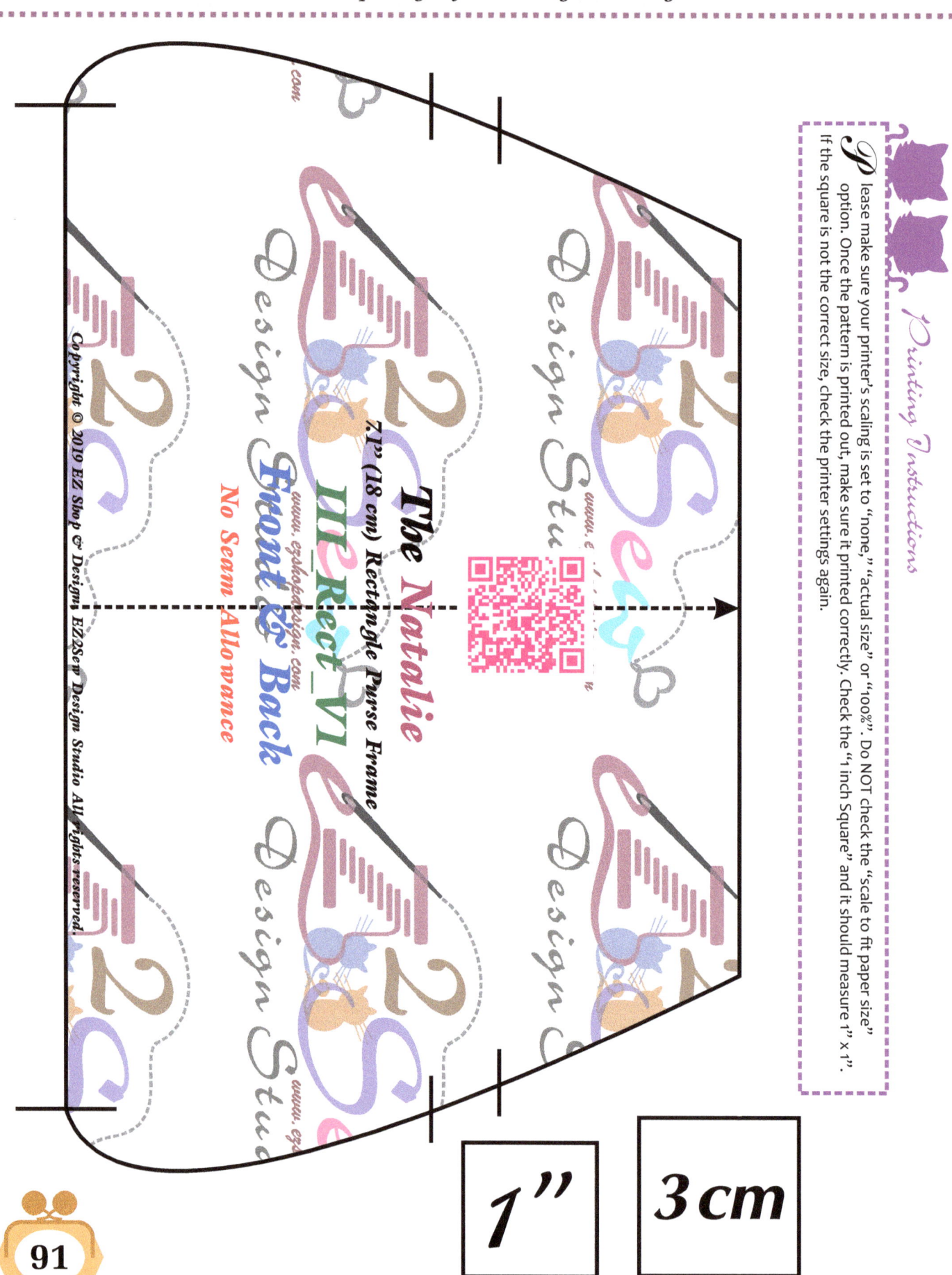

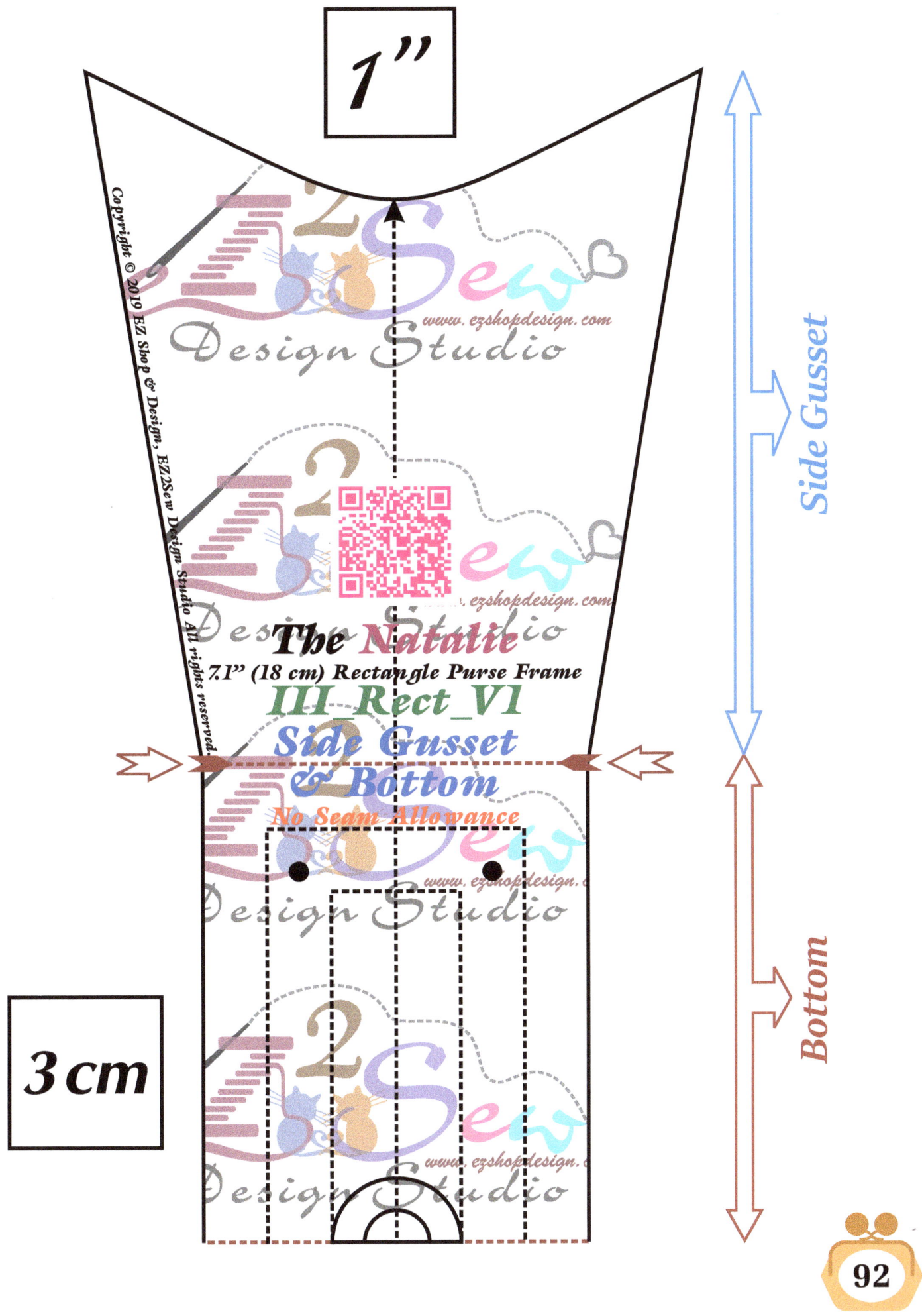

★ **NOTE:** The attached pattern has **NO** seam allowances included. Refer to the Chapter "Understand The Pattern" completely before cutting or sewing! ☺

1"

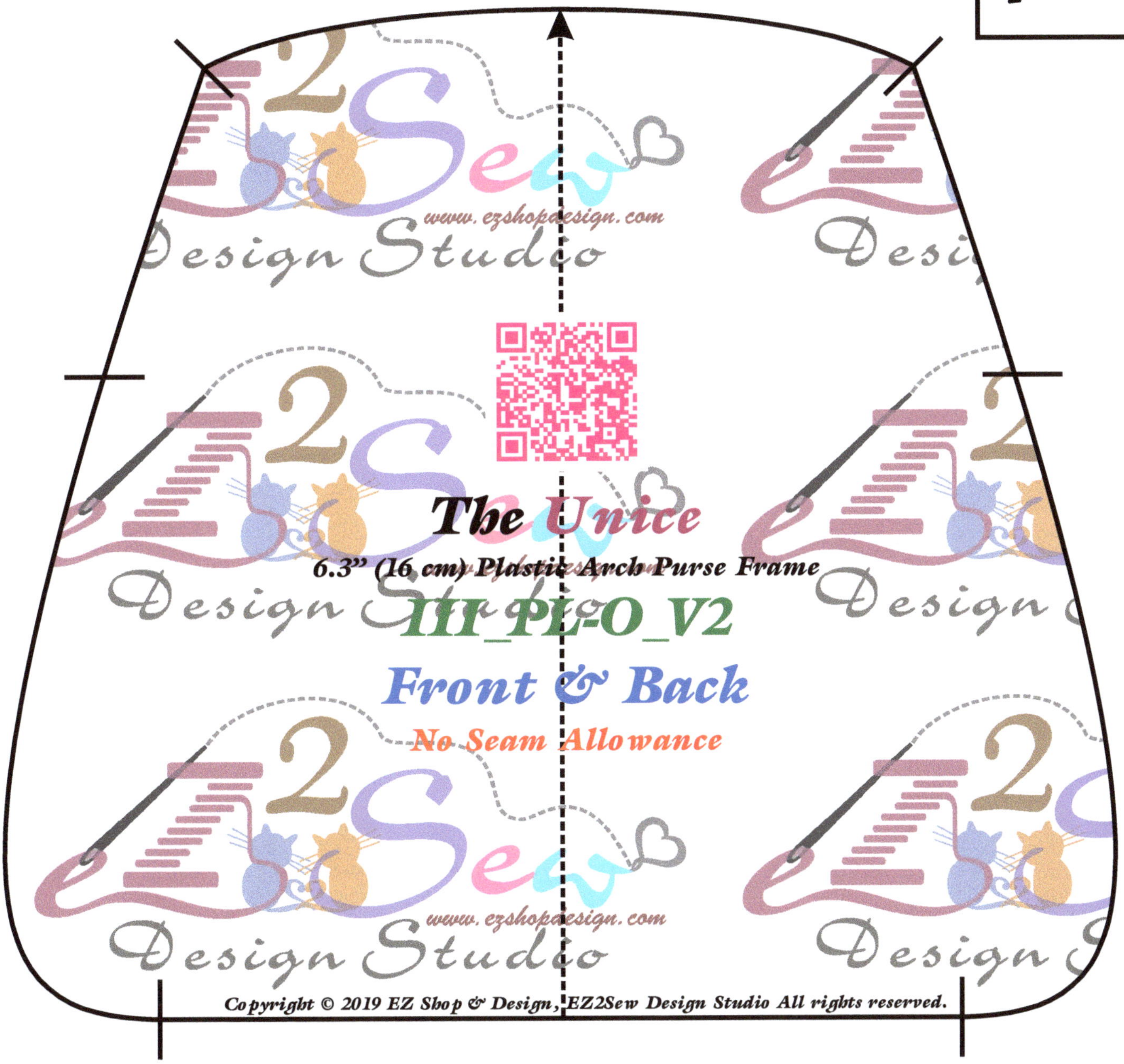

The Unice
6.3" (16 cm) Plastic Arch Purse Frame
III_PL-O_V2
Front & Back
No Seam Allowance

Copyright © 2019 EZ Shop & Design, EZ2Sew Design Studio All rights reserved.

3 cm

🐱🐱 *Printing Instructions*

*P*lease make sure your printer's scaling is set to "none," "actual size" or "100%". Do NOT check the "scale to fit paper size" option. Once the pattern is printed out, make sure it printed correctly. Check the "1 inch Square" and it should measure 1" x 1". If the square is not the correct size, check the printer settings again.

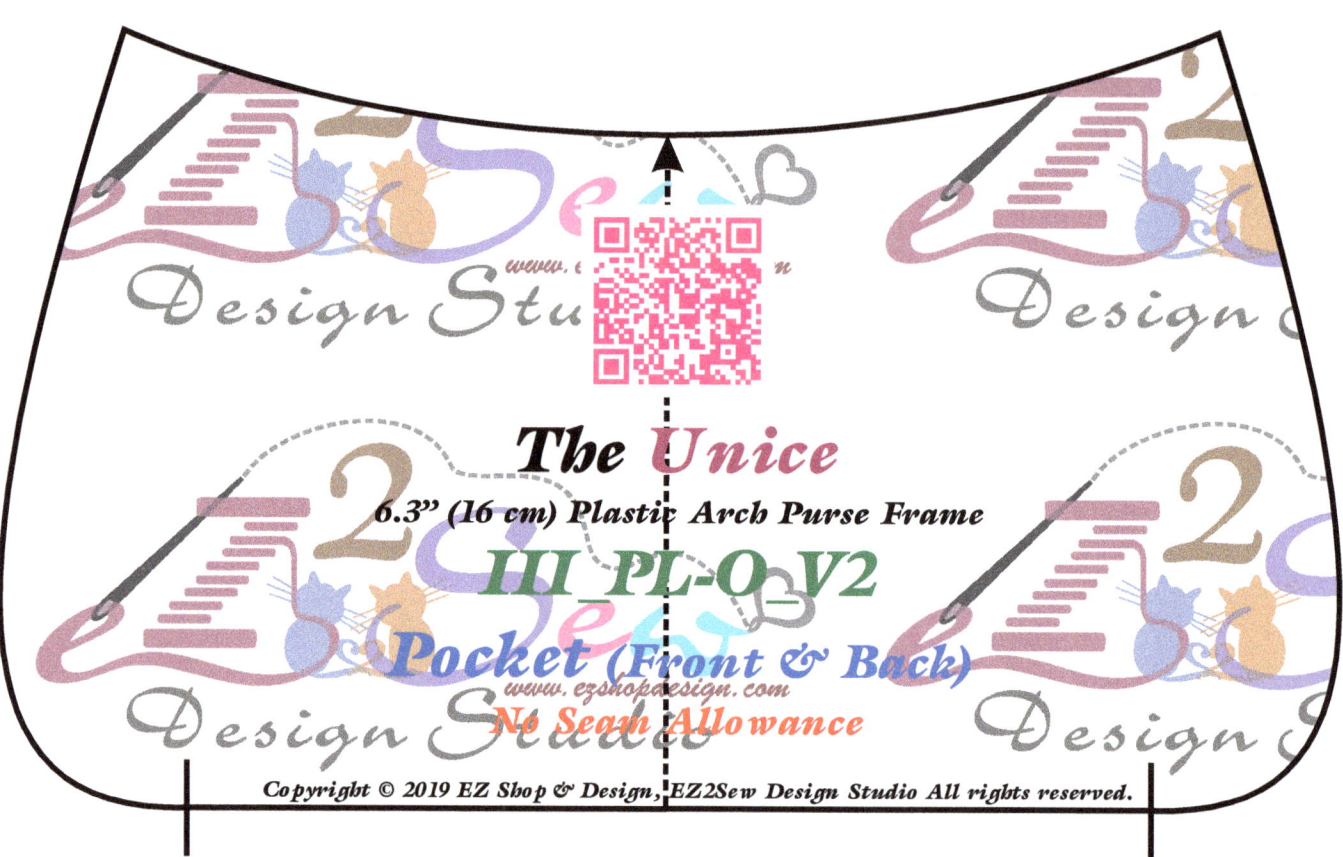

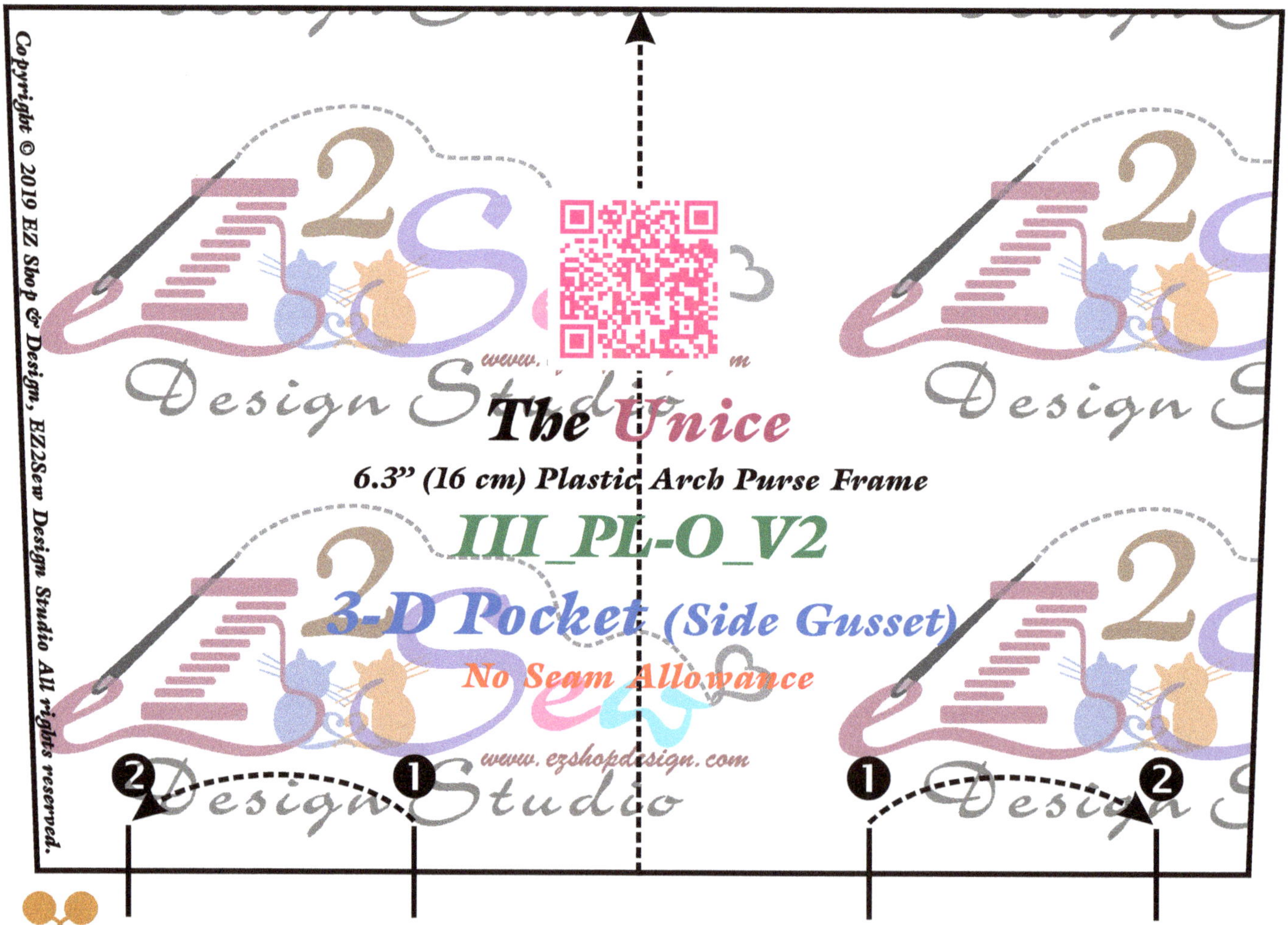

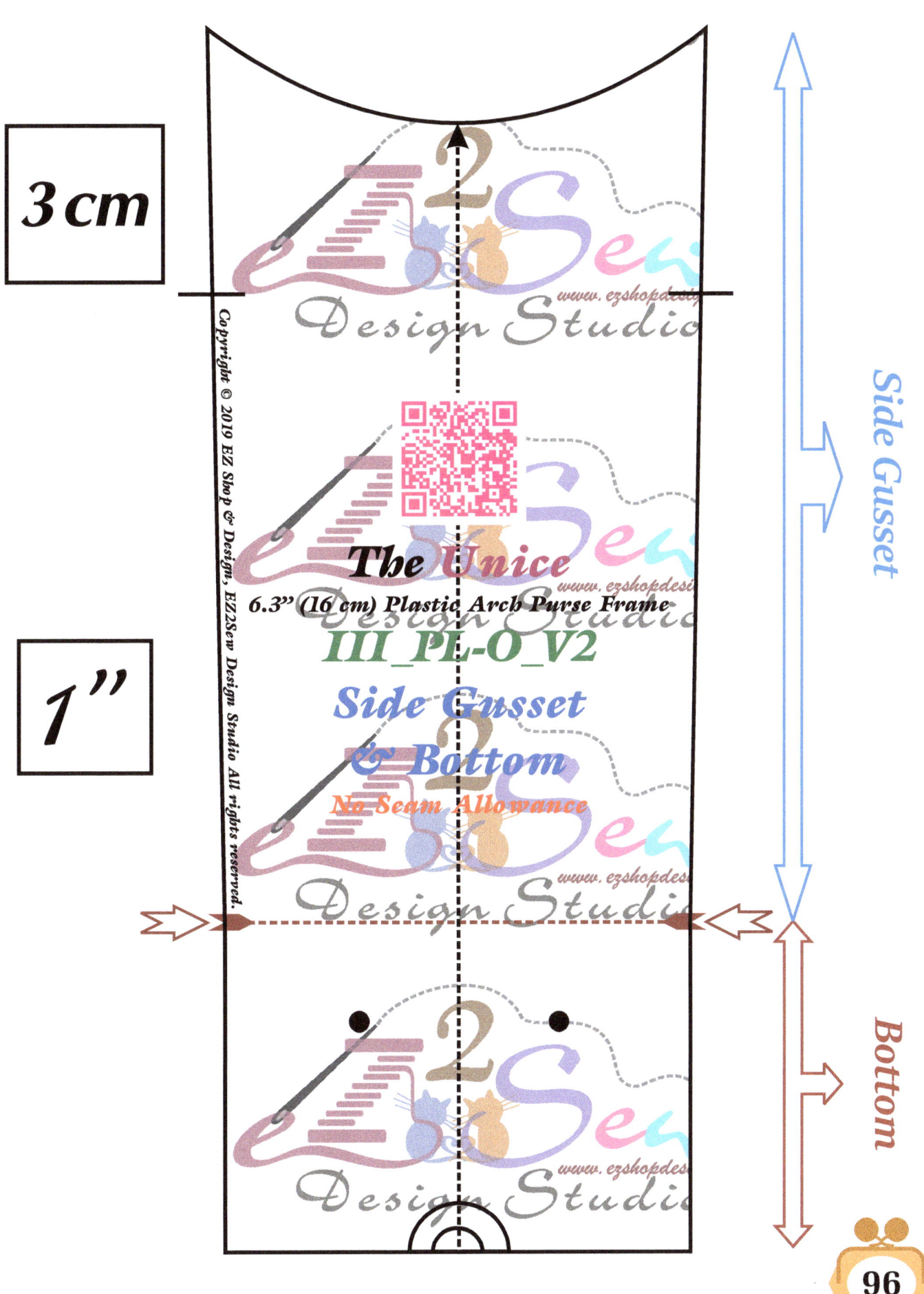

Unice
V1

Helena II
V2 **V1**

97

SEWING SKILL - *Advanced Beginner~Intermediate* ♦♦♦◇◇
DIFFICULT LEVEL - *Easy~Intermediate* ●●●○○

EXHIBIT

Helena II

III_PL-Rect_V1

4.25" (Top W) x 3" (Bottom W)
3.75" (H) x 2.25" (D)

* Top W: the widest part; H: not including the frame;

** Finished Size: (approximate measurements) **

Helena II

III_PL-Rect_V2

4" (Top W) x 2.7" (Bottom W)
2.75" (H) x 2" (D)

* Top W: the widest part; H: not including the frame;

EXHIBIT

Unice

III_PL-Rect_V1

8" (Top W) x 6" (Bottom W)
7" (H) x 3.5" (D)

* *Top W: the widest part; H: not including the frame;*

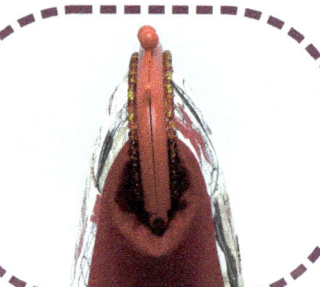

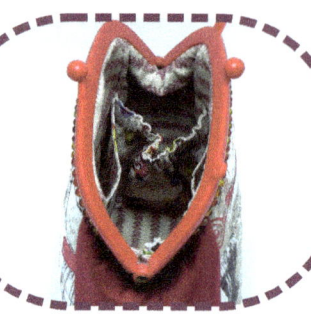

** *Finished Size: (approximate measurements)* **

These three patterns were grouped together because they use the same directions to construct the Exterior and Interior. The differences between these three patterns are the size of the frame and the finished purse piece. The interior pockets of The Helena II (V1 & V2) have the same style. You might want to start from the easiest in difficulty to the more challenging of the three - the Helena II (V1 & V2) and the Unice (V1).

 "The Henela II (V1 & V2)" - Please refer to the chapter **"Basic Bag Construction"**, the section **"Construct the Slip Pocket - Style B"** to construct the interior pockets and in this chapter.

 "The Unice (V1)" - There are three different kinds of pockets in this bag. Please refer to the chapter **"Basic Bag Construction"**, the section **"Construct the Slip Pocket - Style B"** to construct the interior front & back pockets. For details about how to construct the interior side gusset 3-D pockets, please refer to the section **"Construct the 3-D Pocket"**. It's a little challenging to make the exterior front & back pockets, please check the end of this chapter for details. For those who don't want to have the exterior pockets, you may cut the fabric the same way as you cut the interior "Front & Back" piece.

PREPARATION
PREPARING ALL THE MATERIALS

Helena II V1 & V2

✂ **For NON-Directional Fabrics**

Exterior/Interior/Interfacing:

- **Main/Lining** fabric (Pattern B) - "Front & Back" x 1; "Side Gusset" x 2;

- **Interfacing** (Pattern A) - "Front & Back" x 1; "Side Gusset" x 2;

Interior Pocket/Interfacing:

- (Optional) "**Pocket**" - main x 1; lining x 1; interfacing x 1;

✂ **For Directional Fabrics**

Exterior/Interior/Interfacing:

- "**Side Gusset**": the same as non-directional fabrics;

✂ "**Front & Back**":

  ☞ [Option 1] Fold "Front & Back" (Pattern A) in half, add seam allowance all the way around (Pattern B) x 2;

  ☞ [Option 2] "Front & Back" (Pattern B) x 2; "Bottom" (Pattern B) x 1;

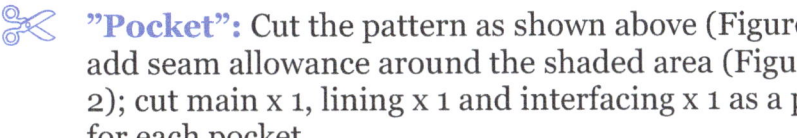

Figure 1

✂ "**Pocket**": Cut the pattern as shown above (Figure 1), add seam allowance around the shaded area (Figure 2); cut main x 1, lining x 1 and interfacing x 1 as a pair for each pocket.

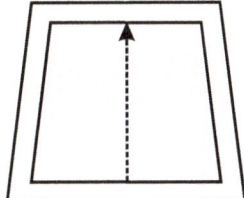

Figure 2

✎ Tip: Do **NOT** apply the interfacing until the "Front & Back" pieces are connected together and become ONE piece.

✎ NOTE: Add seam allowance before cutting any fabric. No seam allowance needed for cutting the interfacing, unless using a sew-in interfacing.

Reference

- ★ Please refer to the Chapter "**Understand The Pattern**" before cutting any fabric and interfacing.
- ★ **Pattern A** - the original pattern which has "*NO Seam Allowance*"
- ★ **Pattern B** - the pattern which has the "*Seam Allowance*" of your choice (1/4", 3/8" or 1/2")

DIRECTIONS

For Directional Fabrics

 If you are using non-directonal fabrics and don't want to make patchwork, you may skip these steps. Please refer to the Chapter "Understand the Pattern".

Prepare the Materials

1 **Cut the fabrics and Connect "Front & Back" together.** If you are using directional fabric on the "Front & Back" and/or making patchwork, you need more than one piece to connect them together (Figure 1).

☞ If you cut the fabric in 2 pieces (fold in half at ①)
- 2 x "Front & Back": Connect both pieces at the bottom edge, Right sides facing together. Sew by using the seam allowance of your choice. (Figure 2)

☞ If you cut the fabric in 3 pieces (fold pattern in half and cut at ②) - 1 x "Front", 1 x "Back" and 1 x "Bottom": Place the bottom of the "Front" (or "Back") and one of the shorter edges of the "Bottom", Right side facing each other, and sew by using the seam allowance of your choice. Repeat the same step on the other side.

2 **Press the seam allowances open.** Press the seam allowances open at the Wrong side. Now, the "Front & Back" is ONE piece.

3 **Get all the fabrics ready and apply interfacing.** Apply interfacing to the Wrong side of the main and lining fabrics, following the manufacturer's instructions. Please refer to the chapter "Fabric & Interfacing" for details.

*For those who use directional fabric and/or make patchwork, you may top stitch 1/8" or 1/16" away from the connecting edge **AFTER** applying the interfacing to the fabric.*

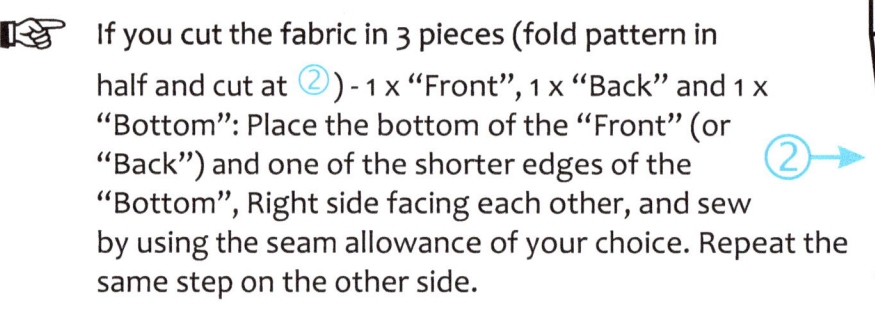

Figure 1

Figure 2

 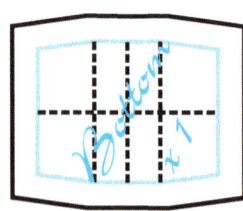 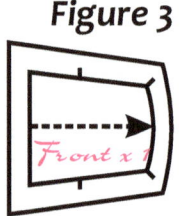

Figure 3

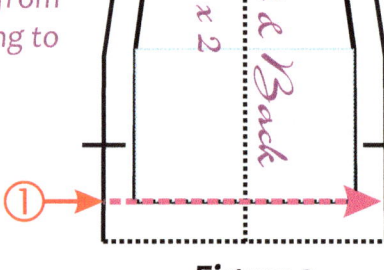

DIRECTIONS

Construct the Interior Pocket (optional)

1 **Get both Pocket main and lining pieces ready to connect.** Place the pocket main and lining pieces Right sides facing each other. Align all the markings, especially the centers.

2 **Sew both shorter edges.** If you would like to add lace to the top of the pocket, sandwich the lace in between the pocket main and lining. Sew only the shorter edges by using the seam allowance of your choice.

3 **Turn Right side out.** Trim the excess of the lace. Turn the pocket piece Right side out through one of the longer edges. Press well and fold the lace on top of the pocket main fabric.

4 **Topstitching.** Top stitch both short edges by using the seam allowance 1/16" (2 mm).

5 **Connect pocket piece to the Lining "Front & Back".** Place the pocket piece on top of the Lining "Front & Back" piece, the pocket main fabric facing up (NOTE: if you are using directional fabric for the Lining "Front & Back", please connect them to become ONE piece first). Align the centers of both pieces at the longer edges. Baste stitching the pocket piece to the Lining "Front & Back" at the longer edges.

6 **Sew the pocket bottom.** Sew two straight seams (please refer to the "Pocket" pattern) to close the pocket bottom.

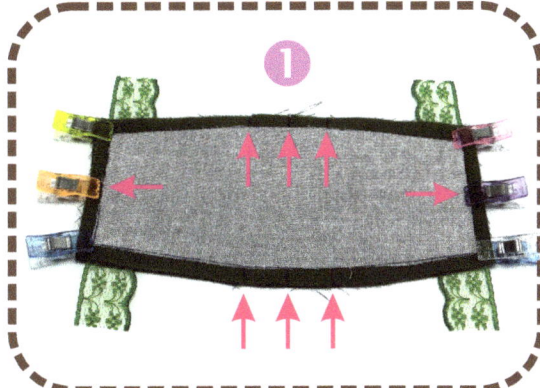

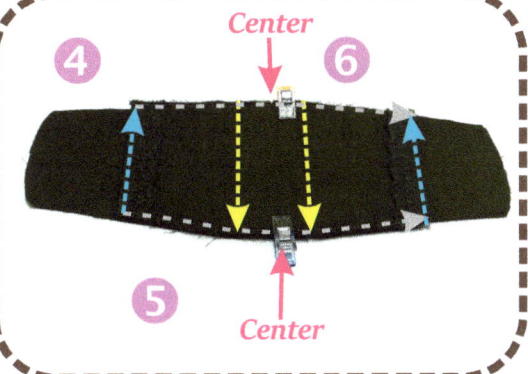

DIRECTIONS

Construct the Interior

 Please refer to the chapter **"Basic Bag Construction"**, section **"Construct a Curved Seam"** to construct the Interior. Please refer to the photos below as well. The circular number indicates the instruction steps mentioned in the section "Construct a Curved Seam".

 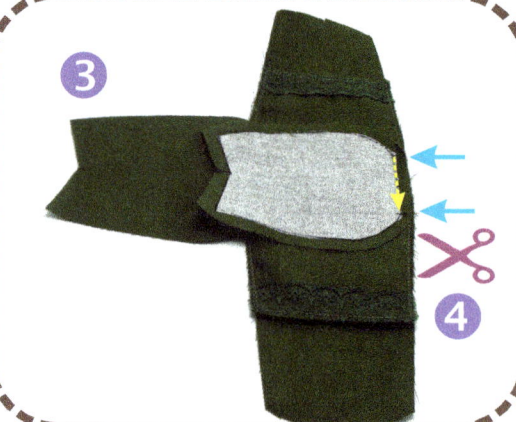

Construct the Exterior

 Use the same steps as constructing the Interior.

DIRECTIONS

Construct the Exterior

Complete the Purse piece

1 **Get Main and Lining pieces. Connect both pieces.** You should have both Main and Lining pieces ready to complete the purse piece. Place the Main piece (Right side out) into the Lining piece (Wrong side out), with the Right sides of both pieces facing each other. Align all 4 center markings.

 *Use chalk or erasable pen to draw the seam line on the Wrong side of the Lining before sewing.*

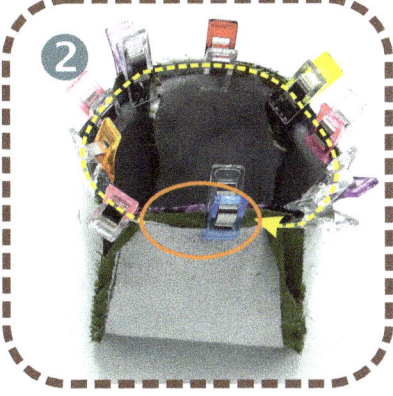

2 **Sew all the way around the top and leave an opening** to connect both pieces with the seam allowance of your choice. Use Pinking Shears to trim the excess or cut notches on the curved seam. Clip the tops of both side seams.

3 **Turn Right side out.** Turn the whole purse piece Right side out through the opening. Use your finger tip or something pointy (but not sharp) to round out the top curved seam.

4 **Press well.** Use an iron to press the purse piece with a bit of steam to remove wrinkles if necessary.

DIRECTIONS

Complete the Purse piece

5 Fold the opening seam allowance inward to the Wrong side. Use clips or pins to hold it in place.

6 Topstitching. Top stitch all the way around the top edge by using 1/16" seam allowance.

✎ *Do NOT use a seam allowance larger than 1/8", even though the top edge will be under the frame; using a seam allowance smaller than 1/8" will work well.*

7 Mark all 4 centers. Press well if needed. Use chalk or erasable pen to mark all 4 centers.

Install the purse frame

1 Install the purse frame. Get the correct size and shape purse frame ready to install to the completed purse piece.

✎ *Please refer to the Chapter "Install the Purse Frame".*

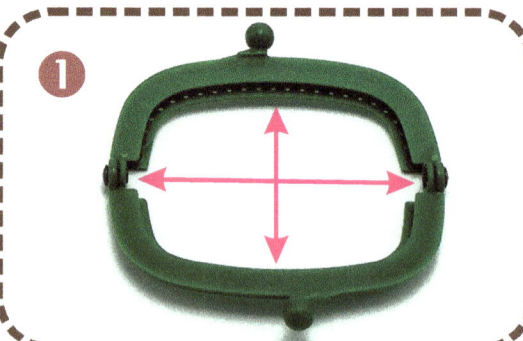

V1

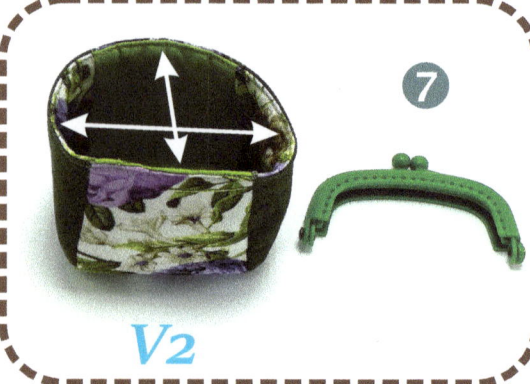
V2

PREPARATION

PREPARING ALL THE MATERIALS

Unice (V1)

 For NON-Directional Fabrics

Exterior/Interior/Interfacing:

- "Side Gusset" (Pattern B) - Exterior: main x 2; Interior: lining x 2; Interfacing (Pattern A): cut 2 for Exterior: main; cut 2 for Interior: lining;

- "Pocket (Interior Front & Back)" (Pattern B) - Interior pocket: main x 2; lining x 2; Interfacing (Pattern A): cut 2;

- "3-D Pocket (Interior Side Gusset)" (Pattern B) - Interior pocket: main x 2; lining x 2; Interfacing (Pattern A): cut 2;

- "Front & Back (Interior) + Bottom" (Pattern B) - Interior: lining x 1; Interfacing (Pattern A): cut 1;

 *Please refer to the chapter **"Understand the Pattern"** before cutting any fabrics.*

 *NOTE: Two options for cutting the exterior front and back piece. If you would like to have two exterior pockets, please check below. If you prefer no pockets on exterior, cut the same way as "**Front & Back (Interior) + Bottom**".*

- Exterior Front & Back with two slip pockets:
    - ✂ **"Front & Back (Exterior) + Pocket (Exterior)"** (Pattern B) - Exterior: main x 2; Interfacing: cut 1 the same as you cut for "Front & Back (Interior) + Bottom";
    - ✂ **"Pocket (Exterior Front & Back) + Bottom"** (Pattern B) - Exterior: main x 1; Interfacing (Pattern A): cut 2 for the pocket area;

✂ **For Directional Fabrics**

- <u>*Exterior/Interior/Interfacing:*</u> *Please refer to the Pattern "**Helena II (V1 & V2)**".*

- ✂ **"Front & Back (Exterior) + Pocket (Exterior)":** Cut the pattern at the marking ✂, add seam allowance before cutting any fabric, and sew to connect all the pieces together.

- ✂ **"Pocket (Exterior Front & Back) + Bottom":** Cut the pattern at the marking ✂, add seam allowance before cutting any fabric, and sew to connect all the pieces together.

DIRECTIONS

Construct the Interior Pocket (optional)

 Please refer to the chapter **"Basic Bag Construction"**, the section **"Construct the Slip Pocket - Style B"** to construct the interior front & back pockets.

 For details about how to construct the interior side gusset 3-D pockets, please refer to the section **"Construct the 3-D Pocket"**. Also, refer to the photos below. The circular number indicates the instruction steps mentioned in the section "Construct the 3-D Pocket".

Construct a slip pocket

Topstitch the top

Create a casing for the elastic

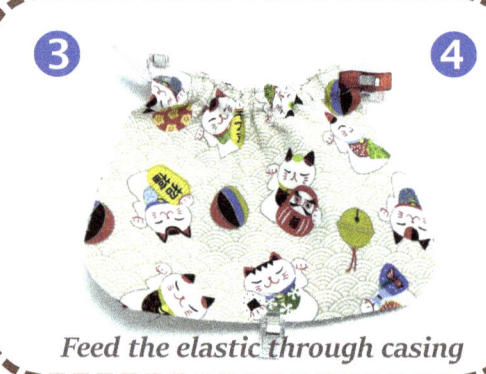
Feed the elastic through casing

Make 3-D folds at the bottom of the pocket

Attach to the side gusset

Construct the Interior

 Please refer to the chapter **"Basic Bag Construction"**, section **"Construct a Curved Seam"** and the **"Helena II"** in this chapter to construct the Interior.

DIRECTIONS

Construct the Exterior

 Option 1 - No exterior pockets: For those who don't want to have the exterior pockets, you may cut the fabric the same way as you cut the interior "Front & Back" piece (Figure 1). If you would like to make patchwork, (1) cut the "Bottom" off and (2) add seam allowances all the way around both the top and bottom pieces. (3) Connect two tops and bottom pieces together and become one piece. (4) Apply interfacing. (5) Connect the side gussets to complete the exterior piece.

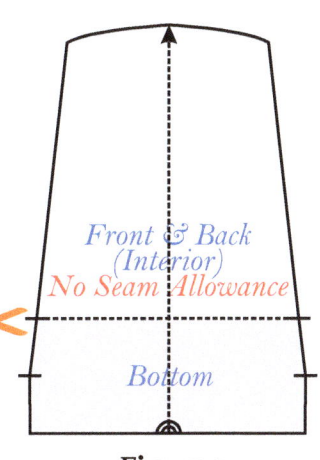

Figure 1

 Option 2 - two exterior pockets: Check the actual size patterns, add seam allowances before cutting the materials:

- ☑ Figure 2: "Front & Back (Exterior) + Front & Back Pocket (Exterior)" x 2
- ☑ Figure 3: "Pocket (Exterior Front & Back) + Bottom" x 1

for Directional fabric: Make sure all the pieces are in the correct direction.

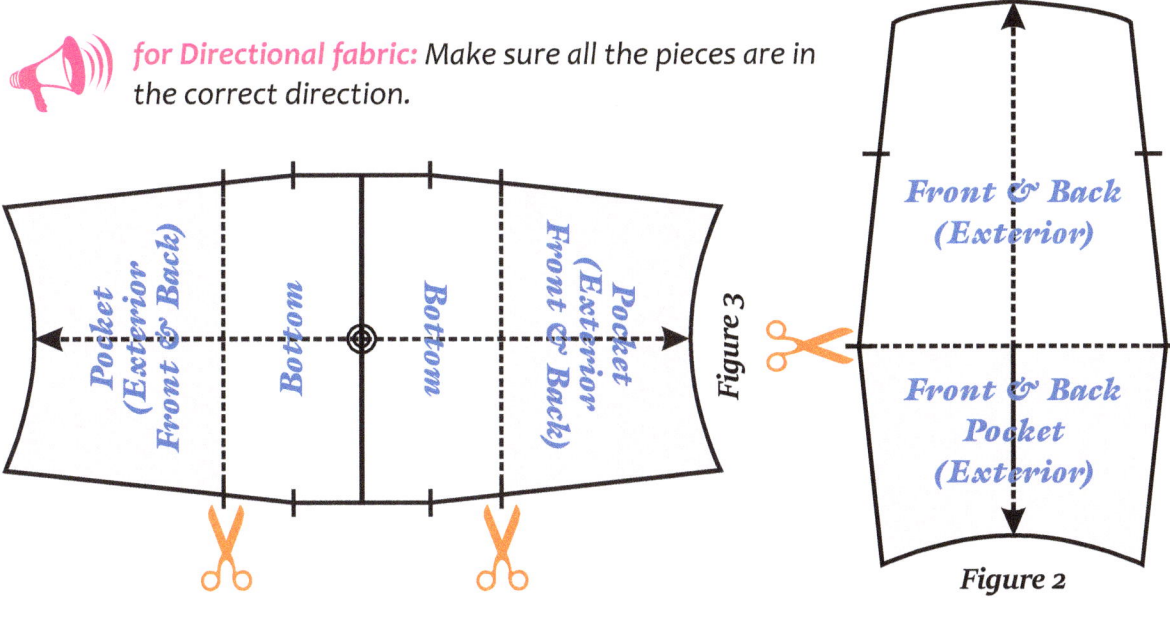

Figure 3

Figure 2

DIRECTIONS

Construct the Exterior

1 **Connect the pocket.** Place the pocket main and lining pieces Right sides facing each other. Align both centers. Sew the top of the pocket by using the seam allowance of your choice.

2 **Turn Right side out, Top stitch, fold and attach the pocket to the base.** Clip the top curved seam allowance. Turn the pocket Right side out. Press well. Top stitch the top of the pocket by using 1/8" or 1/16" seam allowance. Fold the pocket in half at the bottom and baste stitch to attach the pocket to the base piece (Front & Back) - align the markings (check the pattern markings).

3 **Do the same on the other side.** Repeat Step 1 and 2 on the other side. Now, the exterior front & back became one piece.

4 **Install the purse feet at the bottom (optional).** Please refer to the chapter "**Basic Bag Construction**", the section "**Install the Purse feet**".

5 **Apply Interfacing.** Apply interfacing to the wrong side of the exterior Front & Back piece.

DIRECTIONS

Construct the Exterior

6 **Connect Side Gussets to the Front & Back.** Now, you should have one piece of the "Front & Back" and two "Side Gussets" pieces. Connect them the same way as you construct the "**Helena II**".

Complete the Purse piece

 *Please refer to the "**Helena II**" to complete the purse piece and the photos below as well.*

Install the purse frame

1 **Install the purse frame.** Get the correct size and shape purse frame ready to install to the completed purse piece.

 Please refer to the Chapter "Install the Purse Frame".

 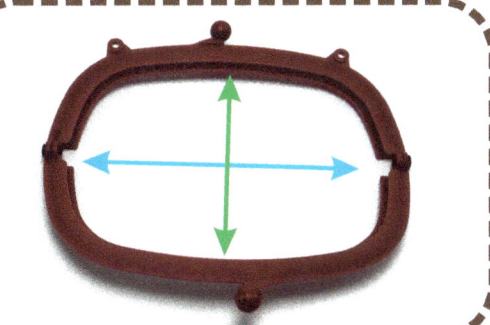

> ★ **NOTE:** The attached pattern has **NO** seam allowances included. Refer to the Chapter "Understand The Pattern" completely before cutting or sewing! ☺

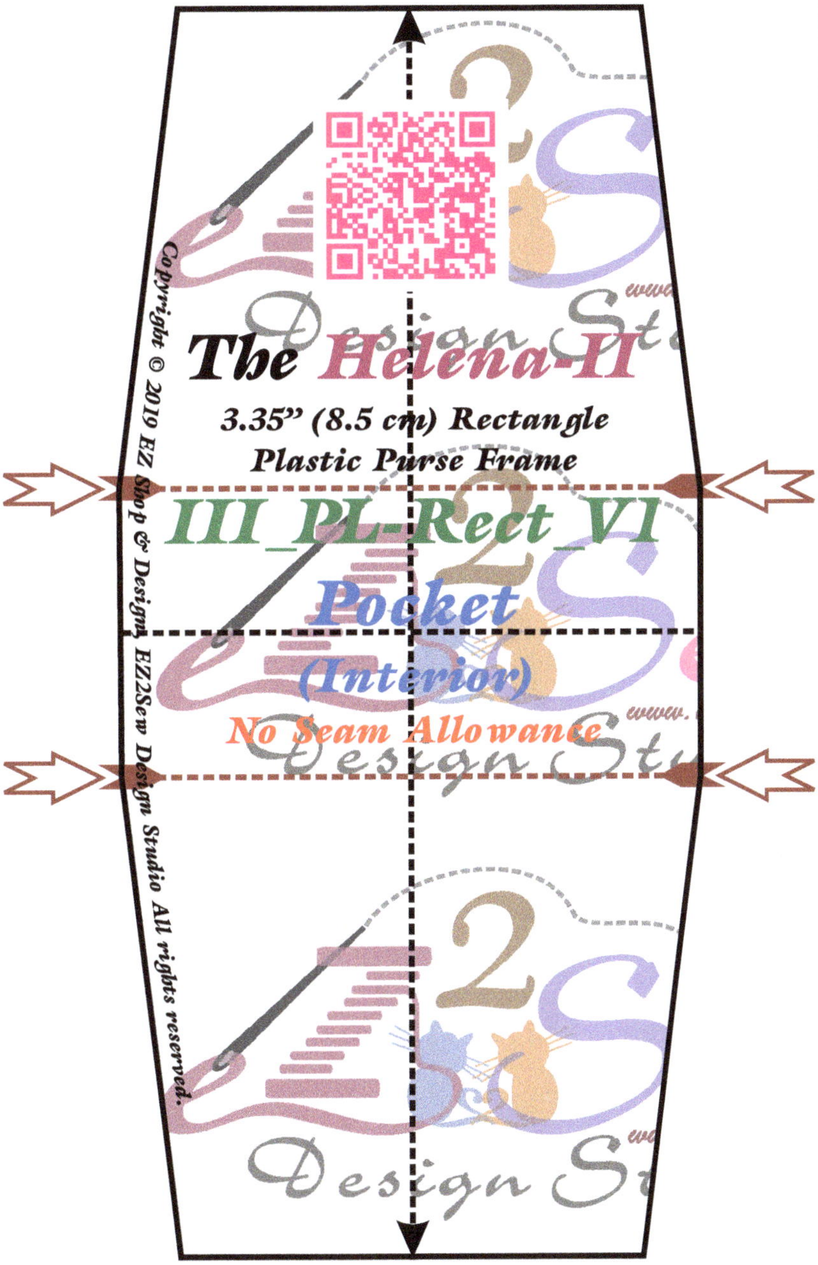

The Helena-II
3.35" (8.5 cm) Rectangle Plastic Purse Frame

III_PL-Rect_VI
Pocket
(Interior)

No Seam Allowance

`1"`

`3 cm`

Printing Instructions

*P*lease make sure your printer's scaling is set to "none," "actual size" or "100%". Do NOT check the "scale to fit paper size" option. Once the pattern is printed out, make sure it printed correctly. Check the "1 inch Square" and it should measure 1" x 1". If the square is not the correct size, check the printer settings again.

3 cm

1"

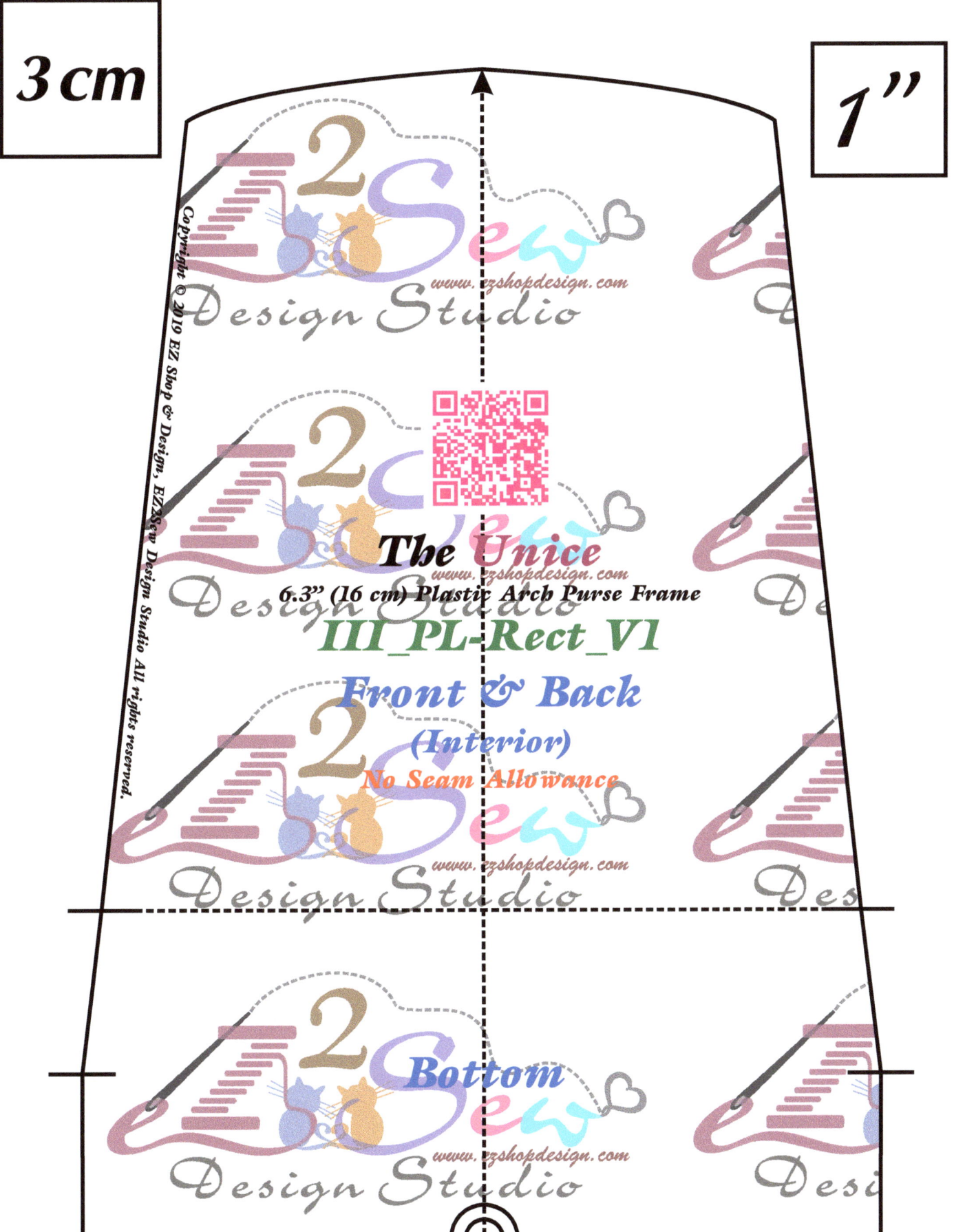

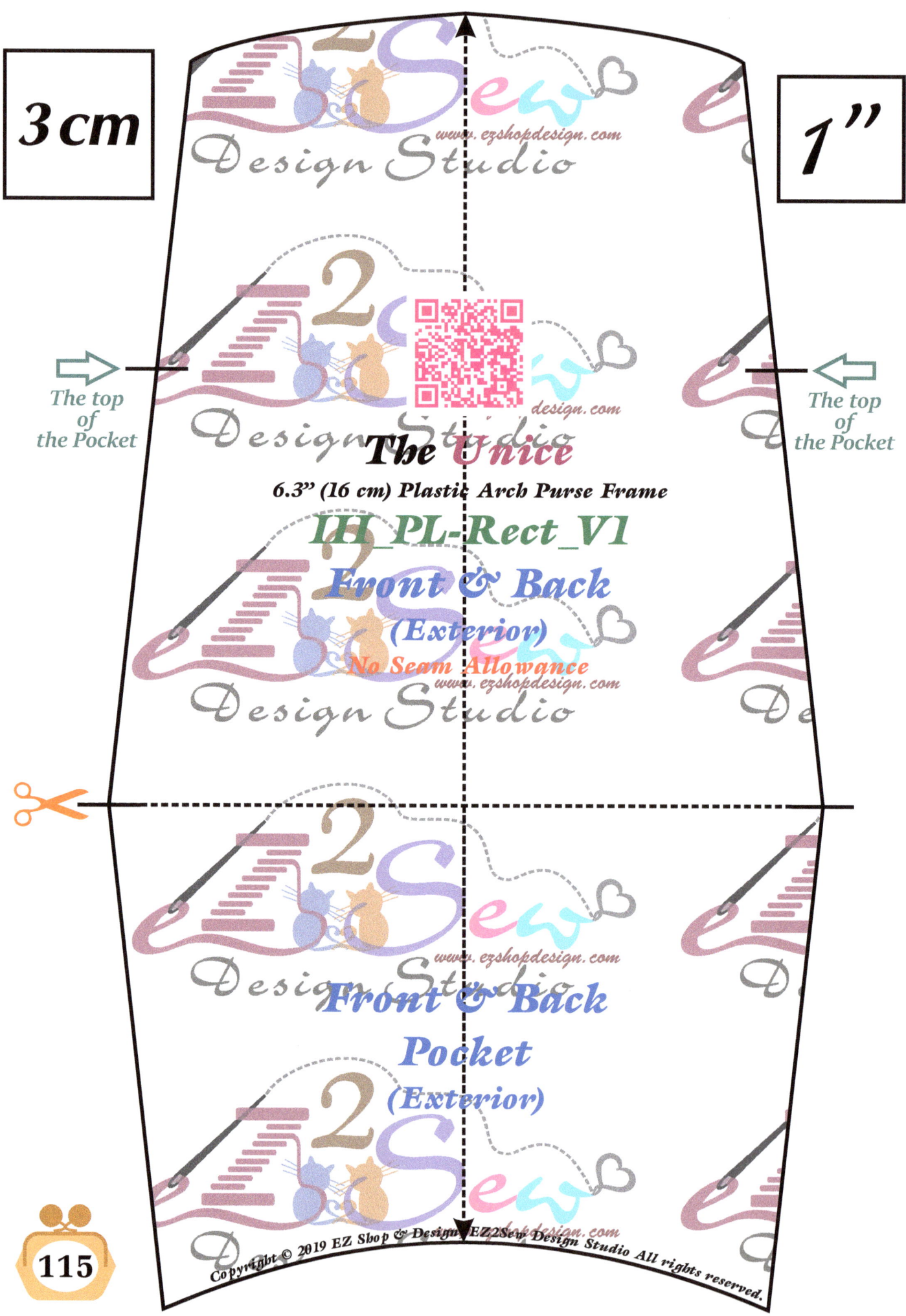

> ☆ **NOTE:** The attached pattern has **NO** seam allowances included. Refer to the Chapter "Understand The Pattern" completely before cutting or sewing! ☺

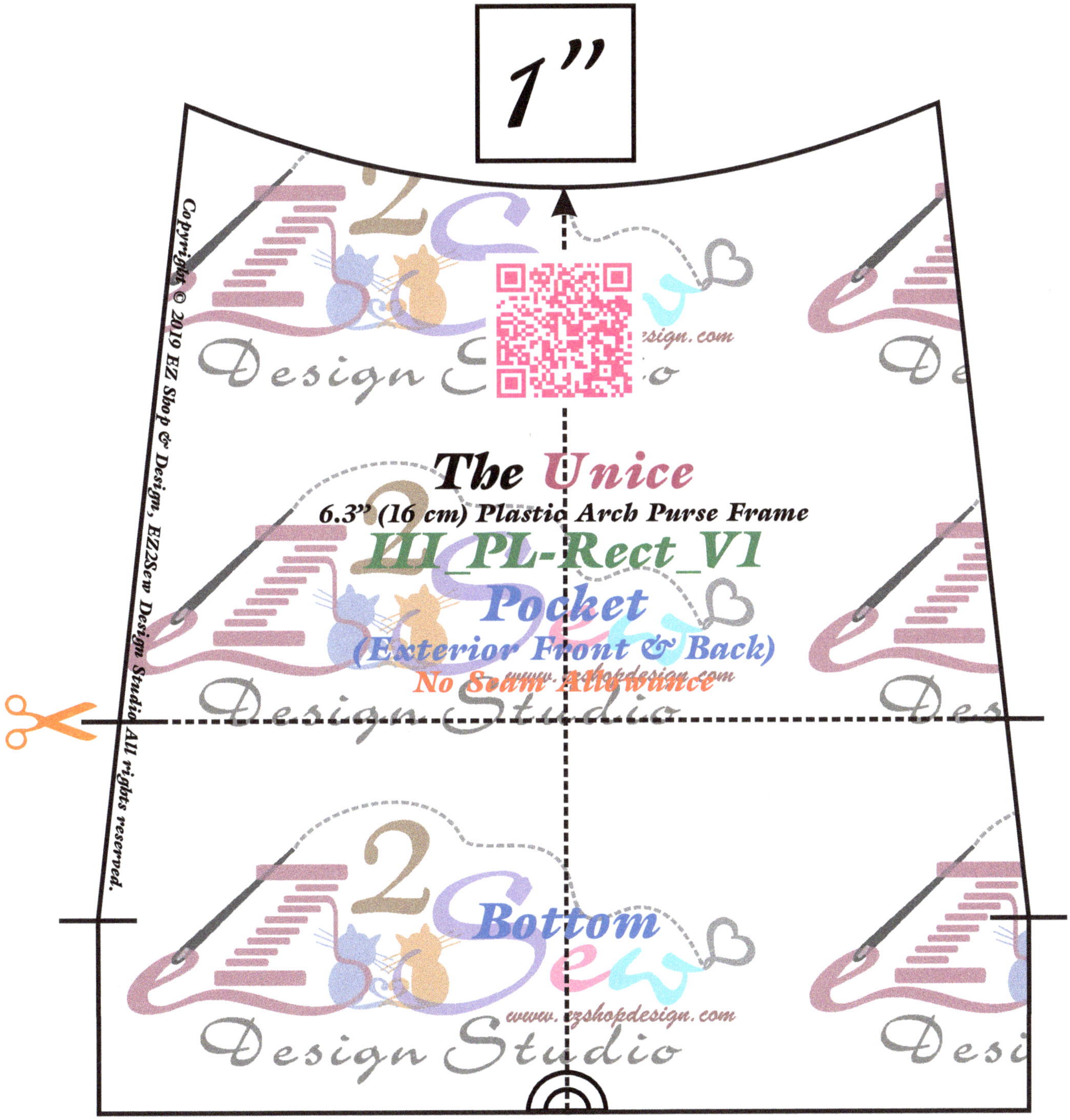

1"

Copyright © 2019 EZ Shop & Design, EZ2Sew Design Studio All rights reserved.

The Unice
6.3" (16 cm) Plastic Arch Purse Frame
III_PL-Rect_V1
Pocket
(Exterior Front & Back)
No Seam Allowance

Bottom

Printing Instructions

Please make sure your printer's scaling is set to "none," "actual size" or "100%". Do NOT check the "scale to fit paper size" option. Once the pattern is printed out, make sure it printed correctly. Check the "1 inch Square" and it should measure 1" x 1". If the square is not the correct size, check the printer settings again.

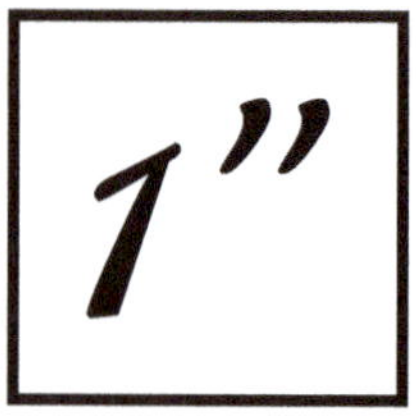

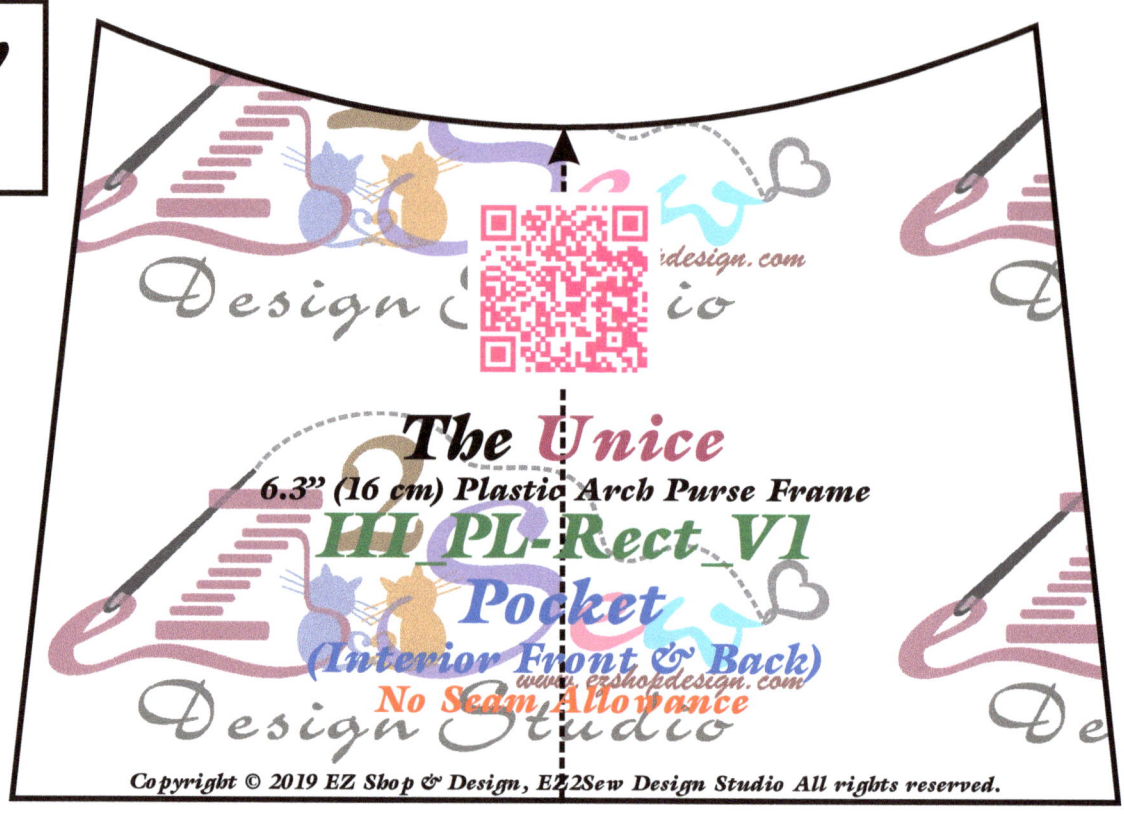

✯ **NOTE:** The attached pattern has **NO** seam allowances included. Refer to the Chapter "Understand The Pattern" completely before cutting or sewing! ☺

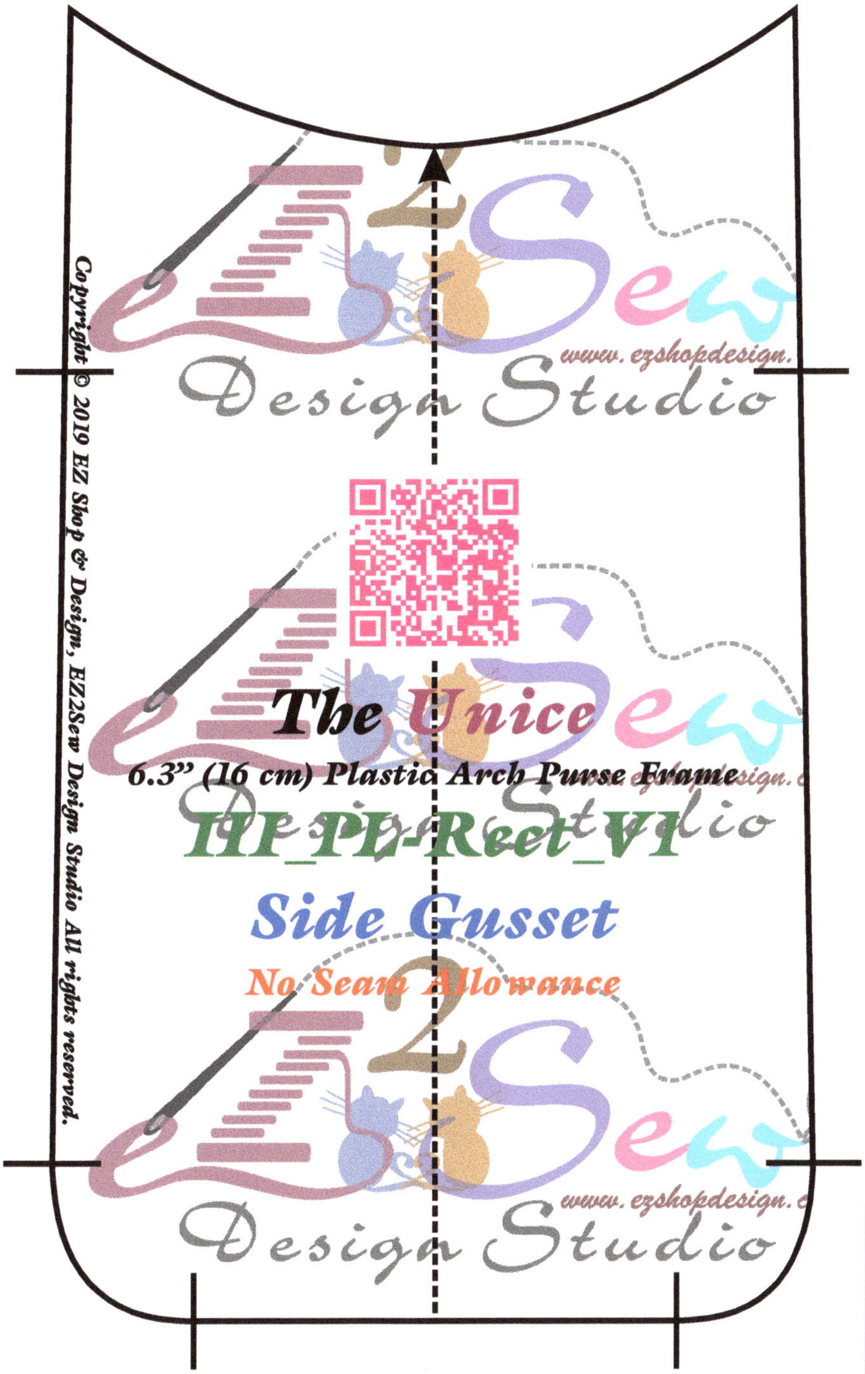

1"

The Unice
6.3" (16 cm) Plastic Arch Purse Frame
HF_PD-Rect_V1
Side Gusset
No Seam Allowance

3 cm

Printing Instructions

Please make sure your printer's scaling is set to "none," "actual size" or "100%". Do NOT check the "scale to fit paper size" option. Once the pattern is printed out, make sure it printed correctly. Check the "1 inch Square" and it should measure 1" x 1". If the square is not the correct size, check the printer settings again.

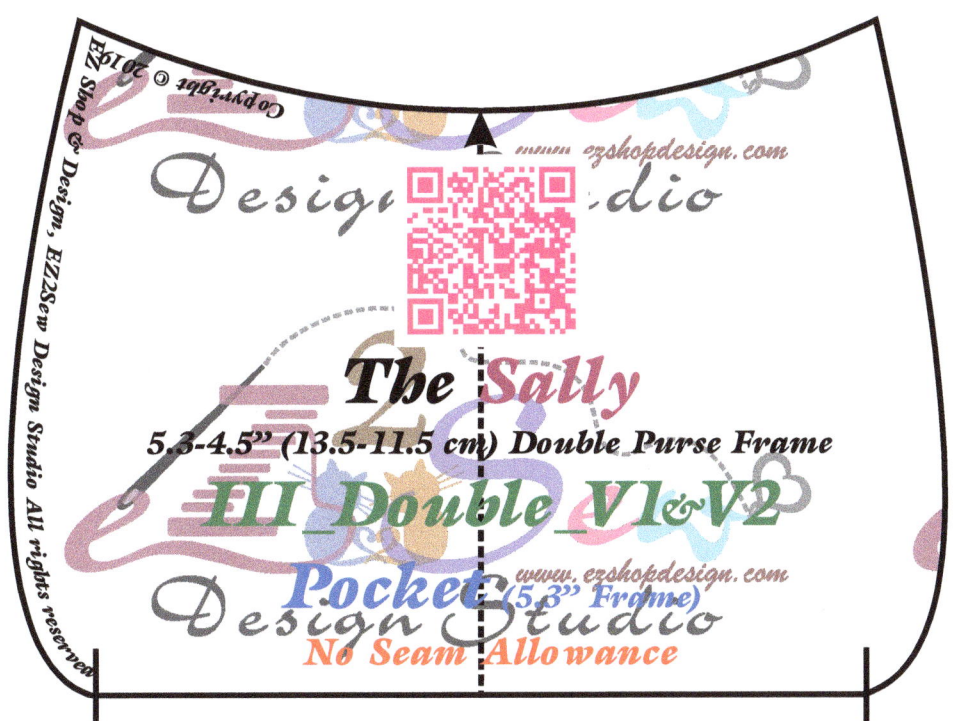

> ✭ **NOTE:** The attached pattern has **NO** seam allowances included. Refer to the Chapter "Understand The Pattern" completely before cutting or sewing! ☺

The Sally
5.3-4.5" (13.5-11.5 cm)
Double Purse Frame
III_Double_V1&V2
Side Gusset
(5.3" Frame)
No Seam Allowance

3 cm

1"

Printing Instructions

> ℘lease make sure your printer's scaling is set to "none," "actual size" or "100%". Do NOT check the "scale to fit paper size" option. Once the pattern is printed out, make sure it printed correctly. Check the "1 inch Square" and it should measure 1" x 1". If the square is not the correct size, check the printer settings again.

Printing Instructions

*P*lease make sure your printer's scaling is set to "none," "actual size" or "100%". Do NOT check the "scale to fit paper size" option. Once the pattern is printed out, make sure it printed correctly. Check the "1 inch Square" and it should measure 1" x 1". If the square is not the correct size, check the printer settings again.

3 cm

1"

☆ **_NOTE:_** The attached pattern has **NO** seam allowances included. Refer to the Chapter "Understand The Pattern" completely before cutting or sewing! ☺

3 cm

1"

Printing Instructions

*P*lease make sure your printer's scaling is set to "none," "actual size" or "100%". Do NOT check the "scale to fit paper size" option. Once the pattern is printed out, make sure it printed correctly. Check the "1 inch Square" and it should measure 1" x 1". If the square is not the correct size, check the printer settings again.

EXHIBIT

Sally

III, I_O_V1

7" (Top W) x 4.75" (Bottom W)
4.75" (H) x 2.5" (D)

* Top W: the widest part; H: not including the frame;

** Finished Size: (approximate measurements) **

Sally

III, II_O_V2

7" (Top W) x 4.75" (Bottom W)
4.75" (H) x 2.5" (D)

* Top W: the widest part; H: not including the frame;

PREPARATION

This is a double frame which has an outer frame (5.3") and an inner frame (4.5") that connects together on both ends. It looks a little challenging to construct, compared to the others, but if you know how to make the Quiana (V1), Lacy, Natalie or Unice (V2), then you will know how to make the outer piece of the Sally (V1 & V2), and if you know how to construct the Helena I, Pearl or Irene, then you have no problem constructing the inner piece of the Sally (V2).

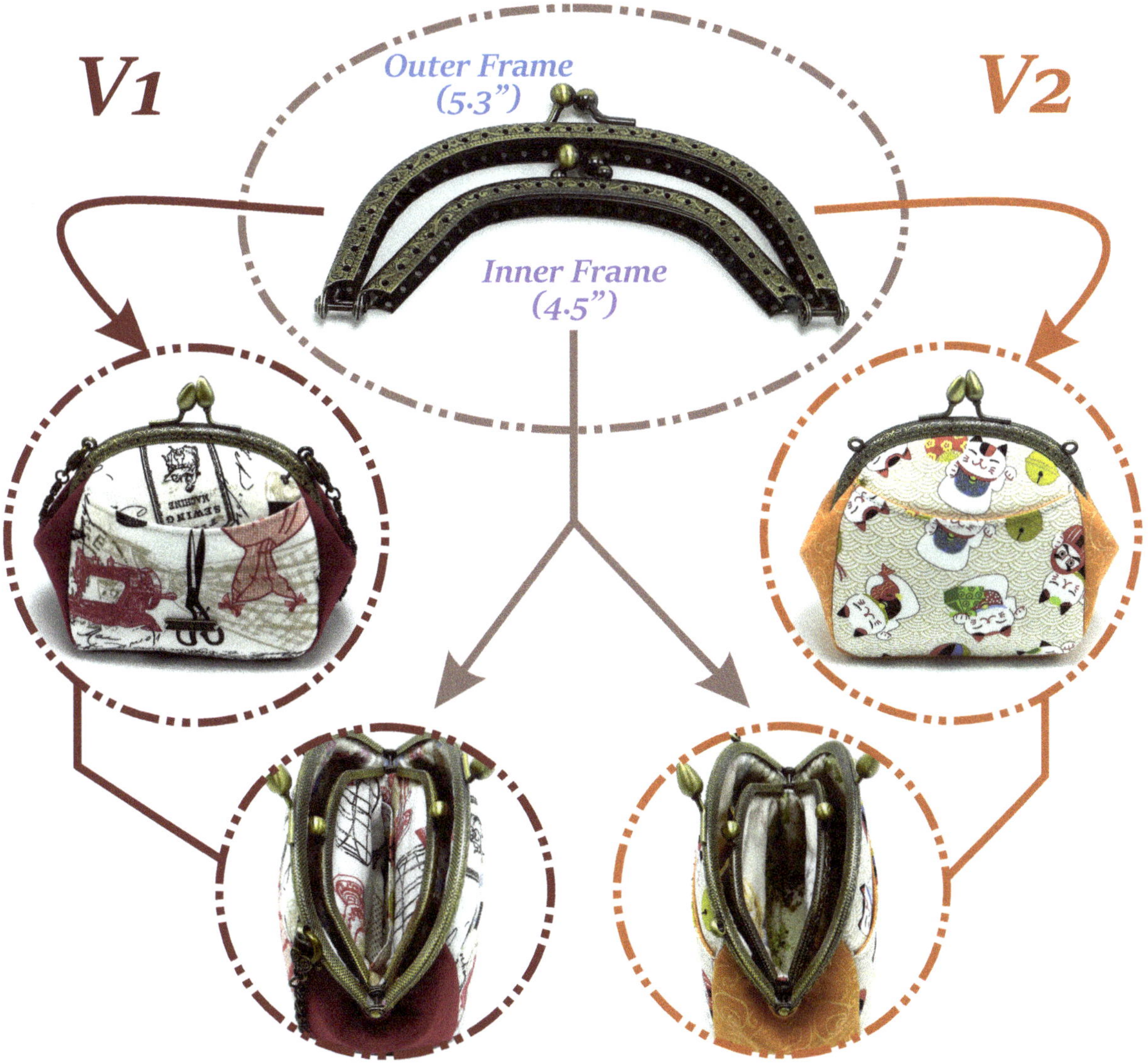

V1 — Outer Frame (5.3") — *V2*

Inner Frame (4.5")

 "The Sally (V1 & V2)" - Please refer to the chapter **"Basic Bag Construction"**, the section **"Construct the Slip Pocket - Style A"** to construct the outer frame exterior/interior pockets.

 "The Sally (V1)" - For details about how to construct the inner frame interior/lining pockets, please refer to the chapter **"Basic Bag Construction"**, the section **"Construct the Slip Pocket - Style C"**.

 "The Sally (V2)" - Please refer to the chapter **"Basic Bag Construction"**, the section **"Construct the Slip Pocket - Style E"** to construct the inner frame interior/lining pockets.

PREPARATION

PREPARING ALL THE MATERIALS - *for both Sally V1 and V2, Outer frame (5.3")*

✂ For NON-Directional Fabrics

Exterior/Interior/Interfacing:

- **Main/Lining** fabric (Pattern B) - "Front & Back" x 2; "Side Gusset & Bottom" x 1;

- **Interfacing** (Pattern A) - "Front & Back" x 2; "Side Gusset & Bottom" x 1;

Pocket/Interfacing: Each pocket is constructed in pairs (Main x 1, Lining x 1); you may make 2 exterior slip pockets and 2 interior slip pockets

- **Pocket (5.3" frame, Style A)**: main x 1, lining x 1; interfacing x 1;

Sally (V1)

✂ For Directional Fabrics

- **"Front & Back"**: the same as non-directional fabrics;

✂ "Side Gusset & Bottom":

☞ [Option 1] Fold "Side Gusset & Bottom" (Pattern A) in half, add seam allowance all the way around (Pattern B) x 2;

☞ [Option 2] "Side Gusset" (Pattern B) x 2; "Bottom" (Pattern B) x 1;

Sally (V2)

✎ *Tip: Do **NOT** apply the interfacing until all the "Side Gusset & Bottom" pieces are connected together. If you are using different fabric for the Bottom piece (for example: cork), apply interfacing to each piece individually.*

✎ NOTE: Add seam allowance before cutting any fabric. No seam allowance needed for cutting the interfacing, unless using a sew-in interfacing.

Reference

★ Please refer to the Chapter "**Understand The Pattern**" before cutting any fabric and interfacing.

★ **Pattern A** - the original pattern which has "NO Seam Allowance"

★ **Pattern B** - the pattern which has the "Seam Allowance" of your choice (1/4", 3/8" or 1/2")

PREPARATION

PREPARING ALL THE MATERIALS - *for Sally V1, Inner frame (4.5")*

For NON-Directional Fabrics

Exterior/Interior/Interfacing:

- **Main/Lining** fabric (Pattern B) - Main: "Front & Back" x 2; Lining: "Front & Back" x 2;

- **Interfacing** (Pattern A) - Main: "Front & Back" x 2; Lining: **No** interfacing;

Pocket/Interfacing:

- **Slip Pocket (Style C)**: "Pocket (4.5" frame)" x 1, interfacing x 1;

For Directional Fabrics

- **"Front & Back"**: the same as non-directional fabrics;

 "Pocket (4.5" frame) x 2

☞ Add seam allowance all the way around, connect both piece at the top first and become one piece.

NOTE: Add seam allowance before cutting any fabric. No seam allowance needed for cutting the interfacing, unless using a sew-in interfacing.

Sally (V1)

Inner Frame (4.5")

★ Please refer to the Chapter *"Understand The Pattern"* before cutting any fabric and interfacing.

★ **Pattern A** - *the original pattern which has "NO Seam Allowance"*

★ **Pattern B** - *the pattern which has the "Seam Allowance" of your choice (1/4", 3/8" or 1/2")*

Reference

PREPARATION

PREPARING ALL THE MATERIALS - *for Sally V2, Inner frame (4.5")*

For NON-Directional Fabrics

Exterior/Interfacing:

- **Main** fabric - "Front & Back" (Pattern B) x 1;
- **Interfacing** - "Front & Back" (Pattern A) x 1; (no seam allowance needed, unless it's a sew-in interfacing)

Interior/Interfacing:

- **Lining** fabric - "Front & Back" (Pattern B) x 1;
- **Interfacing** - "Front & Back" (Pattern A) x 1; (no seam allowance needed, unless it's a sew-in interfacing)

Pocket/Interfacing:

- **Slip Pocket (Style E)**: "Pocket (4.5" frame)" x 1, interfacing x 1;

Sally (V2)

For Directional Fabrics

Exterior/Interfacing:

- **Main** fabric - "Front & Back" (Pattern B) x 2;

 *Connect both pieces at the bottom and become ONE piece; sew by using the seam allowance of your choice.*

- **Interfacing** - "Front & Back" (Pattern A) x 1; (no seam allowance needed, unless it's a sew-in interfacing)

 *Tip: Do **NOT** apply the interfacing until all the Main pieces are connected together.*

Interior/Interfacing: the same as above;

Sally (V2)

Inner Frame (4.5")

DIRECTIONS

The difference between the Sally V1 and V2 is the construction of the inner piece. The inner frame has to be installed before the outer frame, so let's construct the inner piece first.

Sally V1 - the Inner Piece

 There are three parts of the inner piece: Main/Exterior, Lining/Interior and Lining/Interior Pocket (optional). Prepare all the materials and get ready.

Construct the Interior Pocket (optional)

1 Prepare all the materials and apply interfacing to the fabric. Add seam allowance around the patterns before cutting any fabric.

2 Construct the interior Pocket (4.5" frame). Please refer to the chapter **"Basic Bag Construction"**, the section **"Construct the Slip Pocket - Style C"**.

Construct the Interior

1 Connect "Front & Back" pieces. Place both "Front & Back" pieces Right side facing each other, align all the markings. Sew three sides, except the top, by using the seam allowance of your choice.

Construct the Exterior

1 Connect "Front & Back" pieces. Do the same as you construct the interior/lining piece. Turn Right side out.

DIRECTIONS

Complete the Inner Frame Purse piece

1 **Get Main and Lining pieces. Connect both pieces.** You should have both Main and Lining pieces ready to complete the purse piece. Place the Main piece (Right side out) into the Lining piece (Wrong side out), with the Right sides of both pieces facing each other. Align all 4 center markings.

 Use chalk or erasable pen to draw the seam line on the Wrong side of the Lining before sewing.

2 **Sew all the way around the top and leave an opening** to connect both pieces with the seam allowance of your choice. Use Pinking Shears to trim the excess or cut notches on the curved seam. Clip the tops of both side seams.

3 **Turn Right side out.** Turn the whole purse piece Right side out through the opening. Use your finger tip or something pointy (but not sharp) to round out the top curved seam.

4 **Press well.** Use an iron to press the purse piece with a bit of steam to remove wrinkles if necessary.

5 **Fold the opening seam allowance inward to the Wrong side.** Use clips or pins to hold it in place.

6 **Topstitching.** Top stitch all the way around the top edge by using 1/16" seam allowance.

 Do NOT use a seam allowance larger than 1/8", even though the top edge will be under the frame; using a seam allowance smaller than 1/8" will work well.

7 **Mark all 4 centers.** Press well if needed. Use chalk or erasable pen to mark all 4 centers.

DIRECTIONS

Install the Inner Purse frame

1 **Install the inner purse frame.** Get the correct size and shape purse frame ready to install to the completed inner purse piece. Let's put it aside after the installation.

 Please refer to the Chapter "Install the Purse Frame".

Sally V2 - the Inner Piece

 There are three parts of the inner piece: Main/Exterior, Lining/Interior and Lining/Interior Pocket (optional). Prepare all the materials and get ready.

Construct the Interior Pocket (optional)

1 **Prepare all the materials and apply interfacing to the fabric.** Add seam allowance around the patterns before cutting any fabric.

2 **Construct the interior Pocket (4.5" frame).** Please refer to the chapter **"Basic Bag Construction"**, the section **"Construct the Slip Pocket - Style E"**.

Complete the Inner Frame Purse piece

1 **Complete the interior construction.** *Please refer to the directions of* **"The Helena I"** *to complete the interior/lining construction.*

2 **Complete the exterior construction.** *Please refer to the directions of* **"The Helena I"** *to complete the exterior/main construction.*

3 **Complete the inner frame purse piece.** *Please refer to the directions of* **"The Helena I"** *to complete the inner frame purse piece.*

Install the Inner Purse frame

1 **Install the inner purse frame.** Get the correct size and shape purse frame ready to install to the completed inner purse piece. Let's put it aside after installation.

 *Please refer to the Chapter "Install the Purse Frame".*

DIRECTIONS

Sally V1 & V2 - the Outer Piece

 There are three parts of the outer piece: Main/Exterior, Lining/Interior and optional - Exterior (Main)/Interior (Lining) Pockets. Prepare all the materials and get ready.

Construct the Exterior/Interior Pocket (optional)

1 **Prepare all the materials and apply interfacing to the fabric.** Add seam allowance around the patterns before cutting any fabric.

2 **Construct the exterior/interior Pocket (5.3" frame).** Please refer to the chapter **"Basic Bag Construction"**, the section **"Construct the Slip Pocket - Style A"**.

Construct the Interior

1 **Complete the interior construction.** Please refer to the chapter **"Basic Bag Construction"**, the section **"Construct a Curved Seam"** to complete the interior construction.

Construct the Exterior

1 **Complete the exterior construction.** Do the same as how you construct the interior.

DIRECTIONS

Complete the Outer Frame Purse piece

 Please refer to the section **"Complete the Inner Frame Purse piece"** in this chapter to complete the outer frame purse piece and the photos below.

Lining piece   *Main piece*

Sew all the way at the top
Leave an opening

Turn Right Side out Through the opening

Top stitch all the way around

Install the purse frame

 1 **Install the outer purse frame.** Get the purse frame which has already been installed the completed inner purse piece. Let's install the completed outer piece to the frame.

 Please refer to the Chapter "Install the Purse Frame".

SEWING SKILL - Advanced Beginner~Intermediate ♦♦♦◇◇
DIFFICULT LEVEL - Intermediate ●●●○○

EXHIBIT

Helena III

V_Rect_V1

5.25" (Top W) x 3.75" (Bottom W)
3" (H) x 2.5" (D)

Top W: the widest part; H: not including the frame;

** Finished Size: (approximate measurements) **

Melody

V_Rect_V1

9" (Top W) x 7" (Bottom W)
6.75" (H) x 3.75" (D)

Top W: the widest part; H: not including the frame;

✯ **NOTE:** The attached pattern has **NO** seam allowances included. Refer to the Chapter "Understand The Pattern" completely before cutting or sewing! ☺

Printing Instructions

Please make sure your printer's scaling is set to "none," "actual size" or "100%". Do NOT check the "scale to fit paper size" option. Once the pattern is printed out, make sure it printed correctly. Check the "1 inch Square" and it should measure 1" x 1". If the square is not the correct size, check the printer settings again.

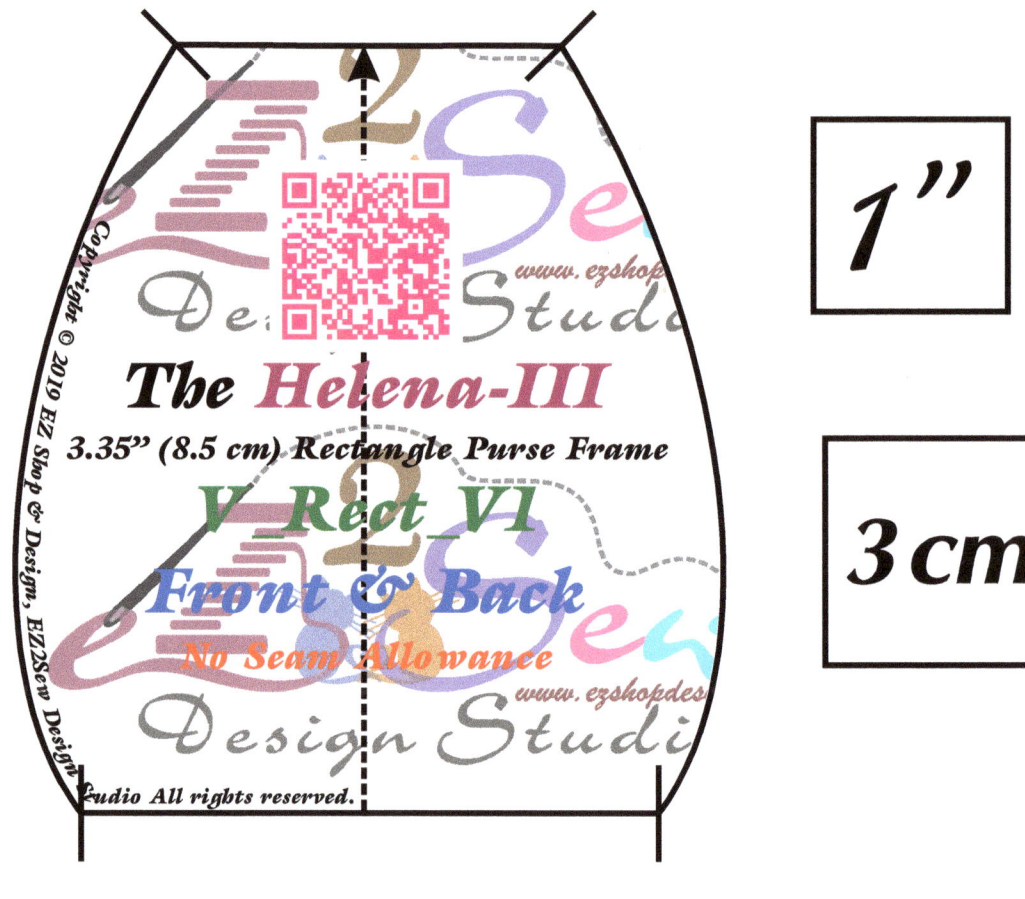

EXHIBIT

Janelle I

V_Rect_V1

7" (Top W) x 5" (Bottom W)
4.5" (H) x 2" (D)

* Top W: the widest part; H: not including the frame;

** Finished Size: (approximate measurements) **

Janelle II

V_Rect_V1

8" (Top W) x 5" (Bottom W)
5" (H) x 3" (D)

* Top W: the widest part; H: not including the frame;

PREPARATION

PREPARING ALL THE MATERIALS

✂ For NON-Directional Fabrics

Exterior/Interfacing:

- **Main** fabric - "Front & Back" (Pattern B) x 2; "Side Gusset" (Pattern B) x 2; "Bottom" (Pattern B) x 1;

- **Interfacing** - "Front & Back" (Pattern A) x 2; "Side Gusset" (Pattern A) x 2; "Bottom" (Pattern A) x 1; (no seam allowance needed)

Interior/Interfacing:

- **Lining** fabric - "Front & Back" (Pattern B) x 2; "Side Gusset" (Pattern B) x 2; "Bottom" (Pattern B) x 1;

- **Interfacing** - "Front & Back" (Pattern A) x 2; "Side Gusset" (Pattern A) x 2; "Bottom" (Pattern A) x 1; (no seam allowance needed)

Helena III

✂ For Directional Fabrics

Exterior/Interfacing:

- **Main** fabric - the same as non-directional fabrics;

- **Interfacing** - the same as above;

Interior/Interfacing:

- **Lining** fabric - the same as non-directional fabrics;

- **Interfacing** - the same as above;

Helena III

Lining   Main

Reference

★ Please refer to the Chapter "**Understand The Pattern**" before cutting any fabric and interfacing.

★ **Pattern A** - the original pattern which has "NO Seam Allowance"

★ **Pattern B** - the pattern which has the "Seam Allowance" of your choice (1/4", 3/8" or 1/2")

DIRECTIONS

For Directional Fabrics

 There is no difference between cutting directional and non-directional fabrics for this 5-piece pattern. If you are using directional fabrics, make sure they are in the correct direction.

Prepare the Materials

1. Cut the fabrics and interfacing. You should have 5 pieces of Main/Exterior (2 x "Front & Back", 2 x "Side Gusset" and 1 x "Bottom"), 5 pieces of Lining/Interior (2 x "Front & Back", 2 x "Side Gusset" and 1 x "Bottom") and all the interfacings ready.

2. Fusing the fabrics. Apply interfacing to the Wrong side of the Main and Lining fabrics, following the manufacturer's instructions. Please refer to the Chapter "Fabric & Interfacing" for details.

Construct the Interior

1. Trace Pattern A on the Wrong side of the fabrics. Trace Pattern A which has NO seam allowance to all the pieces on the Wrong side of the fabric and transfer all the markings to the fabric.

2. Connect the "Front & Back" to the "Bottom". Place the "Bottom" piece Right side up, under one of the "Front & Back" pieces, Wrong side up, align the center markings at the longer edge of the "Bottom" piece.

 *Use pins or clips to hold them in place. Make sure **ALL** the markings are aligned.*

3. Sew. Sew from ① and stop at ② by using the seam allowance of your choice. Connect the other "Front & Back" piece to the other longer edge of the "Bottom" piece.

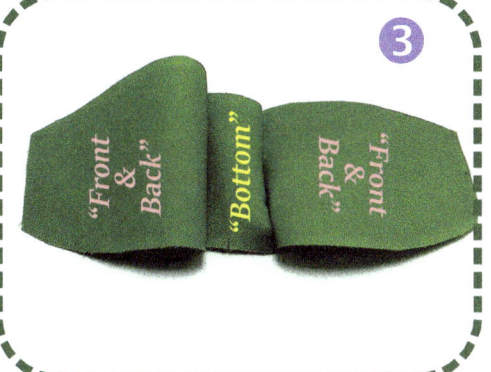

DIRECTIONS

Construct the Interior

4 **Connect the "Side Gusset" to the "Bottom".** Repeat Steps 2 & 3 by connecting the two "Side Gusset" pieces to the shorter edges of the "Bottom" piece.

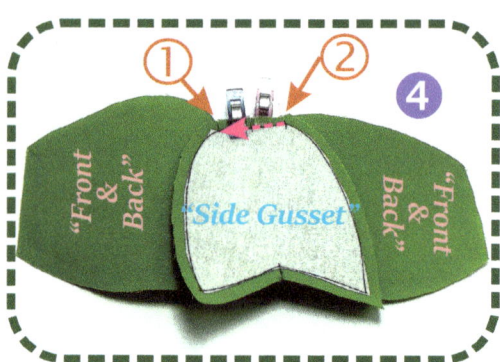

5 **Connect all 4 sides.** Sew all 4 sides by using the seam allowance of your choice to connect all 4 sides together.

6 **Make notches and Press well.** Cut notches at all the curved seams. Press all the seam allowances open, trim the excess if necessary. Put aside the completed Lining piece.

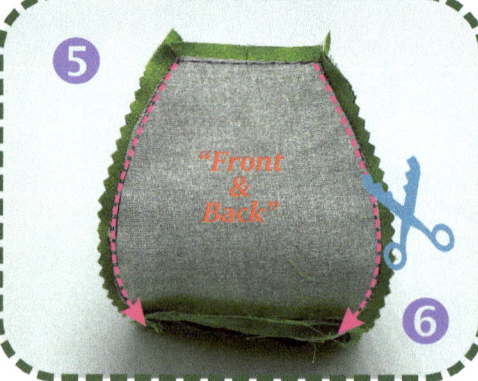

Construct the Exterior

1 **Construct the exterior** using the same process as you did with the Lining. Sew the exterior by using the seam allowance of your choice.

DIRECTIONS

Complete the Purse piece

1 **Get both Main and Lining pieces ready to connect.** You should have both Main and Lining pieces ready to complete the purse piece. Place the Main piece (Right side out) into the Lining piece (Wrong side out), with the Right sides of both pieces facing each other. Align all 4 center markings.

 *Use chalk or erasable pen to draw the seam line on the Wrong side of the Lining **before** sewing.*

2 **Sew all the way around and leave an opening.** Sew all the way around the top edge to connect both pieces with the seam allowance of your choice and don't forget to leave an opening for turning.

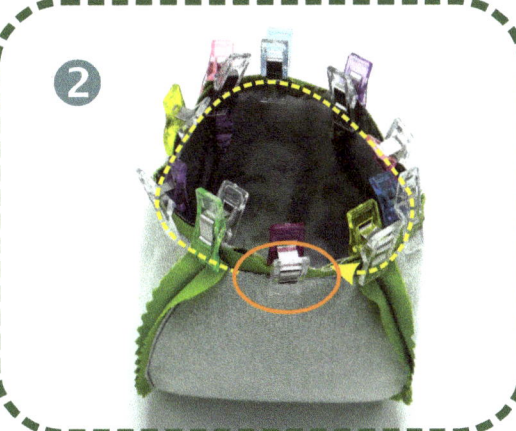

 LEAVE AN OPENING on one of the "Front & Back" pieces that has the **straight** seam for turning the whole piece Right side out later.

3 **Trim.** Use Pinking Shears to trim the excess or make notches at the curved seam allowances. Make a clip on both side gussets where the valley of the "V" shape is; do not cut the thread.

4 **Turn Right side out.** Turn the whole purse piece Right side out through the opening. Use your finger tip or something pointy (but not sharp) to round out the top curved seam.

DIRECTIONS

Complete the Purse piece

5 **Press well.** Use an iron to press the purse piece well with a bit of steam to remove the wrinkles if necessary.

6 **Topstitching.** Top Stitch all the way around the top edge by using 1/16" seam allowance. This will also close the opening.

Do NOT use a seam allowance larger than 1/8", even though the top edge will be under the frame; using a seam allowance smaller than 1/8" will work well.

7 **Mark all 4 centers.** Press well if needed. Use chalk or erasable pen to mark all 4 centers.

Install the purse frame

1 **Install the purse frame.** Get the correct size and shape purse frame ready to install to the completed purse piece.

Please refer to the Chapter "Install Sew-In Purse Frame".

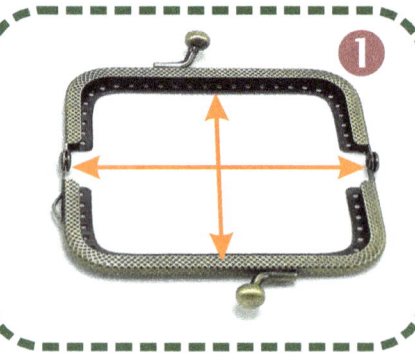

$\mathscr{U}$sing the same directions above to construct the exterior, interior, and complete the purse to the following patterns. The differences among those are the size/shape of the frame, the finished purse piece and with/without the pockets.

*"**The Janelle I and Janelle II**" - Please refer to the chapter "**Basic Bag Construction**", the section "**Construct the Slip Pocket - Style A**" to construct the exterior and/or interior pockets. The Janelle I has an optional pocket cap for the exterior front pocket, please refer to the details later in this chapter.*

*"**The Melody**" - Please also refer to the chapter "**Basic Bag Construction**", the section "**Construct the Slip Pocket - Style A**" to construct the exterior and/or interior pockets. For details about how to construct the interior and exterior side gusset 3-D pockets, please refer to the section "**Construct the 3-D Pocket**".*

PREPARATION

PREPARING ALL THE MATERIALS

Janelle I

✂ **For NON-Directional/Directional Fabrics**

Exterior/Interfacing:

- **Main** fabric - "Front & Back" (Pattern B) x 2; "Side Gusset" (Pattern B) x 2; "Bottom" (Pattern B) x 1;

- **Interfacing** - "Front & Back" (Pattern A) x 2; "Side Gusset" (Pattern A) x 2; "Bottom" (Pattern A) x 1; (no seam allowance needed)

Interior/Interfacing:

- **Lining** fabric - "Front & Back" (Pattern B) x 2; "Side Gusset" (Pattern B) x 2; "Bottom" (Pattern B) x 1;

- **Interfacing** - "Front & Back" (Pattern A) x 2; "Side Gusset" (Pattern A) x 2; "Bottom" (Pattern A) x 1; (no seam allowance needed)

Pocket/Interfacing: Each pocket is constructed in pairs (Main x 1, Lining x 1)

- **Pocket (Style A)**: Main x 1, Lining x 1; Interfacing x 1;
- **Pocket Cap**: Main x 1, Lining x 1; Interfacing x 1; (Optional)

⚬⟜ Accessories and Hardwares

- Magnet set x 1; (Optional: only if you add a pocket cap on top of the pocket)
- Purse feet x 4; (Optional)
- Purse frame x 1;

Reference

★ Please refer to the Chapter *"Understand The Pattern"* before cutting any fabric and interfacing.

★ **Pattern A** - the original pattern which has *"NO Seam Allowance"*

★ **Pattern B** - the pattern which has the *"Seam Allowance"* of your choice (1/4", 3/8" or 1/2")

DIRECTIONS

Construct the Pocket with a Cap

 *If you don't want to add a cap on top of the pocket, you may skip the following steps.*

1 **Cut the "Front & Back" pattern into 2 pieces.** Cut the "Front & Back" (Pattern A) along the dashed line (Figure 1). Add seam allowance of your choice all the way around at both "Top" and "Bottom" patterns (Figure 2).

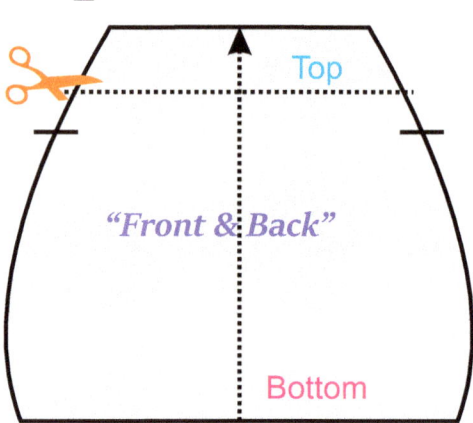
Figure 1

2 **Gather all the materials.** "Front & Back": 1 x "Top", 1 x "Bottom", and 1 x interfacing; "Pocket": 1 x main, 1 x lining and 1 x interfacing; "Pocket Cap": 1 x main, 1 lining and 1 x interfacing; Hardware: 1 set of magnet.

3 **Construct the pocket.** Please refer to the chapter "**Basic Bag Construction**", the section "**Construct the Slip Pocket - Style A**". NOTE: Do **NOT** place the pocket to the "Bottom" base piece yet. Use the pattern as a guide, find the place on the main fabric to install the magnet closure.

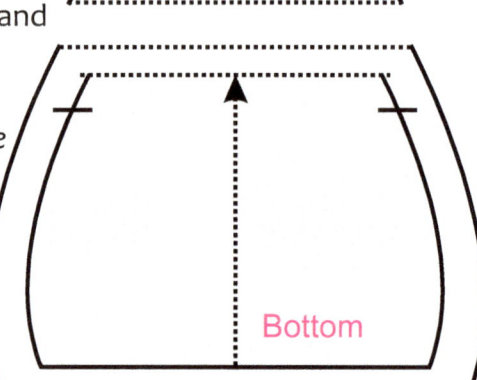
Figure 2

4 **Construct the pocket cap.** Use the pattern as a guide, find the place at the lining to install the magnet closure. Place both cap main and lining pieces Right side facing each other, sew the curved seam by using the seam allowance of your choice, leave the straight seam as an opening for turning the piece right side out. Top stitch, 1/8" seam allowance, on the curved edge, but not on the straight raw edge.

DIRECTIONS

Construct the Pocket with Cap

5 **Install the magnet closure.** *Install the female part of the magnet on the Main fabric of the pocket and the male part to the Lining of the pocket cap.*

6 **Attach the pocket to the base piece.** *Place the pocket piece to the "Bottom" base piece by using baste stitches. Sew all the way around, except the pocket top.*

7 **Attach the pocket cap and apply interfacing.** *Place the pocket cap on top of the pocket and make sure the magnet closure is attached correctly. Place the "Top", Right side facing down, on top of the pocket cap, align the center of the top raw edge of the "Bottom" piece. Sew these three pieces by using the seam allowance of your choice. Flip the "Top" piece to the Right side, top stitch (1/8" seam allowance) on the connected edge. Now, apply the interfacing to the back of the finished front piece.*

✍ **"The Janelle I and Janelle II"** - Use the same directions as the **"Helena III"** to construct the exterior, interior, and complete the purse piece. Please refer to the chapter **"Basic Bag Construction"**, the section **"Construct the Slip Pocket - Style A"** to construct the exterior and/or interior pockets.

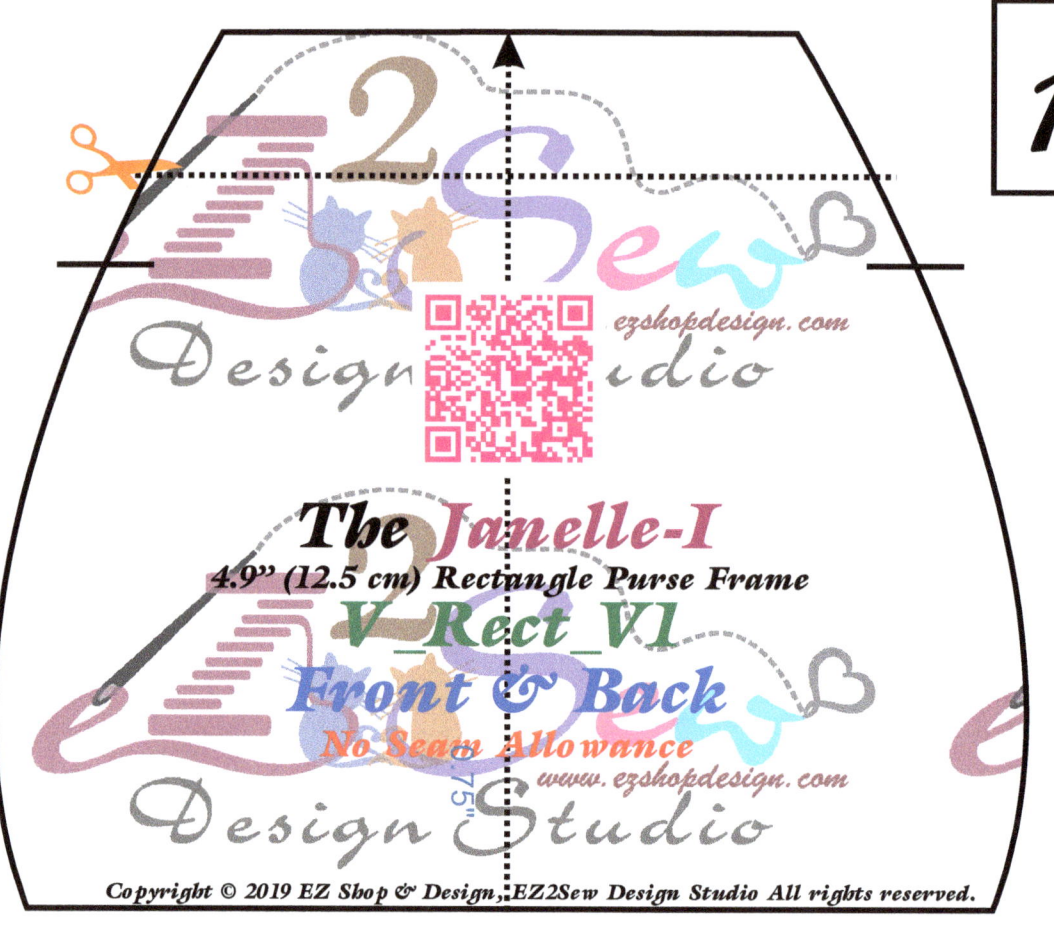

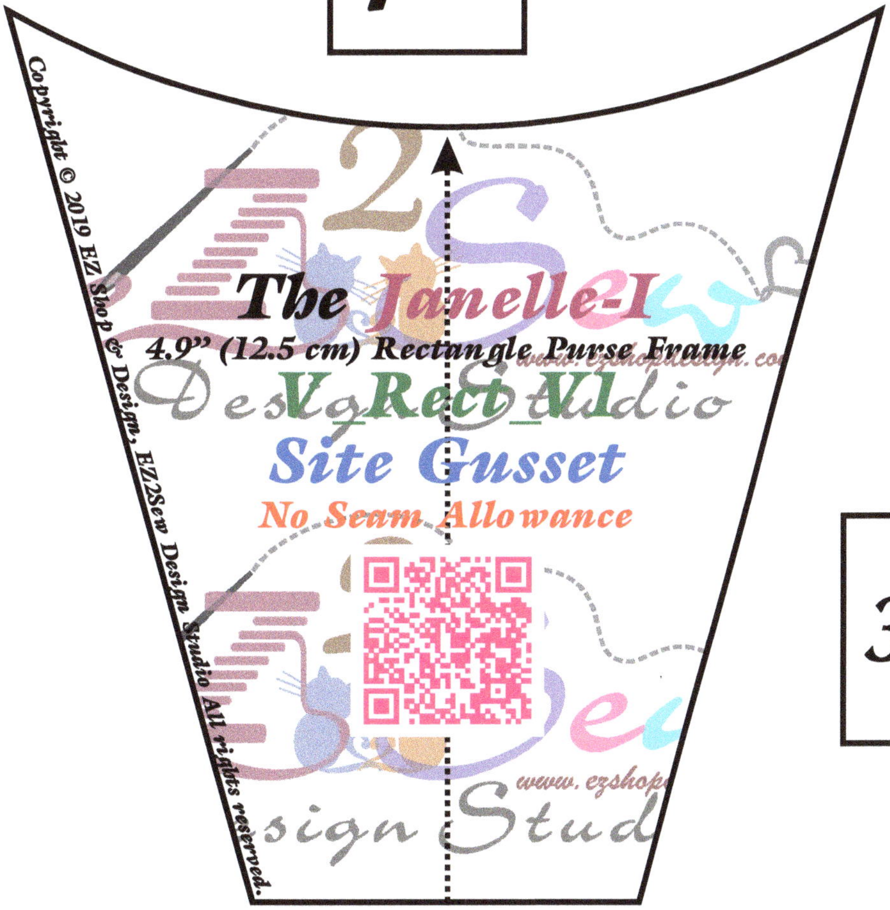

PREPARATION

PREPARING ALL THE MATERIALS

✂ For NON-Directional/Directional Fabrics

Janelle II

Exterior/Interfacing:

- **Main** fabric - "Front & Back" (Pattern B) x 2; "Side Gusset" (Pattern B) x 2; "Bottom" (Pattern B) x 1;

- **Interfacing** - "Front & Back" (Pattern A) x 2; "Side Gusset" (Pattern A) x 2; "Bottom" (Pattern A) x 1; (no seam allowance needed)

Interior/Interfacing:

- **Lining** fabric - "Front & Back" (Pattern B) x 2; "Side Gusset" (Pattern B) x 2; "Bottom" (Pattern B) x 1;

- **Interfacing** - "Front & Back" (Pattern A) x 2; "Side Gusset" (Pattern A) x 2; "Bottom" (Pattern A) x 1; (no seam allowance needed)

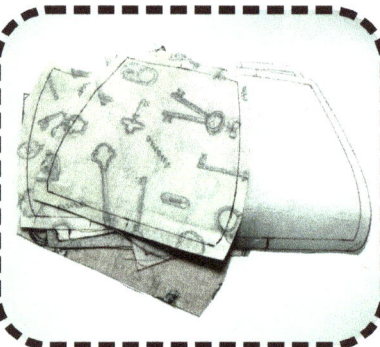

Pocket/Interfacing: Each pocket is constructed in pairs (Main x 1, Lining x 1)

- **Pocket (Style A)**: Main x 1, Lining x 1; Interfacing x 1;

🗝 Accessories and Hardwares

- Purse frame x 1;
- Optional: Lace x 1; Tag x 1; Purse feet x 4;

Reference

★ Please refer to the Chapter "**Understand The Pattern**" before cutting any fabric and interfacing.

★ **Pattern A** - the original pattern which has "NO Seam Allowance"

★ **Pattern B** - the pattern which has the "Seam Allowance" of your choice (1/4", 3/8" or 1/2")

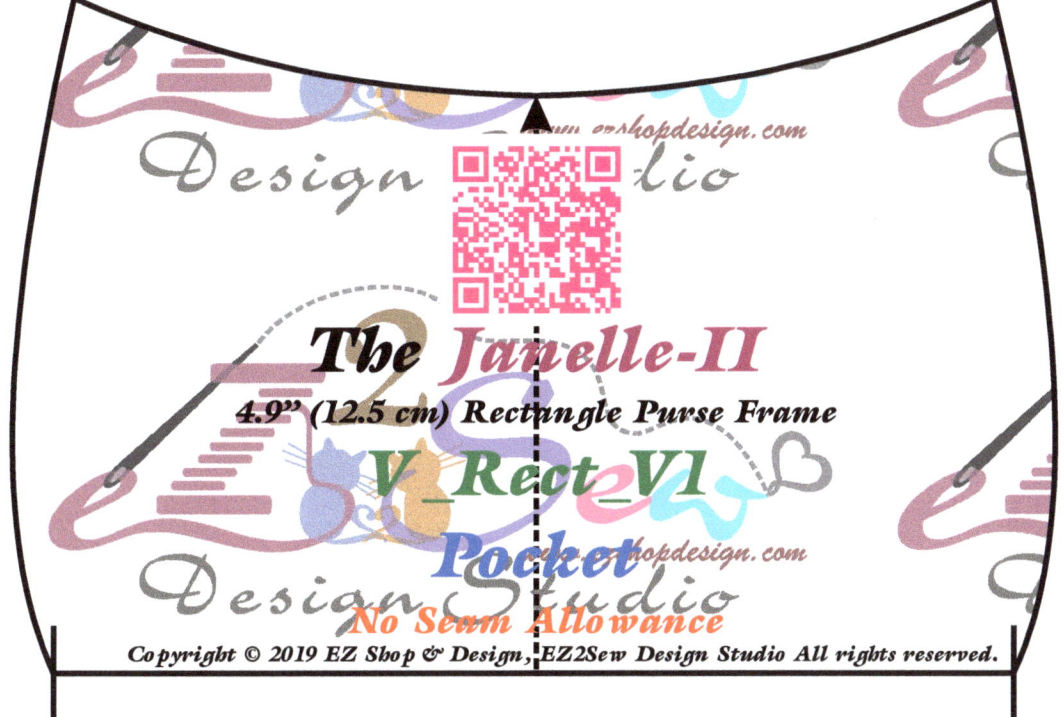

PREPARATION

PREPARING ALL THE MATERIALS

✂ For NON-Directional/Directional Fabrics

Exterior/Interfacing:

- **Main** fabric (Pattern B) - "Front & Back" x 2; "Side Gusset" x 2; "Bottom" x 1;
- **Interfacing** (Pattern A) - "Front & Back" x 2; "Side Gusset" x 2; "Bottom" x 1;

Interior/Interfacing:

- **Lining** fabric (Pattern B) - "Front & Back" x 2; "Side Gusset" x 2; "Bottom" x 1;
- **Interfacing** (Pattern A) - "Front & Back" x 2; "Side Gusset" x 2; "Bottom" x 1;

Pocket/Interfacing: Each pocket is constructed in pairs (Main x 1, Lining x 1)

- **Exterior Pocket (Style A):** Main x 1, Lining x 1; Interfacing x 1;
- **Side Gusset 3-D Pocket:** Main x 1, Lining x 1; Interfacing x 1;
- **Interior 3-D Pocket:** Main x 1, Lining x 1; Interfacing x 1;

🔑 Accessories and Hardwares

- Optional: Purse feet x 4; Lace x 1; Label x 1;
- Optional: Chain Shoulder Strap;
- Purse frame x 1;

Reference

- ★ Please refer to the Chapter **"Understand The Pattern"** before cutting any fabric and interfacing.
- ★ **Pattern A** - the original pattern which has "NO Seam Allowance"
- ★ **Pattern B** - the pattern which has the "Seam Allowance" of your choice (1/4", 3/8" or 1/2")

DIRECTIONS

Construct the Exterior Side Gusset 3-D Pocket

1 **Construct the Side Gusset Pocket.** *Please refer to the chapter* **"Basic Bag Construction"***, the section* **"Construct the Slip Pocket - Style A"** *and* **"Construct the 3-D Pocket"**. **NOTE:** <u>No</u> elastic needed for this 3-D pocket.

2 **Place the 3-D pocket to the "Side Gusset".** *Align all the markings on both the 3-D pocket and the "Side Gusset". Fold the bottom of the 3-D pocket along the markings. Align all the raw edges to the "Side Gusset". Attach the pocket to the Base piece by baste stitching all the way around, except the top of the pocket. Do the same on the other side of the pocket.*

3 **Attach "Side Gusset" to the "Bottom".** *Align the center of the shorter edge of the "Bottom" and the bottom of the "Side Gusset", Wrong side facing each other, sew by using the seam allowance of your choice. Do the same on the other side of the "Side Gusset".*

4 **Apply Interfacing and Install purse feet.** *Apply interfacing to the Wrong side of the finished "Side Gusset" and "Bottom" piece. Optional: Install the purse piece to the "Bottom" by using the pattern as a guide.*

DIRECTIONS

Construct the Interior *and* 3-D Pocket

1 **Construct the 3-D Pocket.** *Please refer to the chapter* **"Basic Bag Construction"**, *the section* **"Construct the 3-D Pocket"**.

2 **Attach the 3-D pocket to the "Front & Back".** *Align all the markings on both the 3-D pocket and the "Front & Back". Attach the pocket to the Base piece by baste stitching all the way around, except the top of the pocket. Repeat on the other side of the pocket.*

3 **Connect "Side Gusset" and the "Bottom".** *Do the same as you construct the exterior "Side Gusset" and "Bottom".*

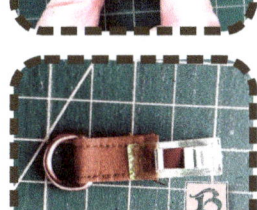

4 **Attach "Front & Back" to the connected "Side Gusset" piece.** *Align all the markings of both "Front & Back" and the finished "Side Gusset" piece. Sew all the way around by using the seam allowance of your choice. Repeat on the other side.*

 NOTE: Leave an **OPENING** at one of the bottom straight seams. Sew the bottom of one of the pockets, using the seam allowance of you choice before attaching the finished "side Gusset" and "Bottom".

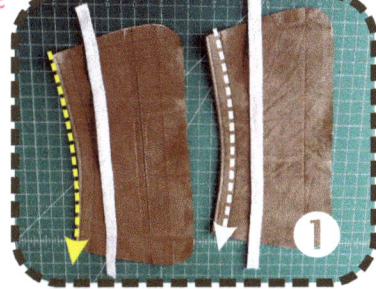 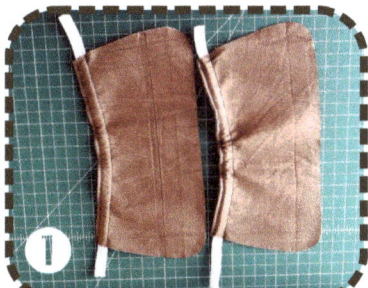

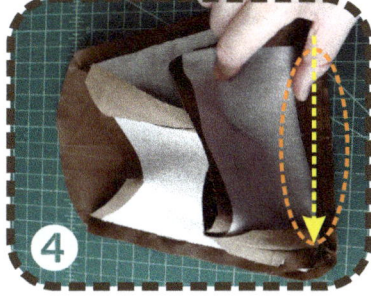  

3 cm

1"

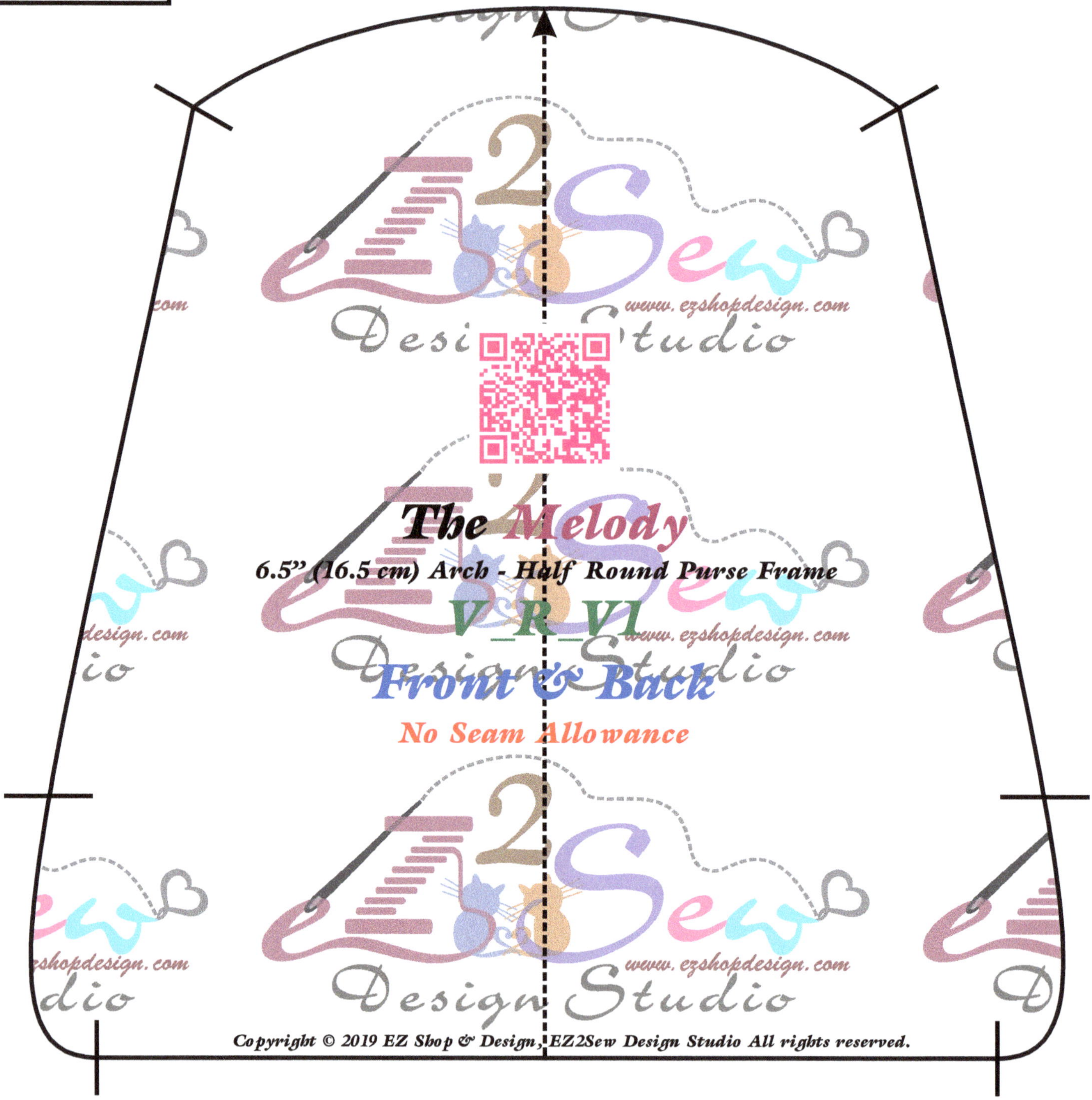

The Melody
6.5" (16.5 cm) Arch - Half Round Purse Frame
V_R_VI
Front & Back
No Seam Allowance

Copyright © 2019 EZ Shop & Design, EZ2Sew Design Studio All rights reserved.

 Printing Instructions

 155

Please make sure your printer's scaling is set to "none," "actual size" or "100%". Do NOT check the "scale to fit paper size" option. Once the pattern is printed out, make sure it printed correctly. Check the "1 inch Square" and it should measure 1" x 1". If the square is not the correct size, check the printer settings again.

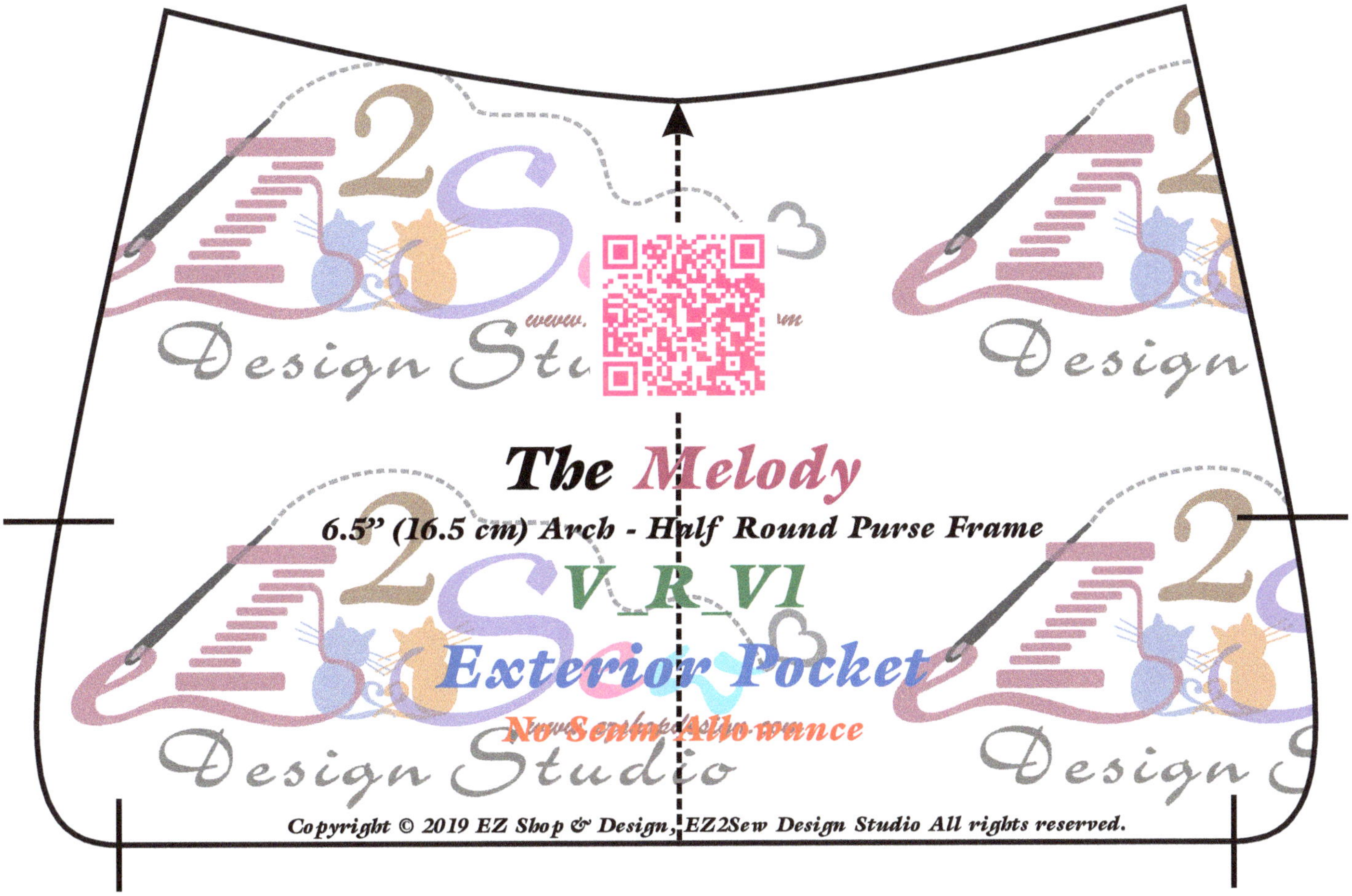

The Melody
6.5" (16.5 cm) Arch - Half Round Purse Frame
V_R_VI
Exterior Pocket
No Seam Allowance

Copyright © 2019 EZ Shop & Design, EZ2Sew Design Studio All rights reserved.

The Melody
6.5" (16.5 cm) Arch - Half Round Purse Frame
V_R_VI
Bottom
No Seam Allowance

Copyright © 2019 EZ Shop & Design, EZ2Sew Design Studio All rights reserved.

Printing Instructions

Please make sure your printer's scaling is set to "none," "actual size" or "100%". Do NOT check the "scale to fit paper size" option. Once the pattern is printed out, make sure it printed correctly. Check the "1 inch Square" and it should measure 1" x 1". If the square is not the correct size, check the printer settings again.

3 cm

1"

Printing Instructions

Please make sure your printer's scaling is set to "none," "actual size" or "100%". DO NOT check the "scale to fit paper size" option. Once the pattern is printed out, make sure it printed correctly. Check the "1 inch Square" and it should measure 1" x 1". If the square is not the correct size, check the printer settings again.

The Melody
6.5" (16.5 cm) Arch - Half Round Purse Frame
Interior 3-D Pocket
V_R_VL
No Seam Allowance

EZ2Sew Design Studio All rights reserved.
Copyright © 2019 EZ Shop & Design.

157

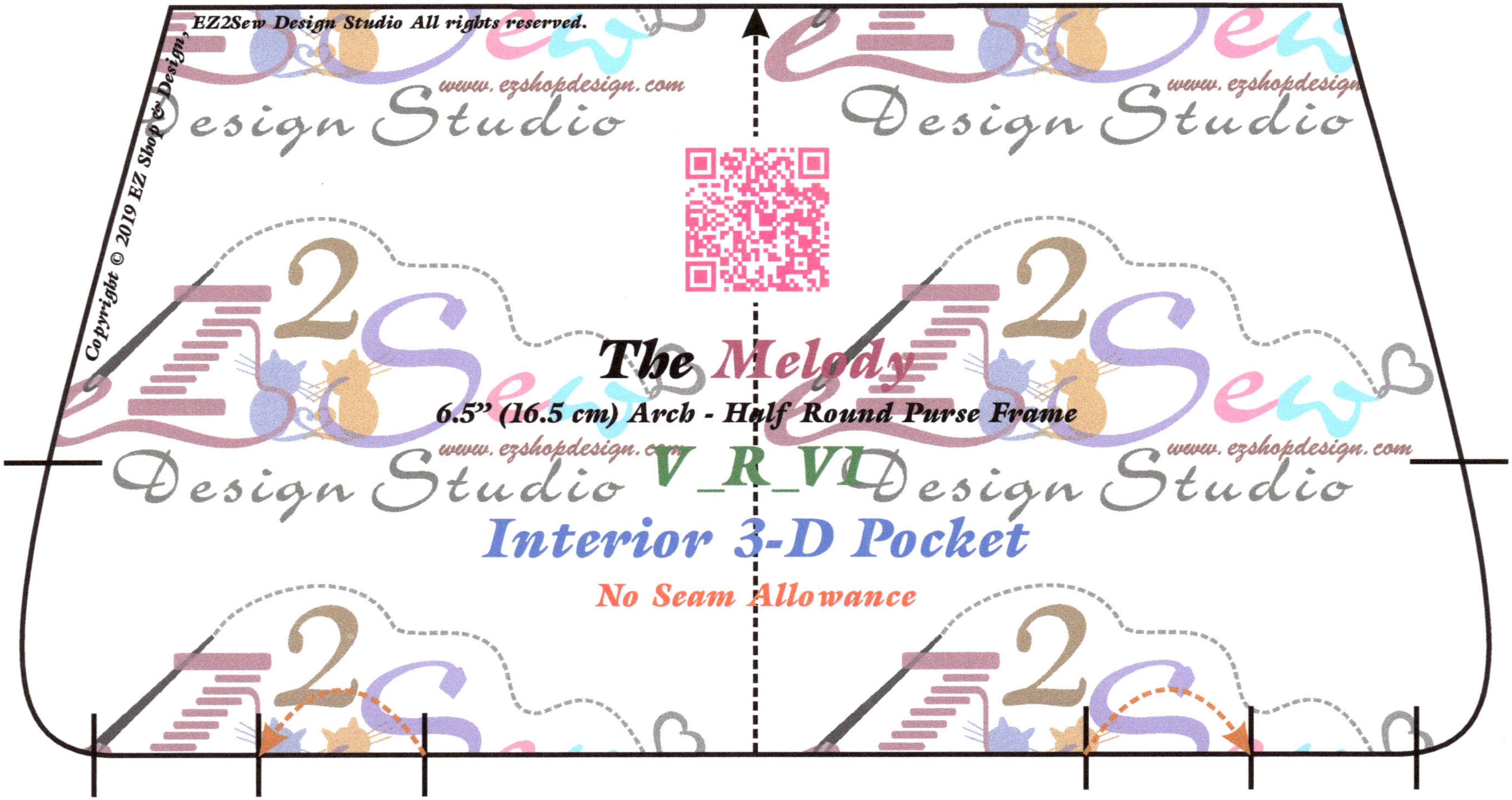

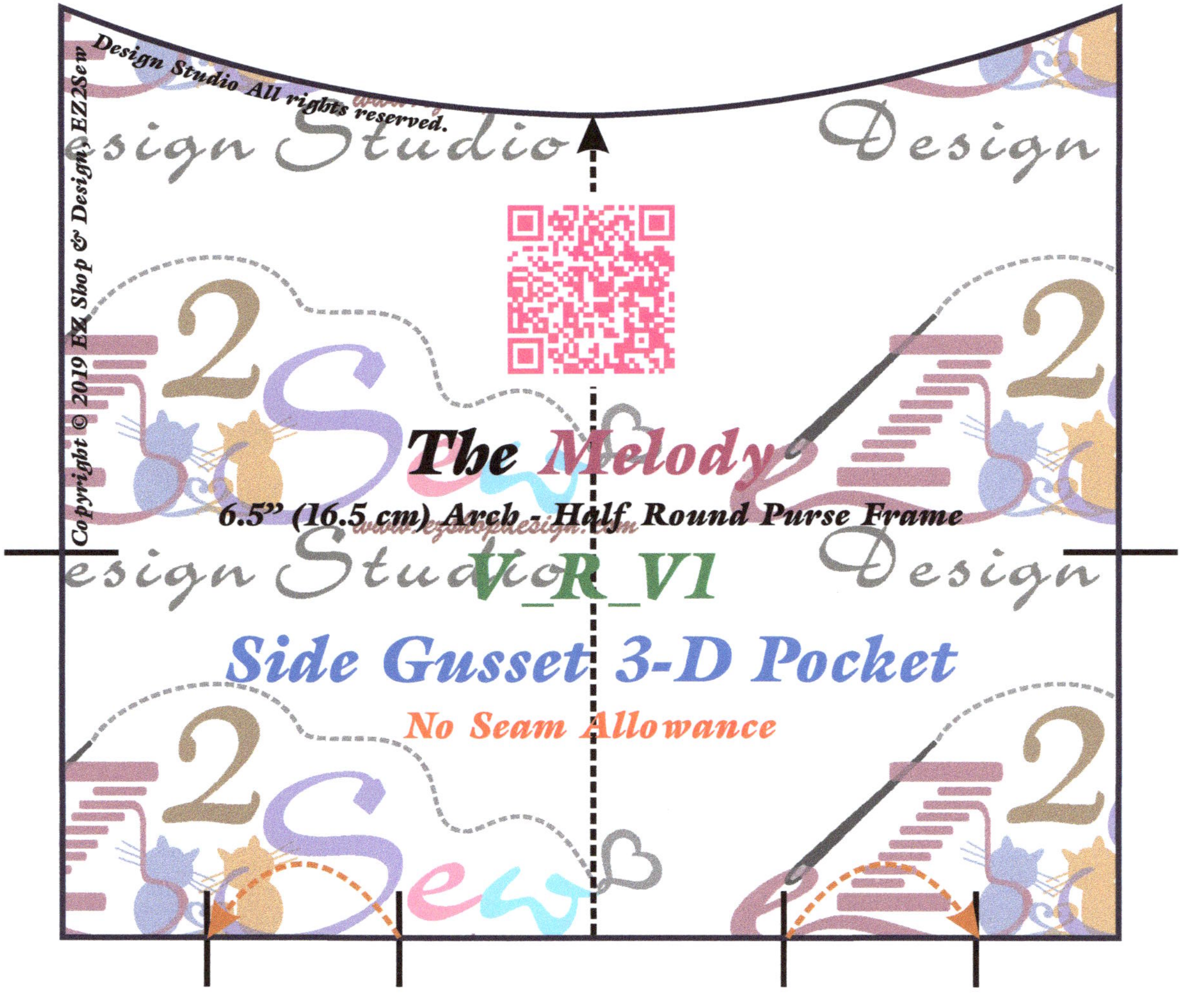

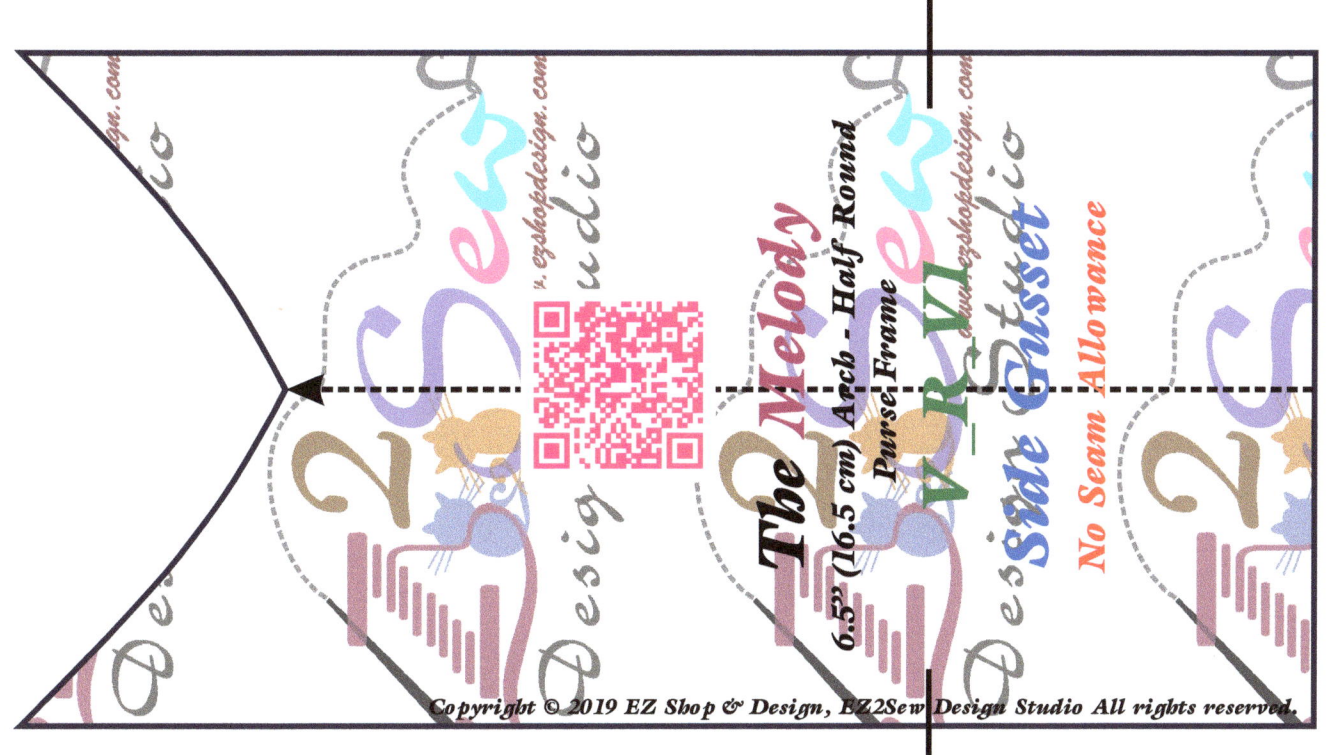

3 cm

1"

EXHIBIT

Tamia

I_Rect_V1

11" (Top W) x 8.25" (Bottom W)
6" (H) x 4" (D)

* Top W: the widest part; H: not including the frame;

** Finished Size: (approximate measurements) **

Tamia

V_Rect_V2

11" (Top W) x 8.25" (Bottom W)
8" (H) x 4" (D)

* Top W: the widest part; H: not including the frame;

PREPARATION

PREPARING ALL THE MATERIALS

 Exterior/Interfacing: *(Connect the pattern first)*

- **Main** fabric (Pattern B) - "Top (Front & Back)" x 2; "Bottom (Front & Back)" x 1; Optional: Lace x 2;

- **Interfacing** (Pattern A) - "Front & Back (Interior)" x 1;

Tamia V1

 Tip: Do **NOT** apply the interfacing until all the Main pieces are connected together and become ONE piece. No seam allowance needed, unless it's a sew-in one.

Interior/Interfacing: *(Connect the pattern first)*

- **Lining** fabric (Pattern B) - "Front & Back (Interior)" x 1;

- **Interfacing** (Pattern A) - "Front & Back (Interior)" x 1;

- **"Pocket (Interior - Front & Back)"** - Main (Pattern B) x 1; Lining (Pattern B) x 1; Interfacing (Pattern A) x 1;

Zipper Flap: *(Connect the pattern first)*

- **Main/Interfacing** fabric - "Zipper Flap" (Pattern B) x 2; Cut 2 for interfacing (Pattern A);

- **Lining** - "Zipper Flap" (Pattern B) x 2; No interfacing needed;

Handle, D-Ring Tab(s) & Hardware:

- **Handle** - 12" x 3" cut 2; (no seam allowance needed)
- **D-Ring Tab** - 2" x 4" (no seam allowance needed) cut 1 for each;
- **Hardware** - (1) 1/2" D-Ring x 2; (2) 16" Zipper x 1; (3) Zipper End x 2; (4) Purse Feet x 4 (optional) (5) Label/Tag x 1 (optional);

Tamia V1

★ Please refer to the Chapter "**Understand The Pattern**" before cutting any fabric and interfacing.

★ **Pattern A** - the original pattern which has "NO Seam Allowance"

★ **Pattern B** - the pattern which has the "Seam Allowance" of your choice (1/4", 3/8" or 1/2")

DIRECTIONS

Tamia V1

There are many elements in this purse, such as, the zipper flap casing, the purse feet installation, the handles, the D-ring tabs, the 3-D pockets, slip pockets and etc.. We will construct those elements one by one and connect them all together. Please refer to the "**Basic Bag Construction**" for more details on some of those elements and photos here. Gather all the materials, accessories and hardware, and let's get started.

Construct the Handle and D-Ring Tab

The Handle and D-Ring Tab - please refer to the chapter "**Basic Bag Construction**", section "**Construct the Handle and D-Ring Tab**" for more details.

Construct the Zipper Flap casing

The Zipper Flap casing - please refer to the chapter "**Basic Bag Construction**", section "**Construct the Zipper Flap casing**" for more details.

DIRECTIONS

Construct the Exterior

1 **Connect both tops and bottom together.** Connect both top pieces with the bottom piece. Place the bottom of the "Top" and one of the flat edges of the "Bottom", Right side facing each other. You may sandwich the lace in between the two pieces (optional) and sew using the seam allowance of your choice.

2 **Apply interfacing and top stitch.** Press seam allowances flat at the Wrong side. The lace can be placed upward or downward, depending on the lace you use and if the lace has direction. Now the Exterior is ONE piece, apply interfacing to the wrong side of the exterior piece. Top stitch at the top piece of the connection.

Top stitch 1/8" or 1/16" away from the connecting edge AFTER applying the interfacing to the fabric. You may add a label/tag at either sides to distinguish the front and back.

Apply one extra layer of interfacing. For example: Pellon 520 Deco-Fuse Firm 4" (W) x 8.25" (L) to the center of the bottom to reinforce.

3 **Install the Purse Feet (optional).** Please refer to the chapter "**Basic Bag Construction**", section "**Install the Purse Feet**".

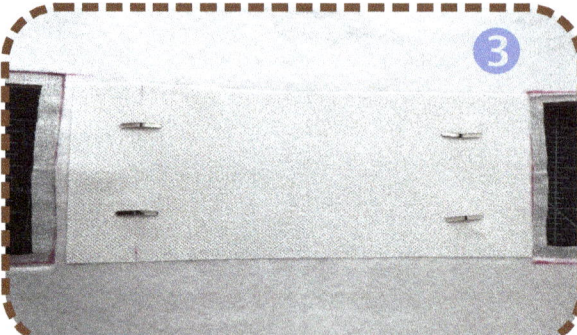

DIRECTIONS

Construct the Exterior

4 **Attach the handles and D-Ring tabs.** Place the handle Right side down at the top of the exterior, 2" away from the center. Attach the D-Ring tab next to the left side of the handle. Do the same step as above at the other side. Baste stitch both handles and tabs to attach them onto the top of the exterior.

5 **Fold the Main fabric in half.** Fold the Main fabric in half, Right side facing together; Align all the markings, top-centers and bottom-centers. Use pins or clips to hold them in place.

6 **Sew both sides.** Sew both sides by using the seam allowance of your choice. Press open the side seam allowances.

7 **Sew box corners.** Fold the box corner, align the center of the side seam and the center marking of the bottom; sew both box corners by using the seam allowance of your choice.

8 **Attach the zipper flap casing.** Turn the exterior piece Right side out. Attach the zipper flap casing Right side facing the top of the exterior piece, aligned at the center (make sure both the handles and D-Right tabs are downward). Use pins or clips to hold them in place and baste stitch both the exterior and zipper flap casing together. We just completed constructing the exterior piece.

DIRECTIONS

Construct the Interior

1 **Construct the interior slip pocket and attach to the Lining.** Please refer to the chapter **"Basic Bag Construction"**, section **"Construct the Slip Pocket - Style D"**.

2 **Sew both sides and box corners.** Do the same as you construct the exterior, from steps 5 to 7.

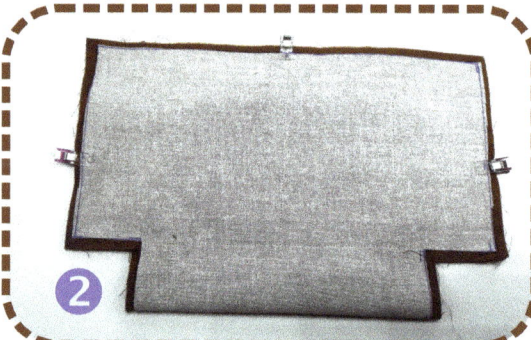 

Complete the Purse piece

1 **Connect both Main and Lining pieces.** You should have both Main and Lining pieces ready to complete the purse piece. Place the Main piece (Right side out) into the Lining piece (Wrong side out), with the Right sides of both pieces facing each other. Align all 4 center markings.

 Use chalk or erasable pen to draw the seam line on the Wrong side of the Lining before sewing.

2 **Sew all the way around the top and leave an opening.** Connect both pieces with the seam allowance of your choice.

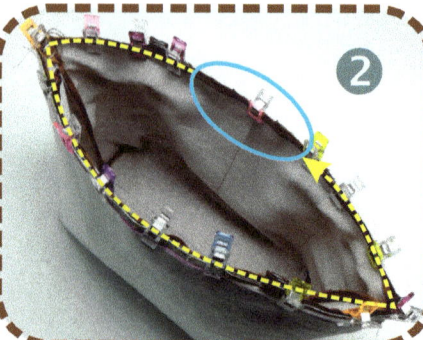 

DIRECTIONS

Complete the Purse piece

3 **Turn Right side out.** Turn the whole purse piece Right side out through the opening.

4 **Press well.** Use an iron to press the purse piece with a bit of steam to remove wrinkles if necessary.

5 **Fold the opening seam allowance inward.** Use 1/4" wide Wonder Tape or Double Stick Fusible Web Tape to hold it in place.

6 **Topstitching.** Top stitch all the way around the connected edge by using 1/16" seam allowance.

Install the purse frame

 **1** **Install the purse frame.** Get the correct size and shape purse frame ready to install to the completed purse piece.

Please refer to the Chapter "Install the Purse Frame". Also, refer to the pattern "Tamia V2" for installing the Metal Zipper Ends.

PREPARATION
PREPARING ALL THE MATERIALS

 Exterior/Pocket/Interfacing:

 Choose the pocket style and follow the cutting instruction below. Add seam allowance before cutting any fabric, no seam allowance needed for the interfacing unless it's a sew-in one.

Tamia V2

- **Slip Pocket**/ea - "Pocket (Front & Back)": main x 1; lining x 1; interfacing x 1;

- **3-D Pocket**/ea - **Magnet**: 1 Set (3/4"); (optional) Lace: 6" L x 1;
  - "3-D Pocket (Front & Back)": main x 1; lining x 1; interfacing x 1; 8.5" L Elastic x 1;
  - "Pocket Cap (Front & Back): main x 1; lining x 1; interfacing x 1;
  - Optional: 2" W x 4" L D-Ring tab x 1; 1/2" D-Ring x 1;

- **Side Gusset** - "Side Gusset" x 2; interfacing x 2;

- **Front & Back** - Interfacing x 1; (optional) Label/Tag x 1;
  - For Slip Pocket/ea: "Front & Back" x 1 for each slip pocket;
  - For 3-D Pocket/ea: "Top" of the 3-D pocket x 1; "Bottom" of the 3-D pocket x 1;

- **Bottom** - "Bottom" x 1; Interfacing x 1; Purse feet x 4 (optional);

- **Zipper Flap** - "Zipper Flap": main x 2; lining x 2; interfacing x 2;

 Interior/Pocket/Interfacing:

- **Front & Back** - "Front & Back" x 2; interfacing x 2;

- **Slip Pocket**/ea - "Pocket (Front & Back)": main x 1; lining x 1; interfacing x 1;

- **Side Gusset** - "Side Gusset" x 2; interfacing x 2;

- **3-D Pocket**/ea - "3D Pocket (Interior Side Gusset)": main x 1; lining x 1; interfacing x 1; 6.5" L Elastic x 1;

- **Bottom** - "Bottom" x 1; Interfacing x 1;

Handle and other accessories:
- **Handle** - Cut 2: 3" W x 12" L; (no seam allowance needed)
- **D-Ring/Tab** - Cut 2: 2" W x 4" L; 2 x D-ring (1/2");
- **Zipper** - 16" L x 1; Zipper End x 2;

Tamia V2

DIRECTIONS

Tamia V2

There are many elements in this purse, such as, the zipper flap casing, the purse feet installation, the handles, the D-ring tabs, the 3-D pockets, slip pockets and etc.. We will construct those elements one by one and connect them all together. Please refer to the **"Basic Bag Construction"** for more details on some of those elements and photos here. Gather all the materials, accessories and hardware, and let's get started.

Construct the Handle and D-Ring Tab

The Handle and D-Ring Tab - please refer to the chapter **"Basic Bag Construction"**, section **"Construct the Handle and D-Ring Tab"** for more details.

Construct the Zipper Flap casing

The Zipper Flap casing - please refer to the chapter **"Basic Bag Construction"**, section **"Construct the Zipper Flap casing"** for more details.

DIRECTIONS

Construct the Interior

1 Construct the interior Front & Back slip pocket and attach to the Lining Front & Back. Please refer to the chapter "**Basic Bag Construction**", section "**Construct the Slip Pocket - Style A**".

2 Construct the interior Side Gusset 3-D pocket and attach to the Lining Side Gusset. Please refer to the chapter "**Basic Bag Construction**", section "**Construct the 3-D Pocket**".

 You might divide the 3-D Pocket by 3 sections. Draw a line, 2.5" away from the bottom center, on each side. Gather the elastic into the center section only. Please refer to the photos.

3 Add a D-Ring to the top of the Lining Front & Back Slip Pocket (optional). Place a D-Ring tab to the top of the Lining Front & Back Slip pocket and baste stitch to attach it to the Lining.

4 Connect the Front & Back to the Side Gussets. Place one of the Side Gusset pieces, Right side facing up, and one of the Front & Back pieces, Right side facing down. Sew one side with the seam allowance of your choice to connect both pieces together.

Connect all 4 pieces together in this order - "Front (& Back)", "Side Gusset", "(Front &) Back", and "Side Gusset".

DIRECTIONS

Construct the Interior

5 **Attach the Bottom to the finished 4-side piece.** Attach the Bottom piece to the finished 4-side panel. Align all 4 centers. Sew all the way around the bottom with the seam allowance of your choice and leave an opening (4" long or longer) on one of the longer sides for turning the whole bag Right side out later.

Construct the Exterior

1 **Install the Purse Feet (optional).** Please refer to the chapter "**Basic Bag Construction**", section "**Install the Purse Feet**".

DIRECTIONS

Construct the Exterior

2 **Construct the 3-D pocket Flap.** If you prefer not to have the pocket flap, you might skip the steps below.

① (Optional) Place a D-Ring tab at the center of the curved seam on the lining flap. The D-Ring points down to the straight seam.

② Use the pattern as a guide to find where to place the male part of the magnet washer, poke and cut two lines using a seam ripper, but do not install the magnet yet. Apply fusible interfacing to the flap main to prevent the hardware from rubbing against the fabric.

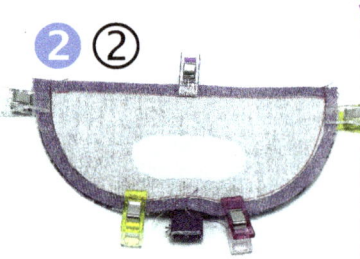

③ Place both flap main and lining Right side facing each other, sew all the way around, except the straight seam, by using the seam allowance of your choice.

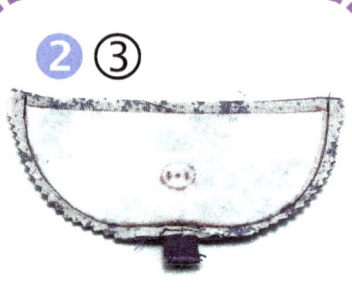

④ Install the male part of the magnet to the flap lining - insert the feet from the Right side of the lining, flatten the magnet feet.

⑤ Turn the flap Right side out through the opening. Top stitch on the curved seam by using 1/8" seam allowance.

3 **Construct the 3-D Pocket.** Please refer to the chapter "**Basic Bag Construction**", section "**Construct the 3-D Pocket**".

Install the female part of the magnet to the main fabric of the 3-D pocket through the bottom opening right after sewing the elastic casing.

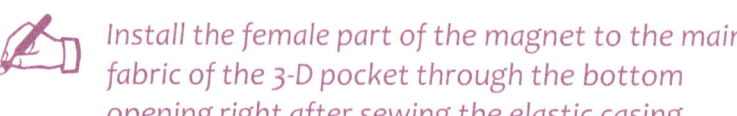

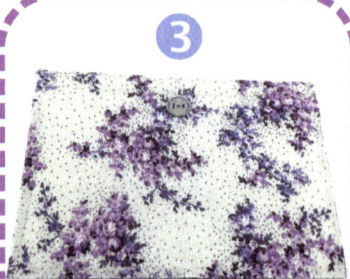  

DIRECTIONS

Construct the Exterior

4 **Attach the Pocket Flap to the pocket.** After attaching the 3-D pocket to the "Bottom" piece, place the pocket flap lining side facing down on top of the 3-D pocket and align the top raw edge of both pieces.

 *Optional: Add lace on one of the longer sides of the "Top" of the 3-D pocket piece, baste stitch to attach both pieces together.*

5 **Completed the 3-D pocket piece.** Place the "Top" of the 3-D pocket piece, Right side (which might have the lace if you added any) facing down, on top of the pocket flap (Right side facing up), the lace side will be aligned at the top raw edge. Sew the three pieces (the "Bottom" of the 3-D Pocket, Pocket Flap and the "Top" of the 3-D Pocket) together by using the seam allowance of your choice on top of the raw edge. Flip the "Top" of the 3-D Pocket piece Right side out. Flip the lace so that it faces the same way as the "Top" of the 3-D Pocket piece. Top stitch 1/8" away from the Pocket Flap.

 Do NOT top stitch onto the Pocket Flap, otherwise the pocket flap won't fully open.

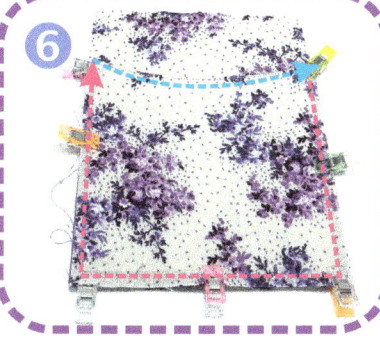

6 **Construct the Slip Pocket.** You may skip steps 2 to 5, if you prefer to have the Slip Pockets at both front and back on your bag.

 Please refer to the chapter "Basic Bag Construction", section "Construct the Slip Pocket - Style A".

DIRECTIONS

Construct the Exterior

7 **Connect the Front & Back to the Side Gussets, then attach to the Bottom.** Place one of the Side Gusset pieces, Right side facing up, and one of the Front & Back pieces, Right side facing down. Sew one side with the seam allowances of your choice to connect both pieces together. Attach the Bottom piece to the finished 4-side panel. Align all 4 centers. Sew all the way around the bottom with the seam allowance of your choice.

 Connect all 4 pieces together in this order - "Front (& Back)", "Side Gusset", "(Front &) Back", and "Side Gusset".

 Top stitch the Side Gusset, 1/16" seam allowance, where the "Front (& Back)" piece and "Side Gusset" connect.

8 **Attach the handles and D-Ring tabs.** Turn the exterior piece Right side out. Place the handle Right side down at the top of the exterior, 2" away from the center. Attach the D-Ring tab next to the left side of the handle. Do the same step as above for the other side. Baste stitch both handles and tabs to attach them onto the top of the exterior.

 Check the "Front & Back" pattern for the handle placement and the "Side Gusset" pattern for the D-Ring Tab placement.

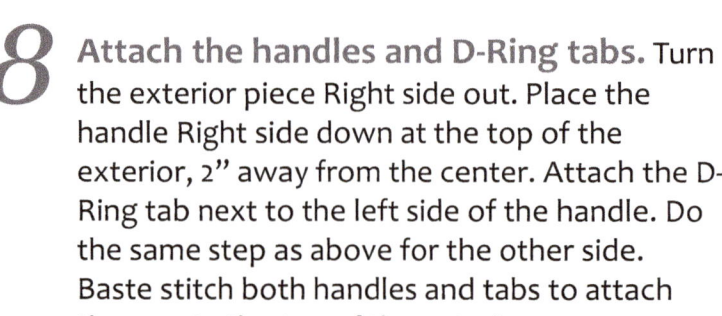

DIRECTIONS

Construct the Exterior

9 **Attach the zipper flap casing.** Place the zipper flap casing Right side facing the top of the exterior piece, make sure all 4 centers are aligned, and both the handles and D-Ring tabs are facing downward. Use pins or clips to hold them in place and baste stitch the exterior and zipper flap casing together. We just completed constructing the exterior piece.

Complete the Purse piece

1 **Connect both Main and Lining pieces.** You should have both Main and Lining pieces ready to complete the purse piece. Place the Main piece (Right side out) into the Lining piece (Wrong side out), with the Right sides of both pieces facing each other. Align all 4 center markings.

Use chalk or erasable pen to draw the seam line on the Wrong side of the Lining before sewing.

2 **Sew all the way around the top** to connect both pieces with the seam allowance of your choice.

3 **Turn Right side out.** Turn the whole purse piece Right side out through the opening at the bottom of the lining.

DIRECTIONS

Complete the Purse piece

4 **Press well.** Use an iron to press the purse piece with a bit of steam to remove wrinkles if necessary.

5 **Topstitching.** Top stitch all the way around the connected edge by using 1/16" seam allowance.

6 **Close the opening.** Close the opening at the bottom of the lining by using blind stitches.

Install the purse frame

1 **Install the purse frame.** Get the correct size and shape purse frame ready to install to the completed purse piece.

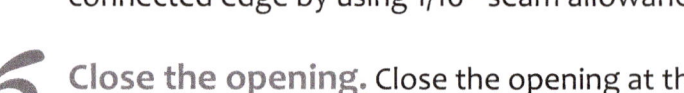

 Please refer to the Chapter "Install the Purse Frame".

 *Install the metal zipper end(s) -* (1) Cut the zipper end to the prefer length. (2) Fold the end of the zipper inward and sew to hold the end in place. (3) Slide the zipper end into the metal. (4) Use a small screw driver to tighten and lock the screw to the zipper.

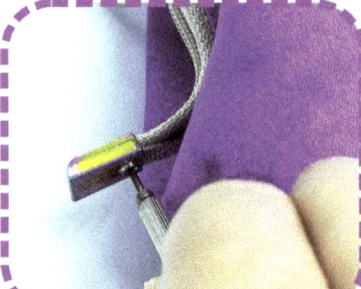

★ **NOTE:** The attached pattern has **NO** seam allowances included. Refer to the Chapter "Understand The Pattern" completely before cutting or sewing! ☺

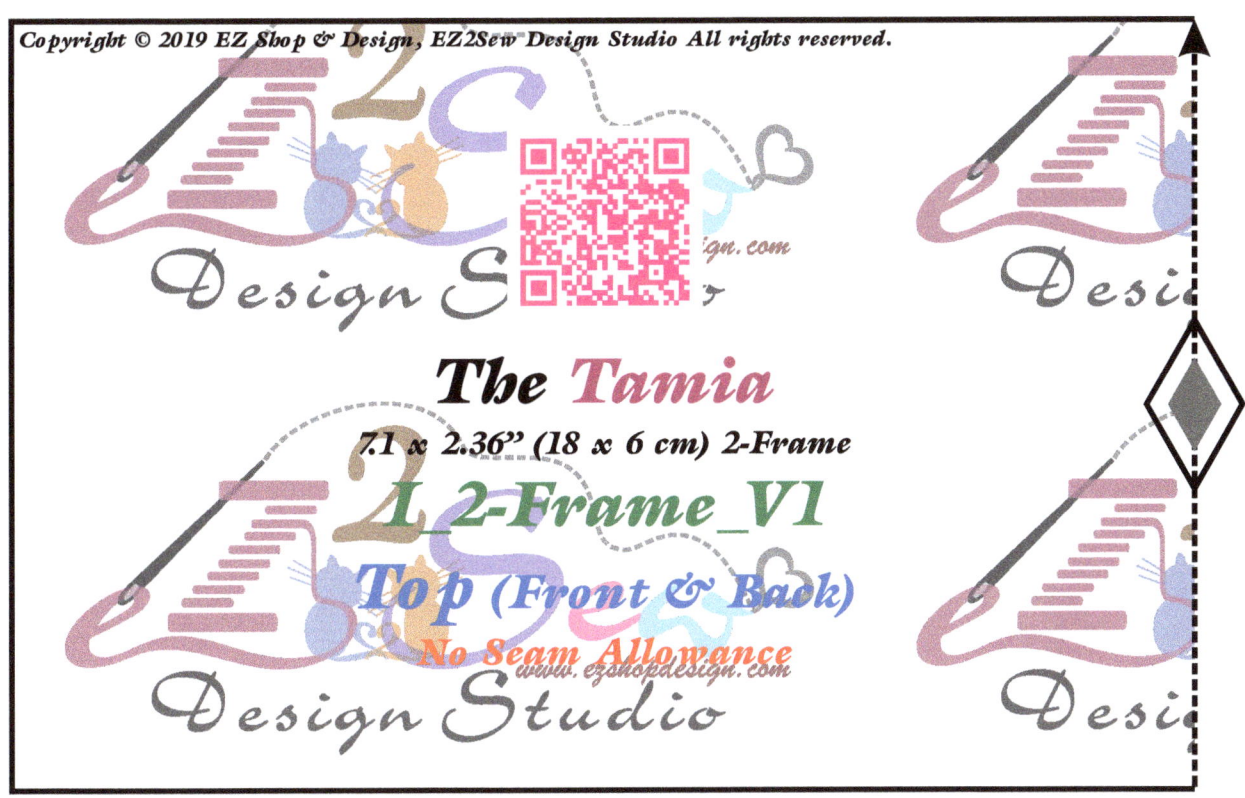

Printing Instructions

Please make sure your printer's scaling is set to "none," "actual size" or "100%". Do NOT check the "scale to fit paper size" option. Once the pattern is printed out, make sure it printed correctly. Check the "1 inch Square" and it should measure 1" x 1". If the square is not the correct size, check the printer settings again.

| 1" | 3cm |

> ★ **NOTE:** The attached pattern has **NO** seam allowances included. Refer to the Chapter "Understand The Pattern" completely before cutting or sewing! ☺

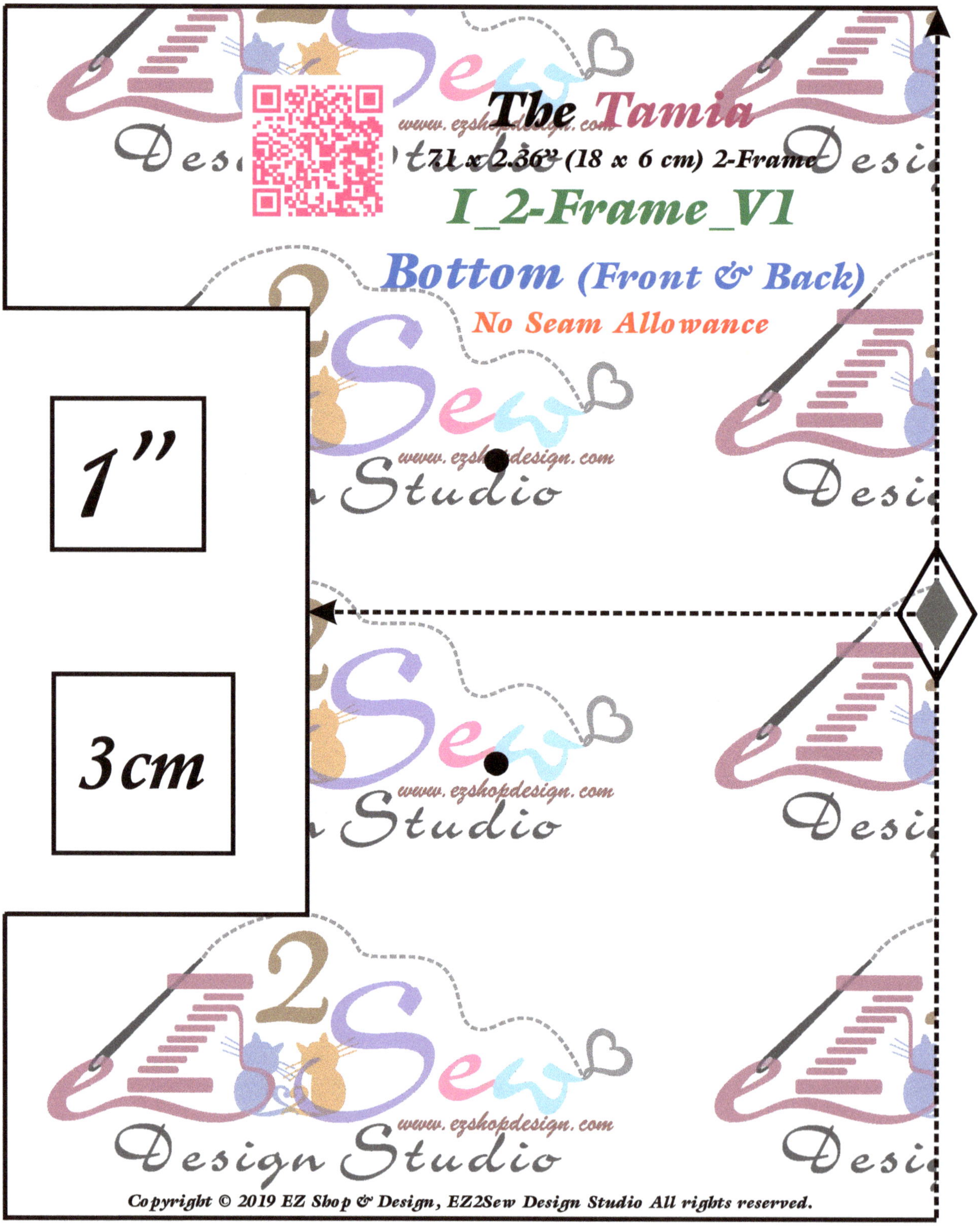

The Tamia
7.1 x 2.36" (18 x 6 cm) 2-Frame
I_2-Frame_V1
Bottom (Front & Back)
No Seam Allowance

1"

3cm

Copyright © 2019 EZ Shop & Design, EZ2Sew Design Studio All rights reserved.

> ✯ **NOTE:** The attached pattern has **NO** seam allowances included. Refer to the Chapter "Understand The Pattern" completely before cutting or sewing! ☺

The Tamia
7.1 x 2.36" (18 x 6 cm) 2-Frame
I_2-Frame_V1
Front & Back (Interior)
No Seam Allowance

3cm

1"

✯ **NOTE:** The attached pattern has **NO** seam allowances included. Refer to the Chapter "Understand The Pattern" completely before cutting or sewing! ☺

The Tamia

7.1 x 2.36" (18 x 6 cm) 2-Frame

I_2-Frame_V1

Pocket

(Interior Front & Back)

No Seam Allowance

Printing Instructions

𝒫lease make sure your printer's scaling is set to "none," "actual size" or "100%". Do NOT check the "scale to fit paper size" option. Once the pattern is printed out, make sure it printed correctly. Check the "1 inch Square" and it should measure 1" x 1". If the square is not the correct size, check the printer settings again.

⭐ **NOTE:** *The attached pattern has <u>NO</u> seam allowances included. Refer to the Chapter "Understand The Pattern" completely before cutting or sewing!* ☺

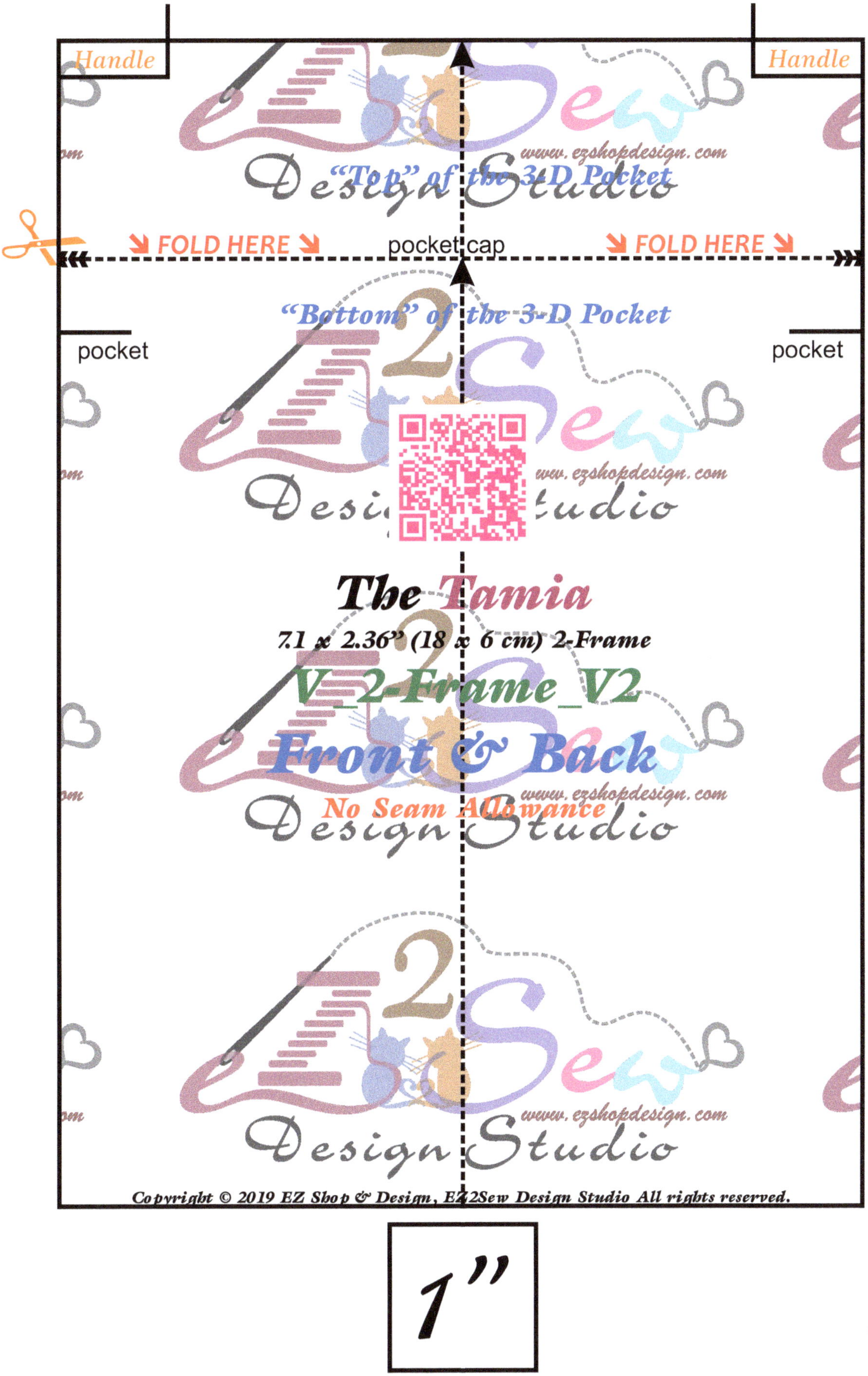

Handle | Handle

"Top" of the 3-D Pocket

✂ ◄◄ ➴ FOLD HERE ➴ pocket cap ➴ FOLD HERE ➴ ►►

"Bottom" of the 3-D Pocket

pocket | pocket

The Tamia
7.1 x 2.36" (18 x 6 cm) 2-Frame

V_2-Frame_V2

Front & Back

No Seam Allowance

Copyright © 2019 EZ Shop & Design, EZ2Sew Design Studio All rights reserved.

1"

> **NOTE:** The attached pattern has <u>NO</u> seam allowances included. Refer to the Chapter "Understand The Pattern" completely before cutting or sewing! ☺

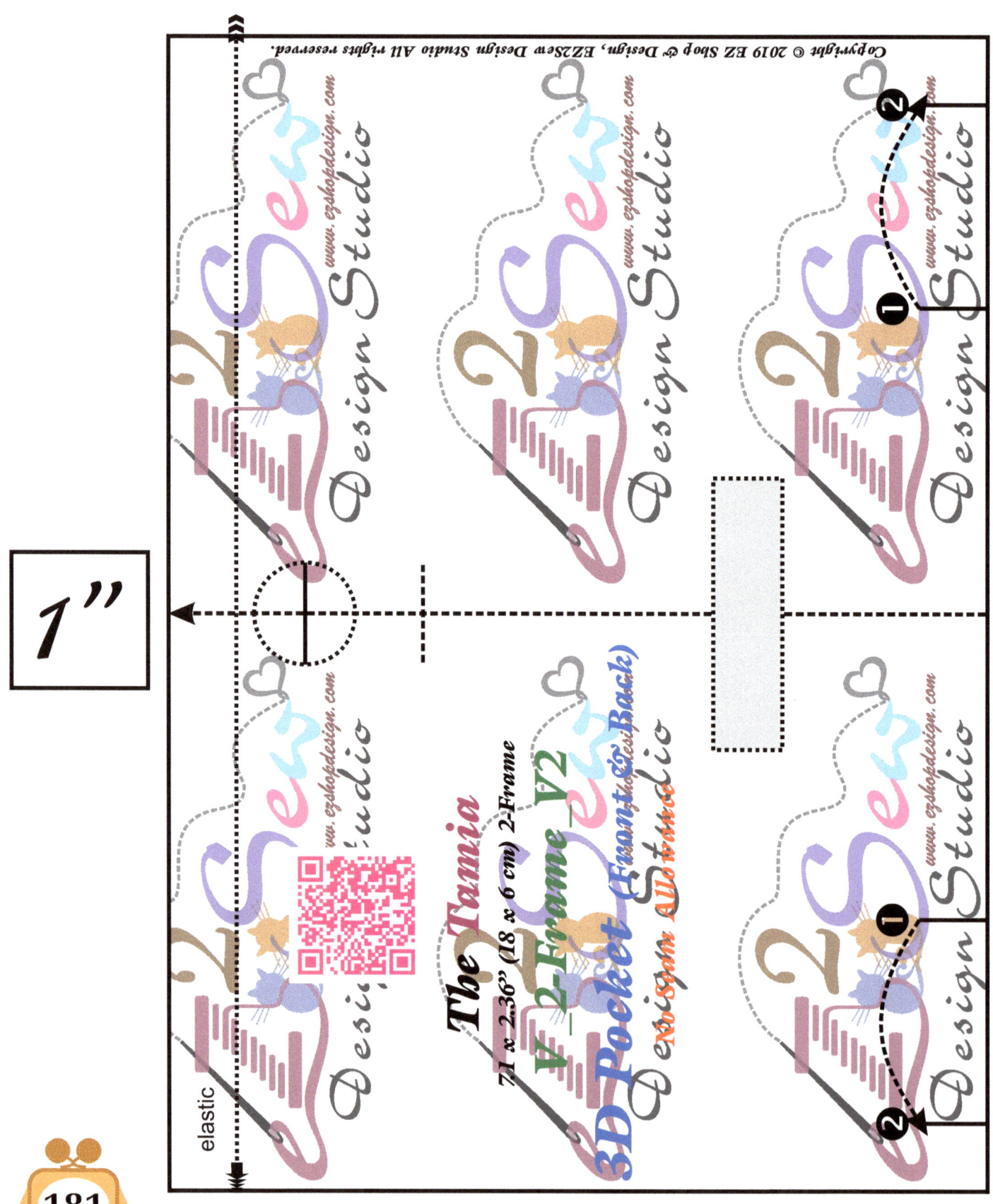

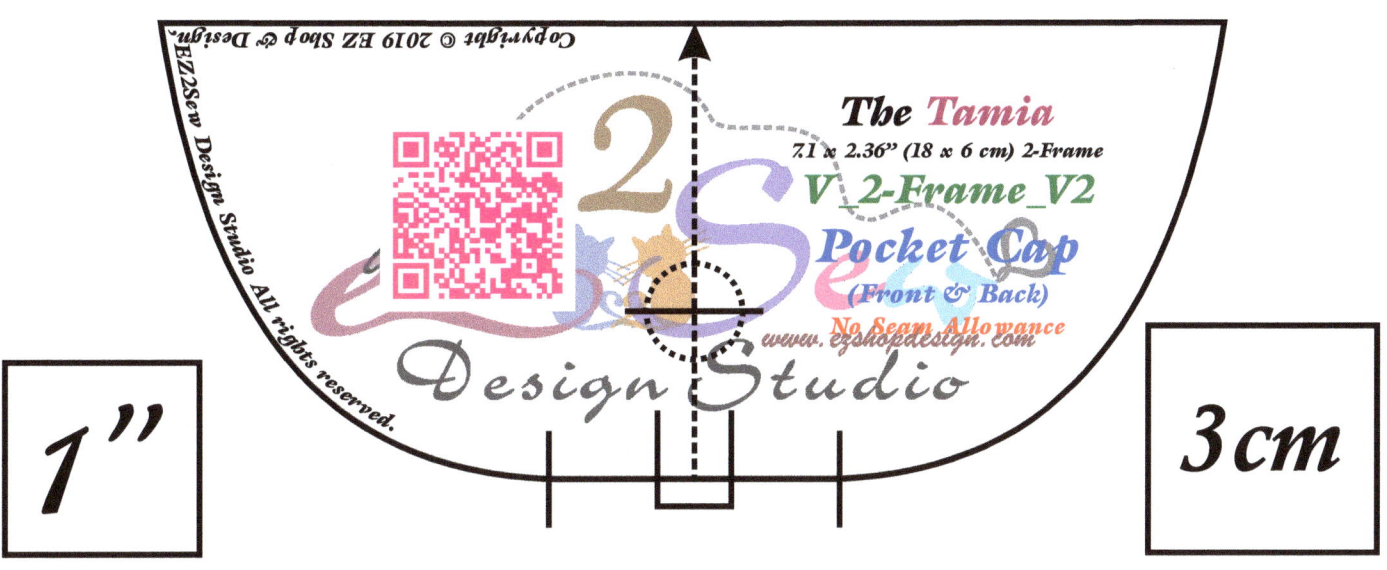

| 3cm |

| 1" |

The Tania
7.1 x 2.36" (18 x 6 cm) 2-Frame
V – 2-Frame V2
3D Pocket
(Interior Side Gusset)
No Seam Allowance

⭐ **NOTE:** The attached pattern has <u>NO</u> seam allowances included. Refer to the Chapter "Understand The Pattern" completely before cutting or sewing! ☺

Copyright © 2019 EZ Shop
©Design, EZ2Sew Design Studio All rights reserved.

Printing Instructions

Please make sure your printer's scaling is set to "none," "actual size" or "100%". Do NOT check the "scale to fit paper size" option. Once the pattern is printed out, make sure it printed correctly. Check the "1 inch Square" and it should measure 1" x 1". If the square is not the correct size, check the printer settings again.

184

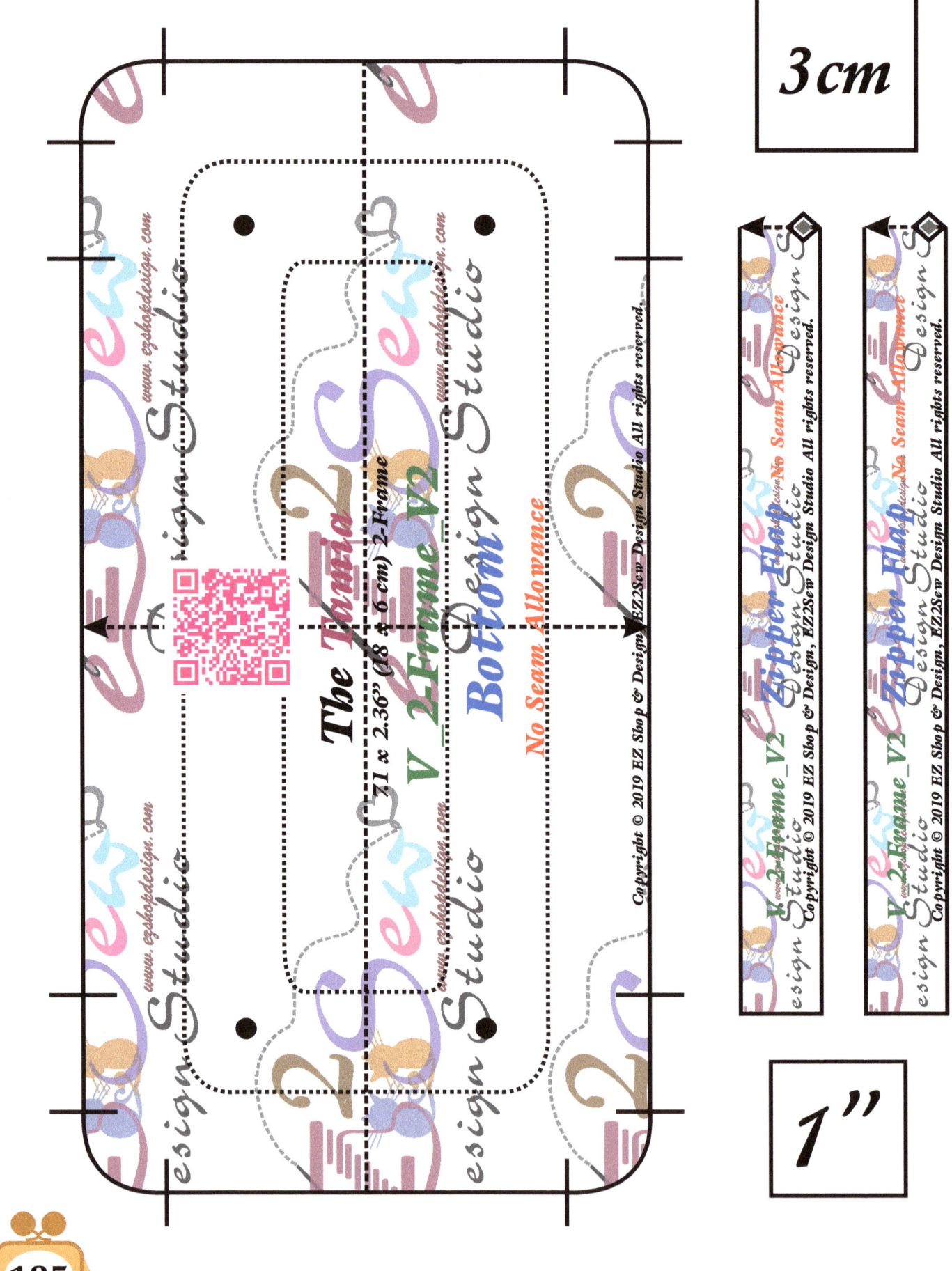